First Workshop on Efficient Benchmarking in NLP (NLP-Power 2022)

Dublin, Ireland
26 May 2022

ISBN: 978-1-7138-6749-4

Printed from e-media with permission by:

Curran Associates, Inc.
57 Morehouse Lane
Red Hook, NY 12571

Some format issues inherent in the e-media version may also appear in this print version.

Printed with permission by Curran Associates, Inc. (2023)

For permission requests, please contact the Association for Computational Linguistics at the address below.

Association for Computational Linguistics
209 N. Eighth Street
Stroudsburg, Pennsylvania 18360

Phone: 1-570-476-8006
Fax: 1-570-476-0860

acl@aclweb.org

Additional copies of this publication are available from:

Curran Associates, Inc.
57 Morehouse Lane
Red Hook, NY 12571 USA
Phone: 845-758-0400
Fax: 845-758-2633
Email: curran@proceedings.com
Web: www.proceedings.com

NLP-Power 2022

The First Workshop on Efficient Benchmarking in NLP

Proceedings of the Workshop

May 26, 2022

The NLP-Power organizers gratefully acknowledge the support from the following sponsors.

In cooperation with

Introduction

NLP Power! is the workshop on efficient benchmarking in NLP.

Benchmarking has become a standard practice for evaluating upcoming models against one another and human solvers; there are still many unresolved issues and methodological concerns. The main idea of the workshop is to bring together researchers that work on benchmarks for natural language processing (NLP) and discuss how benchmarking can be improved to account for computational efficiency, ethical considerations, user preferences, and out-of-domain robustness. The workshop proceedings present the collection of research contributions on the computational efficiency of model evaluation, transfer learning efficiency estimation, evaluation metrics, robustness and bias assessment, and general best practices in benchmarking for NLP.

This is the first time we have organized a workshop with this particular scope of interest. Our workshop is hosted by the 60th Annual Meeting of the Association for Computational Linguistics (ACL 2022). Our program committee consisted of experts from all over the world with years of research experience in the industry and academia. The committee worked hard on every submission and selected 12 research papers to be presented at the workshop in the poster and oral sessions. The workshop program also included one ACL Findings paper. Overall, it resulted in 2 oral presentation sessions, which were intermitted by a poster session, three invited talks, and a round table on the problems of canonic benchmark standards.

NLP Power would not be possible without the dedicated intellectual work of the program committee: their peer review and efforts aimed to improve the work have shaped the scientific community, which is now, for the first time, coming forward with a unified workshop mission. We also express our sincere gratitude to the invited speakers: Anna Rumshiski, He He, and Ulises Mejias, for their contribution to the program. We thank the researchers and NLP practitioners for the engagement and responses and hope to continue to provide a platform for fruitful discussions on various topics, ranging from rethinking benchmarking methods to the reproducibility of the leaderboard results.

You can find more details about the workshop on the website: `http://nlp-power.github.io/`.

Tatiana Shavrina, Valentin Malykh, Ekaterina Artemova, Vladislav Mikhailov, Laura Weidinger, Oleg Serikov, and Vitaly Protasov

Organizing Committee

Program Chairs

Tatiana Shavrina, AIRI, SberDevices
Valentin Malykh, Huawei
Ekaterina Artemova, HSE University, Huawei
Vladislav Mikhailov, SberDevices, HSE University
Oleg Serikov, AIRI, HSE University
Vitaly Protasov, AIRI

Program Committee

Senior Program Committee

Jürgen Schmidhuber, Swiss AI Lab IDSIA, USI, SUPSI

Program Committee

Laura Weidinger, DeepMind
Leonid Zhukov, AIRI
Mikhail Burtsev, AIRI
Nitish Hemant Joshi, CILVR / ML2
Richard Yuanzhe Pang, CILVR / ML2
Adaku Uchendu, Penn State University
Ilya Kuznetsov, TU Darmstadt
Anastasia Bonch-Osmolovskaya, HSE University
Andrey Kravchenko, Oxford University
Daniel Karabekyan, HSE University
Preslav Nakov, QCRI
Suresh Manandhar, Wiseyak, USA
Piotr Piękos, DeepMind
Olga Lyashevskaya, Vinogradov IRL RAS, HSE University
Arjun Akula, Google Research

Secondary Reviewers

Tatiana Shavrina, AIRI, SberDevices
Maria Tikhonova, HSE University, SberDevices
Dina Pisarevskaya, QMUL

Invited Speakers

Ulises A. Mejias, SUNY Oswego
Anna Rumshisky, UMASS, Amazon
He He, CILVR / ML2

Table of Contents

Raison d'être of the benchmark dataset: A Survey of Current Practices of Benchmark Dataset Sharing Platforms

Jaihyun Park *
School of Information Sciences
University of Illinois Urbana-Champaign
jaihyun2@illinois.edu

Sullam Jeoung *
School of Information Sciences
University of Illinois Urbana-Champaign
sjeoung2@illinois.edu

Abstract

This paper critically examines the current practices of benchmark dataset sharing in NLP and suggests a better way to inform reusers of the benchmark dataset. As the dataset sharing platform plays a key role not only in distributing the dataset but also in informing the potential reusers about the dataset, we believe data sharing platforms should provide a comprehensive context of the datasets. We survey four benchmark dataset sharing platforms: HuggingFace, PaperswithCode, Tensorflow, and Pytorch to diagnose the current practices of how the dataset is shared - *which metadata is shared and omitted*. To be specific, drawing on the concept of *data curation* which considers the future reuse when the data is made public, we advance the direction that benchmark dataset sharing platforms should take into consideration. We identify that four benchmark platforms have different practices of using metadata and there is a lack of consensus on what social impact metadata is. We believe the problem of missing a discussion around social impact in the dataset sharing platforms has to do with the failed agreement on who should be in charge. We propose that the benchmark dataset should develop social impact metadata and data curator should take a role in managing the social impact metadata.

1 Introduction

Benchmark datasets play a crucial role in developing the model. Publicly available benchmark datasets serve as a baseline proxy to measure the model's performance and an evaluation as the machine learning (ML) and natural language processing (NLP) scholarship competes for the higher ground. Recent works have started to question the validity of such benchmark datasets regarding their generalizability (Bowman and Dahl, 2021; Paullada et al., 2021), documentation practices (Bender and Friedman, 2018), and social impact (Hovy and Spruit, 2016; Sap et al., 2021), amongst others. Paullada et al. (2021) focus on the way how benchmark datasets are collected and used and advocate cautious understanding of data in order to address ethical issues of using such datasets. Bowman and Dahl (2021) suggest the criteria benchmarks should qualify, namely the robustness, statistical power, and considerations of social impact. However, despite the fact that the documentation of benchmark datasets and the role of the dataset sharing platform are pivotal not only in informing the users about the benchmark dataset but also soliciting a safe use, it has been relatively understudied. We believe that critically examining the current practices of dataset sharing platforms - which metadata is documented and omitted - and suggesting desiderata for data sharing platforms can serve as a practical guide for users and researchers in encouraging a safe environment.

Our findings show that current practices of dataset sharing platforms are highly centered on *reusable* purpose, which focuses on the convenience of the users in making use of the dataset. For example, it provides detailed explanations of how to load the dataset into actual development, how the test and train split are made. It was hard, on the other hand, to find the documentation of the limitations of the dataset (e.g. which societal impacts it may bring); even if there were, the concepts and definitions were often elusive. We introduce the concept of *social impact metadata* which is the documenting practice done in Library and Information Science in order to advocate mitigating possible social harms.

We propose desiderata for documenting benchmark datasets. Beyond descriptive and administrative metadata, the documents of the metadata should also include the social impact metadata. To make it possible, we highly encourage developing

* Both authors contributed equally to this research.

Proceedings of NLP Power! The First Workshop on Efficient Benchmarking in NLP, pages 1 - 10
May 26, 2022 ©2022 Association for Computational Linguistics

the social impact metadata (e.g. demographic statistics of the data) and also emphasize a role of the data curator who is responsible for documenting in terms of the data sharing platforms.

2 Definitions

In order to narrow down the conceptual difference that may conflict between the ML (and NLP) community and Library and Information Science community, we introduce the definition of the key terms that will be used throughout the paper.

Data documentation Data documentation (sometimes called a "codebook") is helpful in understanding and interpreting the dataset (Vardigan et al., 2008). A document can be defined as 'anything in which knowledge is recorded' and documentation is 'any process which serves to make a document available to the user after knowledge.' (Woledge, 1983). With this sense, Data Documentation Initiatives (DDI) defines data documentation as 'document and manage data across the entire data life cycle, from conceptualization to data publication, analysis and beyond' (DDI, 2020). ML community defines the data documentation as 'annotating various demographic characteristics for disaggregated testing, gathering representative data, and providing documentation pertaining to the data gathering and annotation process' (Jo and Gebru, 2020).

Benchmark dataset Benchmark dataset refers to the typical set of datasets that are commonly used for evaluating the model's baseline performance on specific tasks (Bowman and Dahl, 2021). Some of the widely used benchmark datasets in NLP are GLUE (Wang et al., 2018) and SuperGLUE (Wang et al., 2019) for natural language understanding, SQuAD (Rajpurkar et al., 2016) for question and answering, and Seteroset (Nadeem et al., 2021), CrowS (Nangia et al., 2020) for checking biased natural language models, amongst others.

Data sharing platform We consider a data-sharing platform, that provides access to the datasets or the metadata of the datasets. Normally the benchmark datasets are shared through the third party provider rather than the data creators themselves. Generally, the data sharing platforms offer the users direct access to the datasets by their pre-defined methods that are compatible with their libraries used for developing NLP models (e.g. HuggingFace, PyTorch, Tensorflow). Apart from the concept of data curator, who collects, selects, and participates in the data creation process, contributors are the ones that upload and document the dataset to the data-sharing platform. This could be voluntary individuals (e.g. HuggingFace), or in part supported by automated algorithms (e.g. PaperswithCode).

Descriptive metadata Descriptive metadata is considered to contain information that can help users to find, identify, select, and obtain the resource. Title, creator, keywords, subject, type of resource, and other attributes that describe what the resource is about are considered as descriptive metadata (Liu and Qin, 2014; Pomerantz, 2015). In practice, descriptive metadata in the archives can be used to catalog entities, events, time, and space to answer the queries that the users want to find (Dobreski et al., 2020). Descriptive metadata in the benchmark dataset can be derived from variables inside of the dataset. The domain (e.g., social media, news media), scope (e.g., the topic covered by the dataset) can be additional descriptive metadata of the benchmark dataset.

Administrative metadata Administrative metadata is required to house information about managing and administering collections. Administrative metadata includes information about rights, versions, and preservation (NISO, 2004). For the benchmark dataset, the version can be appropriate administrative metadata.

3 Social Impact of Benchmark Dataset Sharing Platforms

Once the benchmark dataset is made available for others, *data friction* comes into play. *Data friction* explains a point of resistance where data can be garbled, misinterpreted, or lost (Edwards et al., 2011). As Edwards et al. (2011) argue, researchers' main interest is in *using* data, not in *describing* the dataset for the benefit of invisible, unknown future users. The problem of benchmark dataset sharing arise because text-as-data and computation is no longer exclusive field of NLP and ML (Monroe et al., 2008). The benchmark dataset can be easily used by researchers outside of NLP and ML community. For instance, now in the name of digital humanities, researchers in humanities also use computational approaches and technologies with historical text data (Connolly, 2020; Soni et al., 2021; Smith et al., 2014).

Likewise, if the benchmark dataset is shared through the sharing platforms, ML and NLP researchers will make derivative models based on the benchmark dataset and this will lead the researchers outside of ML and NLP to indirectly impacted by benchmark dataset without knowing the social impact of the dataset. Even though humanists and social scientists may not fine-tune the parameters of the model itself, their research will be impacted by how the benchmark dataset is designed and constructed. The use of pre-trained model from NLP community by researchers outside of NLP and ML can be found in the case of *politeness detection* model. The original idea of developing a NLP model for detecting politeness from language is from Danescu-Niculescu-Mizil et al. (2013). As the automatic scoring of the politeness in the language has benefits regardless of the field, Hoffman et al. (2017) attempted to reproduce and validate Danescu-Niculescu-Mizil et al. (2013). In doing so, Hoffman et al. (2017) applied the same model to Wikipedia, which is the identical domain and found unexpected results that led them to question the quality of the dataset. Their conclusion called for an investigation on research which reused the dataset that Danescu-Niculescu-Mizil et al. (2013) developed. If the quality of dataset is spurious, then it is hard to say the following research building on the questionable dataset can avoid critics. Nonetheless, the politeness corpus of Danescu-Niculescu-Mizil et al. (2013) is now incorporated into the R package (Yeomans et al., 2018), allowing researchers from outside of ML community can easily load the package and analyze the data. There are some papers already utilized politeness corpus from outside of NLP and ML for social science research purpose (Sun et al., 2021; G Moore et al., 2020). At this point, we do not know how to measure the social impact of politeness detection dataset and the derivative package will bring.

For ML and NLP researchers, identifying who is responsible for assessing the social impact and alarming the benchmark dataset reusers is now more than important. We can find another example of social impact of malfunctioned benchmark dataset in the recent development of a chatbot called 'Lee ruda'. 'Lee ruda' showed how artificial intelligence systems can jeopardize sexual minorities by exposing them to toxic communication space (McCurry, 2021). If the data documentation process is not shared in the benchmark dataset sharing platforms and discussion around social impact of the dataset is not mature enough to alert reusers, the social impact of benchmark dataset can be catastrophic. In this vein, Hovy and Spruit (2016) also emphasizes how naive use of the datasets may cause problems on the society by directly deploying the trained model into the society.

4 Current Practices of Benchmark Dataset Sharing Platforms

We investigated the platforms that practitioners and researchers largely accessed for datasets. This resulted in four main platforms: HuggingFace[1], PaperswithCode [2], Tensorflow [3], and PyTorch [4]. We focused on whether it provides users easy access to datasets along with its metadata. As for PaperswithCode, it did not provide direct access to datasets however, it offered detailed information of data such as the papers that used (cited) the datasets. We excluded the platforms that were managed by the users themselves, such as Github, as it was mostly uploaded by the data creators themselves, rather than other contributors that curated the dataset for ease of use.

HuggingFace HuggingFace provides an infrastructure so ML researchers can easily leverage models and datasets. The idea of HuggingFace is similar to Github, where the codes and data are shared. In HuggingFace, it is the language model trained by different groups of researchers in NLP that is shared. Of many language models available in HuggingFace, what made HuggingFace famous is Transformers, which enabled loading thousands of deep learning frameworks (PyTorch, Tensorflow, JAX) as well as language models (e.g., BERT, RoBERTa, GPT) with a single line of code.

[1] https://huggingface.co/
[2] https://paperswithcode.com/
[3] https://www.tensorflow.org/datasets
[4] https://pytorch.org/text/stable/datasets.html

The Dataset card for social impact, biases, and unknown limitations is developed to reflect the growing concern around the social impact of the ML benchmark dataset (McMillan-Major et al., 2021).

PaperswithCode PaperswithCode organizes the research works from the ML community by providing three access points: tasks, datasets, and methods. PaperswithCode do not house the datasets but rather provide a reference point where you can find the research worked on the specific benchmark dataset. The Dataset section was organized with brief information about the dataset, relevant papers which reused the benchmark dataset, on which tasks the benchmark dataset was used, and where researchers can find the benchmark dataset. For instance, PaperswithCode introduces GLUE dataset with additional information that it can be found from Hugging Face and Tensorflow.

Tensorflow Tensorflow is an open-source library that helps the users to develop and train ML models developed by the Google Brain Team. It serves as the core platform and library for machine learning by allowing the users to customize their own models. In addition to the model library, Tensorflow also provides datasets as a collection of ready-to-use libraries. Ranging from audio, graphs, image, and texts, it offers widely used datasets including benchmarks (e.g. GLUE, SQuAD). The merit of Tensorflow datasets lies in their easy-to-use nature, as users can simply load and make use of the datasets by importing the library, except for a few exceptions that require a manual download.

PyTorch Analogous to the Tensorflow library, PyTorch is an open-source tensor library for deep learning using GPUs and CPUs, primarily developed by Facebook's AI research lab. In addition to the modules for operation, it also provides datasets and tools that make data loading easy, mainly for usability purposes. The dataset it provides is the most widely used benchmark, such as WikiText-2, CoNLL2000Chunking, for a variety of tasks including language modeling, sequence tagging, and text classification amongst others.

5 Results

As one would expect, the essential role of these platforms was focused on helping the users easily fetch the dataset and use it without putting in an extra endeavor. For example, the datasets were well-curated into train and test set splits, so that users can readily reproduce, and custom it to their own task. However, when it came to sharing auxiliary information (*metadata*) regarding the dataset, such as its limitations, and societal impacts, a large portion of the platforms lacked providing detailed information. In this section, we introduce the metadata types used in benchmark dataset sharing platforms and summarized in Table 1 of Appendix A.

5.1 Confusing concepts in terminology and metadata

HuggingFace placed 'Personal and Sensitive Information' into the big category called Dataset Creation. However, given that dataset creation includes information about source and annotation, Dataset Creation is the section for descriptive metadata. Following HuggingFace's rule of categorization, it is hard to identify whether 'Personal and Sensitive Information' is descriptive metadata that can be recorded directly from the dataset. Furthermore, the terminology that HuggingFace is using can be misleading. HuggingFace uses 'Curators' to show *"people involved in collecting the dataset and their affiliation(s)"* [5]. Using the term 'curator' to indicate people who created (collected) the dataset can be confusing. In Library and Information Science (especially the documentation field), the museum curators are people establishing collecting policies to guide the future acquisition of objects (Roberts and Light, 1980). With this sense, HuggingFace is equivalent to a museum where the virtual place houses multiple objects (datasets) and curators are people who put the dataset in the benchmark dataset sharing platform. We believe the confusing concept of curator stems from the fact that the dataset is also collected from various sources. However, a curator is the person who works at the museum or library to facilitate access or circulation of the object, not the writer or creator of the book

[5] https://github.com/huggingface/datasets/blob/master/templates/README_guide.md

or object.

5.2 Lack of documenting the limitations of the benchmark datasets

Among the platforms we investigated, only a few platforms provided the information of limitations of the benchmark datasets. HuggingFace data cards have a section that links the contributors, those who upload the dataset to the platform to write down what the data curation rationale is and how the annotations were made. However, when it comes to the limitations of the benchmark datasets, the detailed explanations about what the limitations are unclear. It is hard to find coherent concept of what limitation should be addressed. For example, one of the datasets mentioned the contextual limitation - monolingual dataset as the limitation *"(the) issue is the focus on English language and lack of multilingual hate speech."* (*hatexplain*[6]) - while the other noted the technical issue, the data size, as its limitation *"The dataset is relatively small and should be used combined with larger datasets."* (*ethos*[7]).

Similar to the Hugging Face, PaperswithCode showed the related papers, however, as the related papers were based on the citation information - whether the dataset was cited in the paper or not - it did not explicitly distinguish the papers that mentioned the limitations of the datasets. Even though one particular paper cited the dataset, it does not necessarily mean that the paper used the dataset for improving their own models. It could have been the paper discussing the caveats of using the dataset. However, this demarcation was not clear to help reusers notice whether there is a potential harm of leveraging this dataset.

As Tensorflow and PyTorch were focused more on its technical use of the datasets, only the information pertaining to how to practically use the datasets was documented. For example, the test and train splits, and the functions that were used to load the data. This different metadata recording practice in benchmark dataset sharing platforms shows that there is no consensus on what metadata to use to inform the reusers of the benchmark dataset.

[6] `https://huggingface.co/datasets/hatexplain`

[7] `https://huggingface.co/datasets/ethos#other-known-limitations`

5.3 Discussions of social impacts

We denote two prominent points when investigating the platforms overall regarding the discussions of social impacts. First, the platforms that documented the social impacts of the benchmark datasets barely existed. Even if there were sections for limitations, it was not clear whether the section is for discussing the social impact of dataset or technical aspect of dataset. Second, the definition of what social impacts it is referring to was obscure if there were any sections allocated to document it. For Tensorflow and PyTorch, as the main focus of these platforms are on redistribution, and enhancing the reusability of the users, the documentation did not include any discussions of the social impacts of the datasets. PaperswithCode has its unique feature, 'leaderboard' that demonstrates the state-of-the-art models that were tested on the given datasets. It allows the users to easily check the model performance based on this leaderboard. This practice, however, is far from discussing the social impacts the datasets and it does not provide the audience with potential caveats that may arise when using the dataset.

HuggingFace, on the other hand, provided the data cards which is the format the contributors need to fill when sharing the dataset, and there is a section that deals with the possible social impact of the dataset. According to the HuggingFace data card guidelines, the range of what social impact is broad ranging from positive impact to potential risks it may have to the society. One of the dataset explanations mentioned the positive social impact it can bring: *"The dataset could prove beneficial to develop models which are more explainable and less biased."* (*hatexplain*[8]), while the others focused on the functional effectiveness: *"This dataset is part of an effort to encourage text classification research in languages other than English."* (*amazon reviews*[9]), and few on the negative impacts: *"..it necessarily requires confronting online content that may be offensive or disturbing but argue that deliberate avoidance does not eliminate such problems"* (*social bias frames*[10]). This lack

[8] `https://huggingface.co/datasets/hatexplain#social-impact-of-dataset`

[9] `https://huggingface.co/datasets/amazon_reviews_multi#social-impact-of-dataset`

[10] `https://huggingface.co/datasets/social_bias_frames#social-impact-of-dataset`

of consensus on what limitation is with respect to benchmark dataset and social impact the benchmark dataset can bring can lead to haphazard organization of benchmark dataset and in turn lead to the failed control of managing implicit bias slipping into derivative NLP models and the findings of the scholars who simply utilize the NLP models.

6 Desiderata of Data Sharing Platforms

The caveat of using benchmark dataset and *vis-à-vis* social impact is gaining attention from the ML community (Hovy and Spruit, 2016; Sap et al., 2021). However, we believe the benchmark dataset sharing platform is not currently up-to-date because the current discussion around the benchmark dataset is missing. We acknowledge that the endeavor of dataset creators is crucial in developing a safe benchmark ecosystem, however, in this work we typically focus on the data sharing platforms. From our analysis, there are many loopholes to fill. PaperswithCode, Tensorflow, and PyTorch emphasized descriptive and administrative metadata while neglecting the importance of the social impact that the benchmark dataset can bring. We want to reiterate that even though data documentation recorded the entire process of dataset creation perfectly, *data friction* (Edwards et al., 2011) could happen when it was made available for others for reuse purposes. Therefore, dataset sharing platforms should take initiative to inform the social impact of the benchmark datasets by critically assessing the datasets. From a data curation perspective, it is unclear who is responsible for organizing the information of social impact, biases, and other limitations.

6.1 Beyond descriptive and administrative metadata

Metadata for administrative purposes which does not describe the dataset itself but may be of use to clarify rights and version were well-developed in four platforms. Although administrative metadata that each platform used was varied, we were able to identify that platforms tried to record licenses (HuggingFace, PaperswithCode) and versions (Tensorflow). However, metadata for social impact were absent in PaperswithCode, Tensorflow, and PyTorch. This may indicate that the discussion around the social impact of reusing the benchmark datasets stays in scholarly communication. Practitioners (both in the ML community and outside of the community) deserve the right to know the potential social impact that the benchmark dataset they are using can bring.

6.2 Data curator for social impact metadata

The next will be answering who is responsible for providing social impact metadata. We propose that the data curator specialists working for the benchmark dataset sharing platform should take a role to announce and organize the social impact of the dataset. As we discussed in the 5. Results section, the role of a curator is to manage the dataset and critically assess the social impact of reuse. It is a lack of understanding the importance of metadata and the role of the curator that made the climate of putting less emphasis on sharing social impact information. HuggingFace placed 'personal and sensitive information' into descriptive metadata section (Dataset Creation), confusing who is responsible for filling out the field of 'personal and sensitive information'. We believe sensitive information is an aspect of the dataset after critically reviewing it. Additional information can either be detected during the collection or after it is completed collecting process. However, it is more likely that sensitive information can slip into the dataset without dataset creators' notice. This makes the nature of 'personal and sensitive information' fall under metadata that needs to be addressed afterward, which is far from descriptive metadata. For instance, if the dataset was collected from social media, data curators should critically assess the dataset to identify if it contains personally identifiable information and complete the metadata section for it.

6.3 Developing social impact metadata

The benchmark dataset may have an impact on society with *exclusion* and *overgeneralization* (Hovy and Spruit, 2016). Hovy and Spruit (2016) explain that the exclusion of certain demographics in the dataset may exacerbate as the models overfit these factors. For example, models that are overfitted to *standard white English* may have the propensity to fail when applied to the products by marginalizing other demographics and their use of language can be overgeneralized. Concretely, below we list some of the possible social impact metadata that needs to be included: *which* metadata should be included, and *why* it should be considered important in terms of social impact.

Demographic statistics is about *the population from whom the data comes.* As the data for NLP deals with language, it carries contextual information beyond its face value. For example, text data retrieved from news wire may represent a typically white, educated, middle-upper class man (Garimella et al., 2019) while text data retrieved from certain social media platforms may convey the language spoken by the platform users. Likewise, the data itself may represent certain socio-demographic groups for the language models to be trained on. Thus, it is important to document the demographic statistics of the dataset. Resonating our recommendation, there is a scholarship claiming the importance of ensuring demographic variation in order to mitigate potential bias upon deployment (Hovy and Prabhumoye, 2021; Rogers et al., 2021; Ardehaly and Culotta, 2014).

Annotators demographics is about *the population who added values (labels) on top of the collected raw data.* Recording metadata about annotators demographics is related to *selection bias* and demographics of annotators accord with *label bias* (Hovy and Prabhumoye, 2021). As annotators (e.g. crowdsource workers) contribute to form the labels, their social norms can be systematically encoded in the dataset, inducing a label bias. Sap et al. (2021) demonstrates how the annotations are highly dependent on the annotator's demographics. To be specific, the task of annotating whether the text is a type of hate speech or not is hinged much on the annotators' ethnic group. It is important to document the annotators' demographics, not only because it informs the users about the representation of annotators but also it also steers future data creators to take into consideration when crowdsourcing annotators.

Besides these items, we also note the initiatives of NAACL (*the discussion of the broader impacts*[11]) and GDPR (*privacy issues of collected data*[12]) are also highly recommendable for starting a discussion on making a consensus about what social impact metadata the benchmark dataset sharing platforms should reflect.

[11] `https://2021.naacl.org/ethics/faq/`

[12] `https://eur-lex.europa.eu/legal-content/EN/TXT/HTML/?uri=CELEX:32016R0679`

7 Conclusion

We believe the documentation of the benchmark dataset plays an important role as it introduces the pitfalls as well as the usage of the dataset. To this end, we examine current practices of widely accessed benchmark dataset sharing platforms - *what is documented and what is omitted* -. Our findings suggest the need for documenting the social impact of the benchmark dataset as well as assigning the data curators for data sharing platforms to be in-charge of documenting relevant metadata.

References

Ehsan Mohammady Ardehaly and Aron Culotta. 2014. Using county demographics to infer attributes of twitter users. In *Proceedings of the joint workshop on social dynamics and personal attributes in social media*, pages 7–16.

Emily M. Bender and Batya Friedman. 2018. Data statements for natural language processing: Toward mitigating system bias and enabling better science. *Transactions of the Association for Computational Linguistics*, 6:587–604.

Samuel Bowman and George Dahl. 2021. What will it take to fix benchmarking in natural language understanding? In *Proceedings of the 2021 Conference of the North American Chapter of the Association for Computational Linguistics: Human Language Technologies*, pages 4843–4855.

Randy Connolly. 2020. Why computing belongs within the social sciences. *Communications of the ACM*, 63(8):54–59.

Cristian Danescu-Niculescu-Mizil, Moritz Sudhof, Dan Jurafsky, Jure Leskovec, and Christopher Potts. 2013. A computational approach to politeness with application to social factors. In *Proceedings of the 51st Annual Meeting of the Association for Computational Linguistics (Volume 1: Long Papers)*, pages 250–259.

DDI. 2020. Ddi lifecycle 3.3.

Brian Dobreski, Jaihyun Park, Alicia Leathers, and Jian Qin. 2020. Remodeling archival metadata descriptions for linked archives. In *International Conference on Dublin Core and Metadata Applications*, pages 1–11.

Paul N Edwards, Matthew S Mayernik, Archer L Batcheller, Geoffrey C Bowker, and Christine L Borgman. 2011. Science friction: Data, metadata, and collaboration. *Social studies of science*, 41(5):667–690.

Sarah G Moore, Gopal Das, and Anirban Mukhopadhyay. 2020. Emotional echo chambers: Observed emoji clarify individuals' emotions and responses to social media posts. *ACR North American Advances*.

Aparna Garimella, Carmen Banea, Dirk Hovy, and Rada Mihalcea. 2019. Women's syntactic resilience and men's grammatical luck: Gender-bias in part-of-speech tagging and dependency parsing. In *Association for Computational Linguistics*.

Erin R Hoffman, David W McDonald, and Mark Zachry. 2017. Evaluating a computational approach to labeling politeness: Challenges for the application of machine classification to social computing data. *Proceedings of the ACM on Human-computer Interaction*, 1(CSCW):1–14.

Dirk Hovy and Shrimai Prabhumoye. 2021. Five sources of bias in natural language processing. *Language and Linguistics Compass*, 15(8):e12432.

Dirk Hovy and Shannon L Spruit. 2016. The social impact of natural language processing. In *Proceedings of the 54th Annual Meeting of the Association for Computational Linguistics (Volume 2: Short Papers)*, pages 591–598.

Eun Seo Jo and Timnit Gebru. 2020. Lessons from archives: Strategies for collecting sociocultural data in machine learning. In *Proceedings of the 2020 conference on fairness, accountability, and transparency*, pages 306–316.

Xiaozhong Liu and Jian Qin. 2014. An interactive metadata model for structural, descriptive, and referential representation of scholarly output. *Journal of the Association for Information Science and Technology*, 65(5):964–983.

Justin McCurry. 2021. South korean ai chatbot pulled from facebook after hate speech towards minorities.

Angelina McMillan-Major, Salomey Osei, Juan Diego Rodriguez, Pawan Sasanka Ammanamanchi, Sebastian Gehrmann, and Yacine Jernite. 2021. Reusable templates and guides for documenting datasets and models for natural language processing and generation: A case study of the huggingface and gem data and model cards. In *Proceedings of the 1st Workshop on Natural Language Generation, Evaluation, and Metrics (GEM 2021)*, pages 121–135.

Burt L Monroe, Michael P Colaresi, and Kevin M Quinn. 2008. Fightin'words: Lexical feature selection and evaluation for identifying the content of political conflict. *Political Analysis*, 16(4):372–403.

Moin Nadeem, Anna Bethke, and Siva Reddy. 2021. Stereoset: Measuring stereotypical bias in pretrained language models. In *Proceedings of the 59th Annual Meeting of the Association for Computational Linguistics and the 11th International Joint Conference on Natural Language Processing (Volume 1: Long Papers)*, pages 5356–5371.

Nikita Nangia, Clara Vania, Rasika Bhalerao, and Samuel Bowman. 2020. Crows-pairs: A challenge dataset for measuring social biases in masked language models. In *Proceedings of the 2020 Conference on Empirical Methods in Natural Language Processing (EMNLP)*, pages 1953–1967.

NISO. 2004. Understanding metadata. *National Information Standards Organization*, 20.

Amandalynne Paullada, Inioluwa Deborah Raji, Emily M Bender, Emily Denton, and Alex Hanna. 2021. Data and its (dis) contents: A survey of dataset development and use in machine learning research. *Patterns*, 2(11):100336.

Jeffrey Pomerantz. 2015. *Metadata*. MIT Press.

Pranav Rajpurkar, Jian Zhang, Konstantin Lopyrev, and Percy Liang. 2016. Squad: 100,000+ questions for machine comprehension of text. In *Proceedings of the 2016 Conference on Empirical Methods in Natural Language Processing*, pages 2383–2392.

D Andrew Roberts and Richard B Light. 1980. Progress in documentation: museum documentation. *Journal of documentation*.

Anna Rogers, Timothy Baldwin, and Kobi Leins. 2021. 'just what do you think you're doing, dave?'a checklist for responsible data use in nlp. In *Findings of the Association for Computational Linguistics: EMNLP 2021*, pages 4821–4833.

Maarten Sap, Swabha Swayamdipta, Laura Vianna, Xuhui Zhou, Yejin Choi, and Noah A Smith. 2021. Annotators with attitudes: How annotator beliefs and identities bias toxic language detection. *arXiv preprint arXiv:2111.07997*.

David A Smith, Ryan Cordel, Elizabeth Maddock Dillon, Nick Stramp, and John Wilkerson. 2014. Detecting and modeling local text reuse. In *IEEE/ACM Joint Conference on Digital Libraries*, pages 183–192. IEEE.

Sandeep Soni, Lauren F Klein, and Jacob Eisenstein. 2021. Abolitionist networks: Modeling lan guage change in nineteenthcentury activist newspapers. *Journal of Cultural Analytics*, 1(1):43.

Shujing Sun, Yang Gao, and Huaxia Rui. 2021. Chronic complainers or increased awareness? the dynamics of social media customer service. In *Proceedings of the 54th Hawaii International Conference on System Sciences*, page 6525.

Mary Vardigan, Pascal Heus, and Wendy Thomas. 2008. Data documentation initiative: Toward a standard for the social sciences. *International Journal of Digital Curation*, 3(1).

Alex Wang, Yada Pruksachatkun, Nikita Nangia, Amanpreet Singh, Julian Michael, Felix Hill, Omer Levy, and Samuel Bowman. 2019. Superglue: A stickier benchmark for general-purpose language understanding systems. *Advances in neural information processing systems*, 32.

Alex Wang, Amanpreet Singh, Julian Michael, Felix Hill, Omer Levy, and Samuel Bowman. 2018. Glue: A multi-task benchmark and analysis platform for natural language understanding. In *Proceedings of the 2018 EMNLP Workshop BlackboxNLP: Analyzing and Interpreting Neural Networks for NLP*, pages 353–355.

Geoffrey Woledge. 1983. Historical studies in documentation:'bibliography'and 'documentation': words and ideas. *Journal of Documentation*.

Michael Yeomans, Alejandro Kantor, and Dustin Tingley. 2018. The politeness package: Detecting politeness in natural language. *R Journal*, 10(2).

A Appendix

Platforms	Metadata type	Items
HuggingFace	Descriptive metadata	Dataset Creation: Curation Rationale, Source Data, Annoatations
	Social impact metadata	Dataset Creation: Personal and Sensitive Information Considerations for Using the data: Social Impact of dataset, Discussions of Biases, Other known Limitations
	Administrative metadata	Additional Information Dataset: Curators, Licensing Information, Citation Information, Contributions
PaperswithCode	Descriptive metadata	Description
	Social impact metadata	
	Administrative metadata	Homepage (Link to paper), Usage (Number of papers using this dataset by year), Benchmark Leader Board (Task, Dataset variant, Best Model, Paper, Code), License, List of papers
Tensorflow	Descriptive metadata	Description, Download size, Dataset size, Auto-cached, Splits, Supervised keys, Figure
	Social impact metadata	
	Administrative metadata	Homepage (Link to paper), Source code (Example code for deployment), Versions, Examples, Citation
PyTorch	Descriptive metadata	Number of lines per split, Number of classes, Parameters
	Social impact metadata	
	Administrative metadata	Code (example code for deployment)

Table 1: Metadata of benchmark dataset sharing platforms

Towards Stronger Adversarial Baselines Through Human-AI Collaboration

Wencong You and **Daniel Lowd**
University of Oregon
Eugene, OR
{wyou, lowd}@cs.uoregon.edu

Abstract

Natural language processing (NLP) systems are often used for adversarial tasks such as detecting spam, abuse, hate speech, and fake news. Properly evaluating such systems requires dynamic evaluation that searches for weaknesses in the model, rather than a static test set. Prior work has evaluated such models on both manually and automatically generated examples, but both approaches have limitations: manually constructed examples are time-consuming to create and are limited by the imagination and intuition of the creators, while automatically constructed examples are often ungrammatical or labeled inconsistently. We propose to combine human and AI expertise in generating adversarial examples, benefiting from humans' expertise in language and automated attacks' ability to probe the target system more quickly and thoroughly. We present a system that facilitates attack construction, combining human judgment with automated attacks to create better attacks more efficiently. Preliminary results from our own experimentation suggest that human-AI hybrid attacks are more effective than either human-only or AI-only attacks. A complete user study to validate these hypotheses is still pending.

1 Introduction

Humans have used language to deceive each other for millennia. With the advent of NLP systems, humans now work to deceive models and algorithms, from evading email spam filters in the early 2000s to defeating classifiers for social network spam, abusive language, misinformation, and more. More recently, humans have developed automated adversarial attacks that minimally modify text while changing the output of a classifier or other NLP systems (Ebrahimi et al., 2018). These automated attacks have the potential to be much more efficient than humans, helping attackers to find weaknesses in models and helping defenders find and patch those same weaknesses (Xie et al., 2021; Zhou et al., 2019).

Attack	Original → Perturbed Text	Label
PSO	city by the sea swings from one approach to the other , but in the end , it stays in formula – which is a [waste → moor] of de niro , mcdormand and the other good actors in the cast .	Neg. (98%) → Pos. (93%)
BAE	When a set of pre-shooting guidelines a director came up with for his actors turns out to be cleverer , better written and of considerable more interest than the finished film , that 's a [bad → good] sign .	Neg. (97%) → Pos. (95%)
PWWS	[A refreshing → axerophthol review] Korean film about five [female → distaff] high school friends who face an uphill battle when they try to take their relationships into deeper waters.	Pos. (99%) → Neg. (73%)

Table 1: Attack Samples on SST-2

The number of automated attacks continues to grow but their effectiveness remains low — Wang et al. (2021a) found that 90% of automated adversarial attacks changed the semantics of the original input or confused human annotators. We have observed similar behavior, as shown in Table 1. These examples are generated by word-level attack algorithms PSO (Zang et al., 2020), BAE (Garg and Ramakrishnan, 2020), and PWWS (Ren et al., 2019), as implemented in the TextAttack framework (Morris et al., 2020), on the sentiment dataset SST-2 (Socher et al., 2013) against BERT model (Devlin et al., 2019). Although all perturbations change the predicted label, PSO chooses a synonym that is inappropriate in the context, BAE selects a complete antonym, and PWWS picks some rare substitutes that are nonsensical and possibly offensive.

Doubtless, humans can be more effective than these attacks, given their effectiveness against real-world spam and abuse filters. We believe that the next step for adversarial attacks and robust NLP is human-AI collaboration, in which humans work with automated adversarial algorithms to pro-

Proceedings of NLP Power! The First Workshop on Efficient Benchmarking in NLP, pages 11 - 21
May 26, 2022 ©2022 Association for Computational Linguistics

duce effective attacks efficiently. Furthermore, real-world attackers are already doing this. Spammers already use many different technologies to accomplish their tasks, including text spinners to rewrite text, HTML tricks to conceal suspicious text, botnets to scale up and avoid IP bans, and more. A typical spammer does not craft every message individually, but uses semi-automated techniques to generate many different messages[1]. In response, a growing amount of NLP research is now using human expertise through human-in-the-loop (HITL) methods to create new benchmarking datasets for evaluating and improving the robustness of NLP systems to adversarial inputs.

Thus far, human expertise in adversarial NLP tasks has been limited. There is a growing body of work in which humans are asked to craft inputs where a given model will perform poorly, but they receive little support in doing so — sometimes word saliences (Mozes et al., 2021), sometimes model predictions (Kiela et al., 2021), and sometimes even less. Overall, the effort between humans and machines is still largely separate; that is, humans generate adversarial examples alone based on model interpretations, without directly interacting with any attack algorithms.

In this paper, we study the potential of direct human-AI interaction for generating higher-quality adversarial examples for NLP tasks. We work with the state-of-the-art word-level attacks on benchmark datasets for sentiment analysis and abuse detection. We choose word-level attacks as they can be more subtle than character-level attacks, which have obvious misspellings. We design an interactive user interface that enables four types of attacks, including two human-AI collaboration methods. Instead of a pure black-box environment, our interface explains the algorithm's search space and allows humans to modify and improve the perturbations while giving humans immediate feedback from the target NLP model. Along with generated attacks, we collect data for user experience and user preference with regard to different attack approaches. We then further study the collected data and analyze the impact of proposed human-AI collaboration methods and the degree of improvement on the adversarial examples. At present, we have pilot data from using the system ourselves; a full user study is pending IRB approval.

[1]For an example of a spammer script that does this, see https://alexking.org/blog/2013/12/22/spam-comment-generator-script.

We summarize our contributions as follows:

- We propose a novel human-AI collaboration strategy to enable direct human and AI interaction for generating word-level adversarial examples for NLP tasks effectively and efficiently.
- We design a framework with friendly user interface to realize four types of attack methods on benchmark datasets against state-of-the-art NLP models. In addition to helping generate adversarial examples, the framework also collects self- and peer-evaluation of example quality and user feedback about the interface.
- We share initial results based on our own use of the system, while IRB approval for a full study is pending.

The rest of the paper is structured as follows: Section 2 discusses work related to our research. Section 3 introduces our framework, the human-AI collaboration methods and the evaluation metrics. Section 4 gives preliminary results and some brief analysis for our findings. Section 5 explains the stages of experiments for generating and collecting quality data. Finally, we conclude and discuss future work in Section 6.

2 Related Work

We review prior work on automated adversarial attacks for NLP, and HITL in adversarial learning.

Automated adversarial attacks for NLP: With the growth of research that studies adversarial learning in NLP, a variety of attack methods have been developed on multiple levels. From character-level modifications such as HotFlip (Ebrahimi et al., 2018), DeepWordBug (Gao et al., 2018), and VIPER (Eger et al., 2019), to word-level perturbations such as BAE (Garg and Ramakrishnan, 2020), PSO (Zang et al., 2020), PWWS (Ren et al., 2019), and TextFooler (Jin et al., 2020). Many of them have been aggregated and organized by toolchains like TextAttack (Morris et al., 2020) and OpenAttack (Zeng et al., 2021) for easy access to researchers.

For character-level attacks, although they show their effectiveness in many ways, they mainly fall in the following two categories: Some of the character-level modifications can be seen as typos if an algorithm simply influences the embedding space by replacing/inserting/deleting one or a few characters in a word, such as DeepWordBug (Gao et al., 2018), then they may be easily detected by a grammar checker tool, like Grammarly [2]; the others can introduce some unique encoding/decoding methods and transform letters to another form, such as VIPER (Eger et al., 2019) that adds accent signs on top of each letter, and these modification may be easily identified by human. Overall, character-level perturbations tend to be more obvious.

On the other hand, the study of word-level attacks is more popular, as a substitute for a word may significantly impact the semantics of the text. Many attack methodologies have been investigated for searching for the optimal synonym substitutions, including BERT-based contextual prediction (Garg and Ramakrishnan, 2020; Li et al., 2020), gradient-based word swap (Ebrahimi et al., 2018; Wallace et al., 2019), particle swarm optimization (Zang et al., 2020), and greedy word search with saliency scores (Ren et al., 2019).

We summarize three attacks that are included in our framework. **BAE:** BERT-based Adversarial Examples (BAE), a black-box contextual perturbation algorithm based on a BERT masked language model (MLM). BAE masks some part of the text, then replaces and inserts tokens into the text, using the BERT-MLM to generate adversarial examples. **PWWS:** Probability Weighted Word Saliency (PWWS), a black-box greedy algorithm that ranks the importance of words based on the saliency score and calculates the classification probability that are used to determine the synonym substitution. **TextFooler:** TextFooler, a black-box greedy algorithm identifies the important words and replaces them with the words that are most semantically similar and grammatically correct with a higher priority until the prediction is altered.

These automated word-level attacks mostly rely on the knowledge of existing target models and algorithms' intensive search to locate the best synonym substitutions. However, recent work (Xie et al., 2021, 2022) shows that the quality of generated adversarial examples is actually far from satisfactory, with respect to the low attack success rate across domains, incorrect grammar, and distorted meaning.

HITL in adversarial learning: As the capacity of automated algorithms may be limited, many researchers propose incorporating crowd-sourcing into generating and annotating adversarial examples. The Dynabench framework asks humans to manually construct examples where an NLP system would perform poorly (Kiela et al., 2021). A HITL QA system that asks humans to write adversarial questions that break a QA system while remaining answerable by humans (Wallace and Boyd-Graber, 2018). The Adversarial NLI project asks humans to annotate mislabeled data and uses humans as adversaries to create a benchmark natural language inference (NLI) dataset for a more robust NLP model (Nie et al., 2020). The most related work compares the performance of human- and machine-generated word-level adversarial examples for NLP classification tasks (Mozes et al., 2021).

However, existing work falls short of direct collaboration between humans and AI. The advantages of human crowd-sourcing and that of automated algorithms are still quite distinct.

3 Framework

In our framework, we study the potential of direct human-AI collaboration for generating higher-quality adversarial examples. At the time of submission, we have completed the design of the framework, confirmed the details for human-AI collaboration, and implemented the interactive user interface.

3.1 Components & Workflow

Our task is divided into two parts: *generating adversarial examples* and *evaluating adversarial examples*. Figure 1 depicts the workflow. First we feed the input samples to the attack phase where four attack methods are implemented. Human participants then use these attack methods to generate adversarial examples aiming to fool the target model's predictions. Participants are asked to self-evaluate the quality of generated adversarial examples based on grammatical properties, the difficulty of generating those examples, and their experiences with the system in terms of the helpfulness of different HITL strategies. Peer-evaluation is also included for evaluating the grammatical properties, and identifying the source of any given text.

We implement three word-level attacks — BAE, PWWS, and TextFooler from the TextAttack library on sentiment dataset SST-2 and abuse comment dataset Hatebase (Davidson et al., 2017) against the RoBERTa target models (Liu et al., 2019) that are trained on these datasets separately. We use RoBERTa as the target model because it outper-

[2]Grammarly, `https://www.grammarly.com/`.

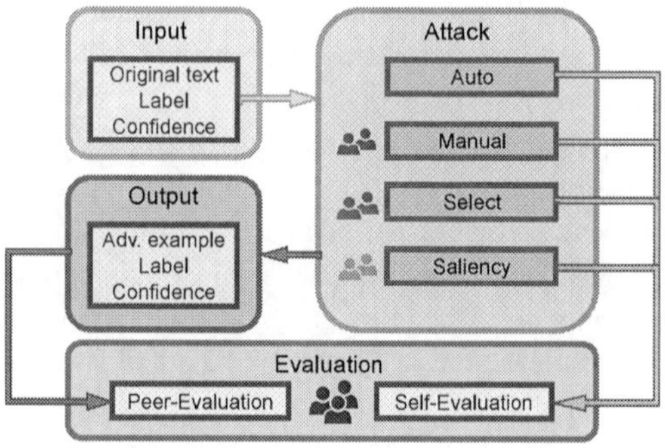

Figure 1: System & Workflow. Human figures in attack phase indicate that there is direct human-AI interaction. Human figures in evaluation phase indicate that humans are involved in both self-evaluation and peer-evaluation.

Attack	Transformation	Operation
BAE	BERT Masked Token Prediction	Replace & Insert
PWWS	WordNet-based synonym swap	Replace
TF	Counter-fitted word embedding swap	Replace

Table 2: A Summary of automated attack algorithms. TF is short for TextFooler.

forms BERT (Devlin et al., 2019) and XLNet (Yang et al., 2019) on various datasets across domains for classification in recent work (Xie et al., 2022). We summarize the characters of these attacks in Table 2. Please refer to Section 2 for a detailed description of them. All attacks share the same Greedy-WIR search method implemented in TextAttack. We make certain modifications to the scripts in the TextAttack library to generate desired intermediate attack results, which are used as interpretable information for HITL adversarial attacks.

3.2 Generating Adversarial Examples

For attack generation, we design an interactive user interface introducing four attack methods:

- **Auto:** Black-box. Participants simply read and evaluate adversarial examples generated by one of the automated attack algorithms. Participants are not provided with any insight on how an automated attack algorithm modifies a sample, but the perturbed example itself. This method is considered as the baseline.

- **Manual:** Black-box. Participants rely on their judgment solely to attack a given sample. The only information they receive is the immediate target model prediction. Once an adversarial example is entered, the target model returns the prediction result to show whether or not the crafted example has successfully flipped the predictive label.

- **Select:** Gray-box. Participants are given intermediate perturbation results from the automated algorithm — specifically, keywords and potential substitution candidates for each keyword. Participants can select the best word substitute using dropdown lists, or enter an alternative word in a text input box. See Figure 5 for the interface. Basically, the Select method relaxes the constraints from the automated algorithm, and allows humans to modify up to five keywords. The immediate predictive label and probability of the selected word combination from the target model is also provided to show whether the chosen words have successfully changed the prediction.

- **Saliency:** Gray-box. Participants are shown a dynamic saliency map as they craft their adversarial examples. A saliency map shows what words the target model identifies as most important that are most likely to affect the prediction, and then marks those words with colors with different intensities. Unlike (Mozes et al., 2021), where the interface displays word saliencies calculated by replacing the word with an out-of-vocabulary token, we implement the built-in method in each automated attack to calculate the saliency score. For example, BAE and TextFooler simply delete the word and calculate the word saliencies, while PWWS replaces each word with an unknown token and calculates the weighted saliency. The corresponding mathematical expressions are provided in A.2 of the Appendix. Overall, the Saliency method grants even more flexibility by allowing humans to change more words if necessary in order to preserve correct grammar and semantics. Participants can adjust their perturbation based on the dynamic saliency map and the target model's immediate prediction, see Figure 6 for the interface.

For each method, participants are given a small number of original samples selected from one of the datasets, perform adversarial attacks on those samples with or without the assistance of the automated algorithms.

3.3 Evaluating Adversarial Examples

To evaluate generated adversarial examples, we consider the following properties:

- **Grammar:** measures whether or not the text contains any syntax errors, and retains the original or similar semantics. This is crucial for identifying if an adversarial attack is successful, as if the perturbation is fundamentally wrong by making the sentence unreadable or flipping the emotion of the message completely, we consider it as a failed attack.

- **Plausibility:** measures whether or not the text is naturally crafted by native speakers. A piece of text is highly plausible if it is natural, logically correct, appropriately worded, and preserving meaningful messages (Wang et al., 2021b). These properties appear as naturalness, correctness, appropriateness and meaningfulness in our user interface.

- **Effort:** reflects the difficulty level for participants to successfully perform adversarial attacks using different attack methods.

- **Helpfulness:** collects the degree of helpfulness of the information provided to participants to assist with generating adversarial examples in different attack methods (i.e., intermediate search results, lists of candidates, saliency maps, and more).

All properties are evaluated on a scale from 1 to 5 where 5 indicates the best quality, the most difficult, or the most helpful, depending on the specific property; see Figure 7.

Participants are required to self-evaluate their own constructed examples using each of the attack methods. Since self-evaluation can be very subjective, to ensure the fairness and to yield a more balanced and less biased analysis and outcome, we also plan to include anonymous peer-evaluation using Amazon Mechanical Turk (AMT) [3] with a group of AMT workers who are excluded from previous attack tasks. Each AMT worker reads a random subset of the adversarial examples, identifies what source an example may come from, and evaluates the grammatical quality (i.e. grammar and plausibility) of that example on the same scales.

[3]Amazon Mechanical Turk, see https://www.mturk.com/

4 Preliminary Results

Our hypotheses are that with minimal human collaboration, compared to automated attacks alone, the attacks would yield more promising results that are meaningful while holding correct grammar and semantics. In our preliminary work, we already see promise for this direction. Table 3 shows an example where PWWS on its own failed to come up with a good attack example, but succeeded in identifying the key text to modify. A human was then able to propose alternative text, which tricked the classifier while maintaining the correct semantics.

OR. Txt	Auto Txt	HITL Txt
4 friends , 2 couples , 2000 miles , and all the Pabst Blue Ribbon beer they can drink - it 's the ultimate road-trip . (Pos. 62%)	4 friends , 2 couples , 2000 miles , and all the Pabst disconsolate Ribbon beer they can drink - it 's the ultimate road-trip . (Neg. 84%)	4 friends , 2 couples , 2000 miles , and all the Pabst cheap beer they can drink - it 's the ultimate road-trip . (Neg. 83%)

Table 3: Original vs. automated attack vs. HITL attack

As a pilot experiment, to test the viability of the framework before recruiting participants, the authors used the framework on themselves to collect 532 unique adversarial examples generated from the SST-2 dataset. By studying these examples, we have seen the following patterns (which we hypothesize will extend to the full experiments):

Success Rate: Figure 2 shows the attack success rate across all attack methods. Though an automated attack may have a higher attack success rate due to the advantage of intensive search and the NLP model-oriented design, humans can achieve comparable attack success rate if provided with better human-AI interaction. Additionally, manually crafted attacks without any assist cannot compete with the those generated through other methods.

Grammar and Plausibility: Figure 3 presents the average scores for grammar and plausibility, where the error bars denote the standard errors of the scores. The scores are aggregated and averaged per the attack method from the self-evaluation results over the 532 adversarial examples. It is obvious that human-generated adversarial examples on average have higher scores considering the grammatical properties and plausibility. Manual attack and HITL methods seem to produce higher-quality adversarial examples with the assistance of automated algorithms, as compared to automated

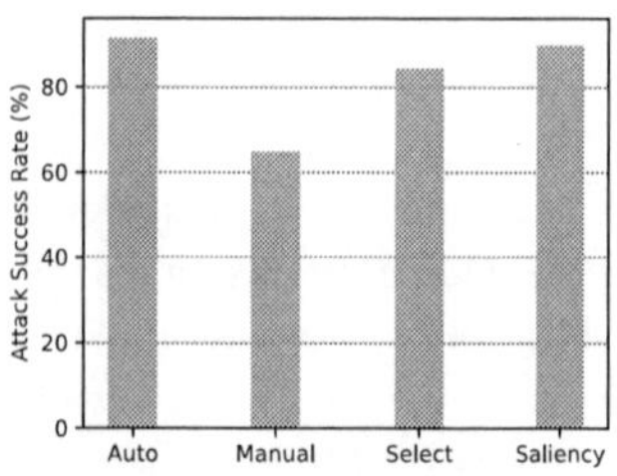

Figure 2: Attack success rate

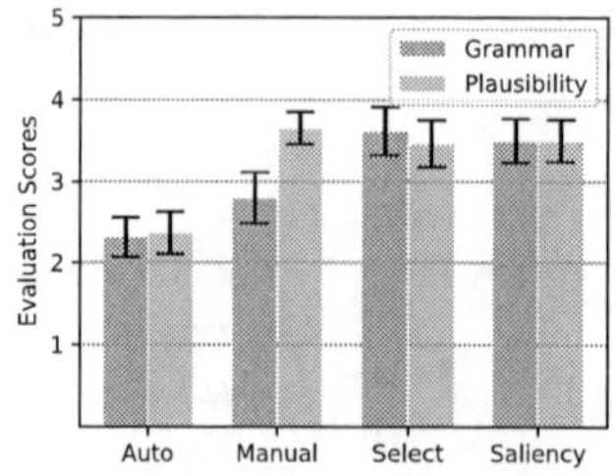

Figure 3: Grammar & plausibility

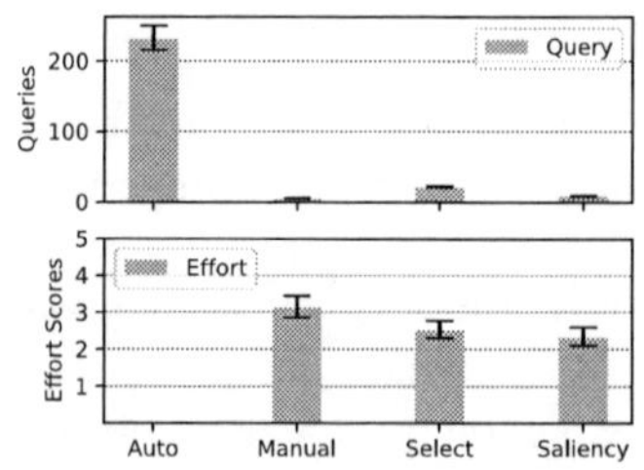

Figure 4: Queries & Effort

attacks, these methods loosen the constraints on various degrees and grant humans more freedom to make more modifications if needed. Therefore humans have more flexibility crafting grammatically correct and plausible adversarial examples.

Queries and Human Effort: The top of Figure 4 displays the number of queries it takes for an automated algorithm or a human to choose their word substitutions. The bottom of the figure gives the average effort scores for each attack method. The error bars denote the standard errors of the scores. The results illustrate that humans are able to perturb an NLP model with more effort but fewer queries, and the gray-box setting, which includes additional information for the participants, is easier to attack than the black-box settings. The extra information provides some insight and explanation about how an automate algorithm understands the NLP model and how an NLP model decides the predictions.

5 Planned Experiments

We plan to hire approximately 54 adult native English speakers, of whom we expect a subset to be experts in NLP or linguistics, from our local university to generate adversarial examples, and additional adult native English speaker AMT workers for peer-evaluation.

Unlike the recent work of Mozes et al. (2021), which relies entirely on online crowd-sourcing on AMT, we carry on in-person experiments for attack generation, where we provide a few examples and detailed instructions to the participants to show how our interface operates, and what the standards/baselines are for evaluating the adversarial examples. We expect to obtain higher-quality data by bringing participants into a more controlled environment where it's easier to provide instruction, answer questions, and receive feedback.

To motivate participants through the process, we have designed an incentive payment plan. Details are included in A.3 of the Appendix.

Stage 1: adversarial example generation and self-evaluation. In each task, each participant is asked to work with approximately 15 examples from a source dataset, generating adversarial examples based on the source examples. We show the same examples to three different participants, who work independently to find their own adversarial examples. This gives us a chance to observe how varied the solutions are; if solutions vary substantially, then a larger group of people may have a better chance to find a good attack.

To increase the quality of the adversarial examples, we plan to have each participant complete the Auto and Manual methods before moving on to our proposed HITL methods. This also serves the purpose of training participants in these tasks, similar to tasks 1-3 by Mozes et al. (2021). By doing so, participants have the chance to get familiar with our user interface, and get a better understanding of the capacity of an automated attack algorithm versus a human, in terms of influencing the target model's predictions. They then closely interact with the automated algorithms and the target model, where they obtain extra interpretable information from both parties that could assist them with more effective perturbations.

To increase the independence of the factors that may potentially impact the experiment results statistically, such as the order of samples and attack tasks being presented to an participant, we mix up the order of samples in each attack method, and we switch the order of attack methods before giving them to the participants.

Each participant at our local university is expected to submit about 45 adversarial examples if they successfully complete all four tasks (the examples are not necessarily all successful attacks). We also collect all the attempts they make between two submissions and consider the total number of attempts as the number of queries. We are hoping to gather at least 2000 unique and quality adversarial examples among participants from all tasks.

Stage 2: peer-evaluation After collecting and organising generated adversarial examples, we will recruit an independent group of AMT workers to annotate the data. Similar to (Mozes et al., 2021), we plan to select AMT workers based on their historical performance. That is, AMT workers who have successfully completed more than 1000 human intelligence tasks, and have an approval rate that is higher than 98% would be selected for peer-evaluation. We present AMT workers with a few adversarial examples (approximately 50 examples) generated by humans and/or automated algorithms, randomly and anonymously. Each example is evaluated by three AMT workers to reduce variance.

We aim to recruit 30 qualified AMT workers and hope to gather 1500 unique peer-evaluation results from them for about 500 examples.

6 Conclusion & Future Work

Humans have excellent intuition about language, but weak intuition about deep networks; automated attacks are often the opposite. Given the weak performance of manual attacks and automated attacks against NLP systems, some type of human-AI collaboration is essential to truly evaluate their robustness, and to be prepared for the inevitable attacks from real-world adversaries.

In the future, we will carry out the experiments as designed, and further include the IMDB movie review dataset curated by (Maas et al., 2011). As the texts in the IMDB dataset are often longer, this dataset may provide participants greater flexibility in modifying the examples.

We believe that further study into collaboration methods will lead to a better understanding of adversarial attacks and more robust NLP models. We hope to provide a new benchmark for HITL adversarial learning while we continue exploring other effective human-AI collaboration methods. We hope that our framework will help researchers and practitioners better evaluate the robustness of NLP models to the best attacks that humans and algorithms can construct, and then improve their models by training on these adversarial examples.

Acknowledgement

This work was supported by a grant from the Defense Advanced Research Projects Agency (DARPA), agreement number HR00112090135. This work benefited from access to the University of Oregon high-performance computer, Talapas.

References

Thomas Davidson, Dana Warmsley, Michael W. Macy, and Ingmar Weber. 2017. Automated hate speech detection and the problem of offensive language. In *ICWSM*, pages 512–515.

Jacob Devlin, Ming-Wei Chang, Kenton Lee, and Kristina Toutanova. 2019. BERT: Pre-training of deep bidirectional transformers for language understanding. In *Proceedings of the 2019 Conference of the North American Chapter of the Association for Computational Linguistics: Human Language Technologies, Volume 1 (Long and Short Papers)*, pages 4171–4186, Minneapolis, Minnesota. Association for Computational Linguistics.

Javid Ebrahimi, Anyi Rao, Daniel Lowd, and Dejing Dou. 2018. HotFlip: White-box adversarial examples for text classification. In *Proceedings of the 56th Annual Meeting of the Association for Computational Linguistics (Volume 2: Short Papers)*, pages 31–36, Melbourne, Australia. Association for Computational Linguistics.

Steffen Eger, Gözde Gül Şahin, Andreas Rücklé, Ji-Ung Lee, Claudia Schulz, Mohsen Mesgar, Krishnkant Swarnkar, Edwin Simpson, and Iryna Gurevych. 2019. Text processing like humans do: Visually attacking and shielding NLP systems. In *Proceedings of the 2019 Conference of the North American Chapter of the Association for Computational Linguistics: Human Language Technologies, Volume 1 (Long and Short Papers)*, pages 1634–1647, Minneapolis, Minnesota. Association for Computational Linguistics.

Ji Gao, Jack Lanchantin, Mary Lou Soffa, and Yanjun Qi. 2018. Black-box generation of adversarial text sequences to evade deep learning classifiers. In *2018 IEEE Security and Privacy Workshops (SPW)*, pages 50–56.

Siddhant Garg and Goutham Ramakrishnan. 2020. BAE: BERT-based adversarial examples for text classification. In *Proceedings of the 2020 Conference on Empirical Methods in Natural Language Processing*, pages 6174–6181, Online. Association for Computational Linguistics.

Di Jin, Zhijing Jin, Joey Tianyi Zhou, and Peter Szolovits. 2020. Is BERT really robust? A strong baseline for natural language attack on text classification and entailment. In *Proceedings of the 34th AAAI Conference on Artificial Intelligence, 32nd Innovative Applications of Artificial Intelligence Conference, and 10th AAAI Symposium on Educational Advances in Artificial Intelligence, New York, NY, USA, February 7-12, 2020*, pages 8018–8025. AAAI Press.

Douwe Kiela, Max Bartolo, Yixin Nie, Divyansh Kaushik, Atticus Geiger, Zhengxuan Wu, Bertie Vidgen, Grusha Prasad, Amanpreet Singh, Pratik Ringshia, Zhiyi Ma, Tristan Thrush, Sebastian Riedel, Zeerak Waseem, Pontus Stenetorp, Robin Jia, Mohit Bansal, Christopher Potts, and Adina Williams. 2021. Dynabench: Rethinking benchmarking in NLP. In *Proceedings of the 2021 Conference of the North American Chapter of the Association for Computational Linguistics: Human Language Technologies*, pages 4110–4124.

Linyang Li, Ruotian Ma, Qipeng Guo, Xiangyang Xue, and Xipeng Qiu. 2020. BERT-ATTACK: Adversarial attack against BERT using BERT. In *Proceedings of the 2020 Conference on Empirical Methods in Natural Language Processing (EMNLP)*, pages 6193–6202, Online. Association for Computational Linguistics.

Yinhan Liu, Myle Ott, Naman Goyal, Jingfei Du, Mandar Joshi, Danqi Chen, Omer Levy, Mike Lewis, Luke Zettlemoyer, and Veselin Stoyanov. 2019. RoBERTa: A robustly optimized BERT pretraining approach. *CoRR*, abs/1907.11692.

Andrew L. Maas, Raymond E. Daly, Peter T. Pham, Dan Huang, Andrew Y. Ng, and Christopher Potts. 2011. Learning word vectors for sentiment analysis. In *Proceedings of the 49th Annual Meeting of the Association for Computational Linguistics: Human Language Technologies*, pages 142–150, Portland, Oregon, USA. Association for Computational Linguistics.

John Morris, Eli Lifland, Jin Yong Yoo, Jake Grigsby, Di Jin, and Yanjun Qi. 2020. TextAttack: A framework for adversarial attacks, data augmentation, and adversarial training in NLP. In *Proceedings of the 2020 Conference on Empirical Methods in Natural Language Processing: System Demonstrations*, pages 119–126, Online. Association for Computational Linguistics.

Maximilian Mozes, Max Bartolo, Pontus Stenetorp, Bennett Kleinberg, and Lewis Griffin. 2021. Contrasting human- and machine-generated word-level adversarial examples for text classification. In *Proceedings of the 2021 Conference on Empirical Methods in Natural Language Processing*, pages 8258–8270, Online and Punta Cana, Dominican Republic. Association for Computational Linguistics.

Yixin Nie, Adina Williams, Emily Dinan, Mohit Bansal, Jason Weston, and Douwe Kiela. 2020. Adversarial nli: A new benchmark for natural language understanding. In *ACL*, pages 4885–4901.

Shuhuai Ren, Yihe Deng, Kun He, and Wanxiang Che. 2019. Generating natural language adversarial examples through probability weighted word saliency. In *Proceedings of the 57th Annual Meeting of the Association for Computational Linguistics*, pages 1085–1097.

Richard Socher, Alex Perelygin, Jean Wu, Jason Chuang, Christopher D. Manning, Andrew Ng, and Christopher Potts. 2013. Recursive deep models for semantic compositionality over a sentiment treebank. In *Proceedings of the 2013 Conference on Empirical Methods in Natural Language Processing*, pages 1631–1642, Seattle, Washington, USA. Association for Computational Linguistics.

Eric Wallace and Jordan Boyd-Graber. 2018. Trick me if you can: Adversarial writing of trivia challenge questions. In *Proceedings of ACL 2018, Student Research Workshop*, pages 127–133, Melbourne, Australia. Association for Computational Linguistics.

Eric Wallace, Shi Feng, Nikhil Kandpal, Matt Gardner, and Sameer Singh. 2019. Universal adversarial triggers for attacking and analyzing NLP. In *Proceedings of the 2019 Conference on Empirical Methods in Natural Language Processing and the 9th International Joint Conference on Natural Language Processing, Hong Kong, China, November 3-7, 2019*, pages 2153–2162. Association for Computational Linguistics.

Boxin Wang, Chejian Xu, Shuohang Wang, Zhe Gan, Yu Cheng, Jianfeng Gao, Ahmed Hassan Awadallah, and Bo Li. 2021a. Adversarial GLUE: A multitask benchmark for robustness evaluation of language models. In *Thirty-fifth Conference on Neural Information Processing Systems Datasets and Benchmarks Track (Round 2)*.

Xiao Wang, Qin Liu, Tao Gui, Qi Zhang, Yicheng Zou, Xin Zhou, Jiacheng Ye, Yongxin Zhang, Rui Zheng, Zexiong Pang, Qinzhuo Wu, Zhengyan Li, Chong Zhang, Ruotian Ma, Zichu Fei, Ruijian Cai, Jun Zhao, Xingwu Hu, Zhiheng Yan, Yiding Tan, Yuan Hu, Qiyuan Bian, Zhihua Liu, Shan Qin, Bolin Zhu, Xiaoyu Xing, Jinlan Fu, Yue Zhang, Minlong Peng, Xiaoqing Zheng, Yaqian Zhou, Zhongyu Wei, Xipeng Qiu, and Xuanjing Huang. 2021b. TextFlint: Unified multilingual robustness evaluation toolkit for natural language processing. In *Proceedings of the 59th Annual Meeting of the Association for Computational Linguistics and the 11th International Joint Conference on Natural Language Processing: System Demonstrations*, pages 347–355, Online. Association for Computational Linguistics.

Zhouhang Xie, Jonathan Brophy, Adam Noack, Wencong You, Kalyani Asthana, Carter Perkins, Sabrina Reis, Zayd Hammoudeh, Daniel Lowd, and Sameer Singh. 2021. What models know about their attackers: Deriving attacker information from latent representations. In *Proceedings of the 4th BlackboxNLP Workshop on Analyzing and Interpreting Neural Networks for NLP*, pages 69–78, Punta Cana, Dominican Republic. Association for Computational Linguistics.

Zhouhang Xie, Jonathan Brophy, Adam Noack, Wencong You, Kalyani Asthana, Carter Perkins, Sabrina Reis, Sameer Singh, and Daniel Lowd. 2022. Identifying adversarial attacks on text classifiers.

Zhilin Yang, Zihang Dai, Yiming Yang, Jaime Carbonell, Russ R Salakhutdinov, and Quoc V Le. 2019. XLNet: Generalized autoregressive pretraining for language understanding. In *Advances in Neural Information Processing Systems*, volume 32. Curran Associates, Inc.

Yuan Zang, Fanchao Qi, Chenghao Yang, Zhiyuan Liu, Meng Zhang, Qun Liu, and Maosong Sun. 2020. Word-level textual adversarial attacking as combinatorial optimization. In *Proceedings of the 58th Annual Meeting of the Association for Computational Linguistics*, pages 6066–6080, Online. Association for Computational Linguistics.

Guoyang Zeng, Fanchao Qi, Qianrui Zhou, Tingji Zhang, Bairu Hou, Yuan Zang, Zhiyuan Liu, and Maosong Sun. 2021. Openattack: An open-source textual adversarial attack toolkit. In *Proceedings of the 59th Annual Meeting of the Association for Computational Linguistics and the 11th International Joint Conference on Natural Language Processing: System Demonstrations*, pages 363–371.

Yichao Zhou, Jyun-Yu Jiang, Kai-Wei Chang, and Wei Wang. 2019. Learning to discriminate perturbations for blocking adversarial attacks in text classification. In *Proceedings of the 2019 Conference on Empirical Methods in Natural Language Processing and the 9th International Joint Conference on Natural Language Processing (EMNLP-IJCNLP)*, pages 4904–4913, Hong Kong, China. Association for Computational Linguistics.

A Appendix

A.1 User Interface

See Figures 5, 6, and 7 on the next few pages.

A.2 Word Saliency for BAE, TextFooler, and PWWS

We now describe the word salience methods used by BAE, TextFooler, and PWWS. These approaches are first described by (Jin et al., 2020; Ren et al., 2019); we summarize their methods below.

Considering a sentence X consisting of n words $X = \{w_1, w_2, \dots, w_n\}$, and its true label y, BAE and TextFooler simply delete a word w_i and measure the word importance $I_{w_i}, \forall w_i \in X$ for contributing to the model predictive score $P(X)$. Denote the sentence without w_i as $X_{\setminus w_i}$, where

$$X_{\setminus w_i} = X \setminus \{w_i\} = \{w_1, \dots, w_{i-1}, w_{i+1}, \dots, w_n\}.$$

The importance score I_{w_i} is calculated as the difference between the predictive scores before and after deleting word w_i, i.e.

$$I_{w_i} = P(X) - P(X_{\setminus w_i}),$$

if $P(X) = P(X_{\setminus w_i}) = y$;

$$I_{w_i} = (P(y|X) - P(y|X_{\setminus w_i})) + (P(\hat{y}|X_{\setminus w_i}) - P(\hat{y}|X)),$$

if $P(X) = y$ and $P(X_{\setminus w_i}) = \hat{y}$, where $y \neq \hat{y}$.

PWWS first replaces a word w_i with a candidate word w_i^* to form a new sentence $X^* = \{w_1, \dots, w_i^*, \dots, w_n\}$, where w_i^* is the best candidate that changes the predictive probability the most, calculated by

$$w_i^* = argmax_{w_i' \in C} P(y|X) - P(y|X'),$$

where $X' = \{w_1, \dots, w_i', \dots, w_n\}$, and w_i' is a candidate token among all substitute candidates C for word w_i. Therefore, the most significant predictive probability change is obtained by

$$\Delta P_i^* = P(y|X) - P(y|X^*).$$

PWWS then calculates the standard saliency by replacing w_i with an unknown token via

$$S(X, w_i) = P(y|X) - P(y|\hat{X})$$

where $\hat{X} = \{w_1, \dots, unknown, \dots, w_n\}$. A saliency vector $\mathbf{S}(X)$ is obtained by calculating the saliency for every word in the sentence. PWWS finally combines the predictive probability and the saliency vector through a dot product to get a probability weighted saliency score (Ren et al., 2019). That is

$$H(X, X^*, w_i) = \phi \mathbf{S}(X) \cdot \Delta P_i^*,$$

where ϕ is a softmax function. $H(X, X^*, w_i)$ eventually determines the word importance for PWWS.

A.3 Incentive Payment Plan

Each participant at the university is expected to complete the adversarial example generation tasks using all four attack methods for consistency. Therefore, we create an incentive payment plan to motivate participants to work through the four tasks: Auto, Manual, Select, and Saliency. The Auto setting is fairly simple, which we expect participants to finish the task in less than 30 minutes, and we pay \$12/person. The Manual setting is slightly more time-consuming and more difficult,

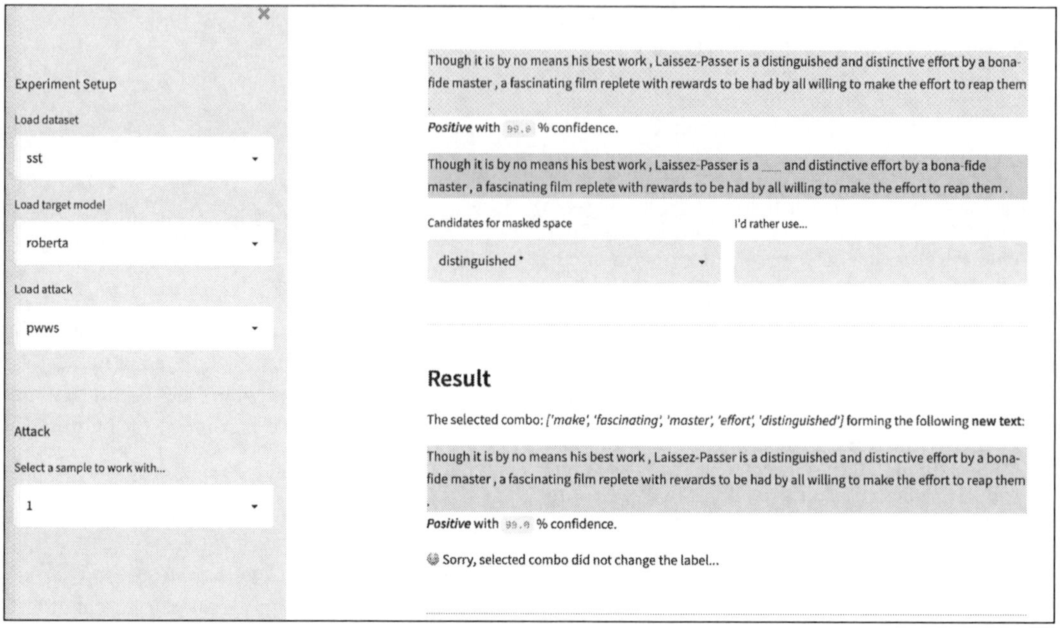

Figure 5: The interface for the Select task

we expect them to finish the task in 60 minutes, and we pay \$28/person. The Select and Saliency may also require some effort and attempts so that we expect them to complete the tasks in 90 minutes, and we pay \$40/person for each task. By doing so, we hope to keep participants interested and motivated throughout the whole process.

We also plan to reward ten participants \$10 who give constructive feedback for our user interface or experiment design through a drawing system. Additionally, we will double the pay for the top three participants who provide the most quality adversarial examples, where the quality is evaluated anonymously on AMT during the peer-evaluation phase.

For peer-evaluation performed on AMT, We will match the market prices and pay \$0.2∼0.25/example to the AMT workers. Peer-evaluation is fairly straightforward, and we estimate that it takes no more than 90 minutes for each AMT worker to complete the task.

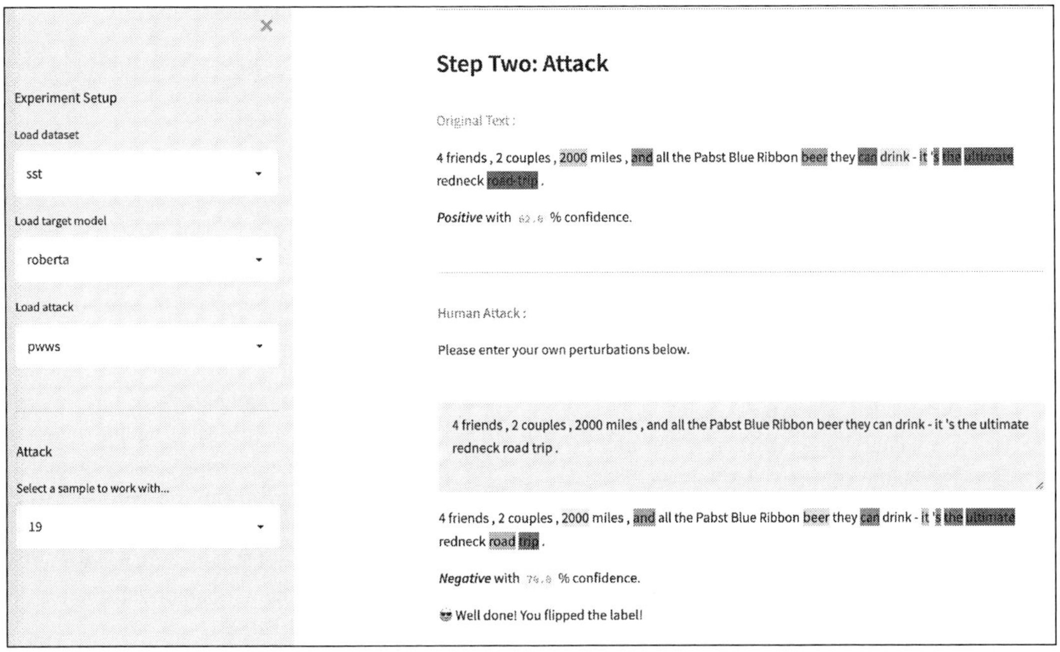

Figure 6: The interface for the Saliency task

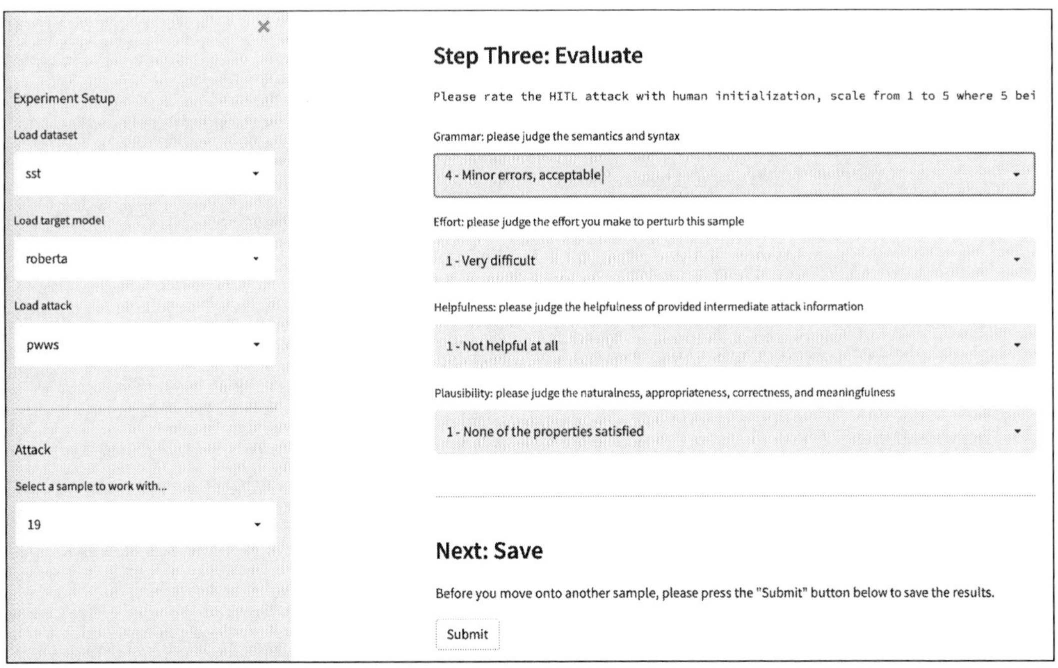

Figure 7: The interface for self-evaluation

Benchmarking for Public Health Surveillance tasks on Social Media with a Domain-Specific Pretrained Language Model

Usman Naseem[1], Byoung Chan Lee[2], Matloob Khushi[1], Jinman Kim[1], Adam G. Dunn[3]
[1]School of Computer Science, University of Sydney, Australia
[2]School of Medicine, University of Sydney, Australia
[3]School of Medical Sciences, University of Sydney, Australia
blee9781@uni.sydney.edu.au
{usman.naseem,matloob.khushi,jinman.kim,adam.dunn}@sydney.edu.au

Abstract

A user-generated text on social media enables health workers to keep track of information, identify possible outbreaks, forecast disease trends, monitor emergency cases, and ascertain disease awareness and response to official health correspondence. This exchange of health information on social media has been regarded as an attempt to enhance public health surveillance (PHS). Despite its potential, the technology is still in its early stages and is not ready for widespread application. Advancements in pretrained language models (PLMs) have facilitated the development of several domain-specific PLMs and a variety of downstream applications. However, there are no PLMs for social media tasks involving PHS. We present and release PHS-BERT, a transformer-based PLM, to identify tasks related to public health surveillance on social media. We compared and benchmarked the performance of PHS-BERT on 25 datasets from different social medial platforms related to 7 different PHS tasks. Compared with existing PLMs that are mainly evaluated on limited tasks, PHS-BERT achieved state-of-the-art performance on all 25 tested datasets, showing that our PLM is robust and generalizable in the common PHS tasks. By making PHS-BERT available[1], we aim to facilitate the community to reduce the computational cost and introduce new baselines for future works across various PHS-related tasks.

1 Introduction

Public health surveillance (PHS) is defined by the World Health Organization[2] as the ongoing, systematic collection, assessment, and understanding of health-related required information for the planning, implementation, and assessment of healthcare (Aiello et al., 2020). PHS aims to design and assist interventions; it acts as a primary warning system in health emergencies (epidemics, i.e., acute events), it reports and records public health interventions (i.e., monitoring health), and it observes and explains the epidemiology of health issues, allowing for the prioritization of necessary details for health policy formulation (i.e., targeting chronic events). Traditional PHS systems are often limited by the time required to collect data, restricting the quick or even instantaneous identification of outbreaks (Hope et al., 2006).

Social media is growingly being used for public health purposes and can disseminate disease risks and interventions and promote wellness and healthcare policy. Social media data provides an abundant source of timely data that can be used for various public health applications, including surveillance, sentiment analysis, health communication, and analyzing the history of a disease, injury, or promote health. Systematic reviews of studies that examine personal health experiences shared online reveal the breadth of application domains, which include infectious diseases and outbreaks (Charles-Smith et al., 2015), illicit drug use (Kazemi et al., 2017), and pharmacovigilance support (Golder et al., 2015). These applied health studies are motivated by their potential in supporting PHS, augmenting adverse event reporting, and as the basis of public health interventions (Dunn et al., 2018).

The use of deep learning in natural language processing (NLP) has advanced the development of pretrained language models (PLMs) that can be used for a wide range of tasks in PHS. However, directly applying the state-of-the-art (SOTA) PLMs such as Bidirectional Encoder Representations from Transformers (BERT) (Devlin et al., 2019), and its variants (Liu et al., 2019; Lan et al., 2019; Sanh et al., 2019; Naseem et al., 2021c) that are trained on general domain corpus (e.g., Bookcorpus, Wikipedia, etc.) may yield poor per-

[1]https://huggingface.co/publichealthsurveillance/PHS-BERT

[2]https://www.euro.who.int/en/health-topics/Health-systems/public-health-services

Proceedings of NLP Power! The First Workshop on Efficient Benchmarking in NLP, pages 22 - 31
May 26, 2022 ©2022 Association for Computational Linguistics

formances on domain-specific tasks. To address this limitation, several domain-specific PLMs have been presented. Some of the well-known in the biomedical field include the following: biomedical BERT (BioBERT) (Lee et al., 2019) and biomedical A Lite BERT (BioALBERT) (Naseem et al., 2020, 2021a). Recently, other domain-specific LMs such as BERTweet (Nguyen et al., 2020) for 3 downstream tasks, i.e., part-of-speech tagging, named-entity-recognition, and text classification and COVID Twitter BERT (CT-BERT) (Müller et al., 2020) for 5 text classification tasks have been trained on datasets from Twitter.

Despite the number of PLMs that have been released, none have been produced specifically for PHS from online text. Furthermore, all these LMs were evaluated with the selected dataset, and therefore their generalizability is unproven. To benchmark and fill the gap, we present PHS-BERT, a new domain-specific contextual PLM trained and fine-tuned to achieve benchmark performance on various PHS tasks on social media. PHS-BERT is trained on a health-related corpus collected from user-generated content. Our work is the first large-scale study to train, release and test a domain-specific PLM for PHS tasks on social media. We demonstrated that PHS-BERT outperforms other SOTA PLMs on 25 datasets from different social media platforms related to 7 different PHS tasks, showing that PHS is robust and generalizable.

2 Related Work

2.1 Pretrained Language Models

Transformer-based PLMs such as BERT (Devlin et al., 2019) and its variants (Liu et al., 2019; Lan et al., 2019) have altered the landscape of research in NLP domain. These PLMs are trained on a huge corpus but may not provide a good representation of specific domains (Müller et al., 2020). To improve the performance in domain-specific tasks, various domain-specific PLMs have been presented. Some of the famous in the biomedical domain are BioBERT (Lee et al., 2019) and BioALBERT (Naseem et al., 2020). Recently, for tasks on social media-specific, other PLMs such as BERTweet (Nguyen et al., 2020), COVID Twitter BERT (CT-BERT) (Müller et al., 2020) have been trained on datasets from Twitter. For various downstream tasks, these domain-specific PLMs were demonstrated to be effective alternatives for PLMs trained on a general corpus for a variety of downstream tasks (Müller et al., 2020). The assumption is that the LMs trained on the user-generated text on Twitter can handle the short and unstructured text in tweets. Despite this progress, their generalizability is unproven, and there is no PLM for public health surveillance using social media.

2.2 NLP for Public Health Surveillance

The use of social media in conjunction with advances in NLP for PHS tasks is a growing area of study (Paul and Dredze, 2017). NLP can assist researchers in the surveillance of mental disorders, such as identifying depression diagnosis, assessing suicide risk and stress identification, vaccine hesitancy and refusal, identifying common health-related misconceptions, sentiment analysis, and the health-related behaviors they support (Naseem et al., 2022a,b).

Rao et al. (2020) presented a hierarchical method that used BERT with attention-based BiGRU and achieved competitive performance for depression detection. For vaccine-related sentiment classification, Zhang et al. (2020) classified tweet-level HPV vaccine sentiment using three transfer learning techniques (ELMo, GPT, and BERT) and found that a finely tuned BERT produced the best results. Biddle et al. (2020) presented a method (BiLSTM-Senti) that leveraged contextual word embeddings (BERT) with word-level sentiment to improve performance. Naseem et al. (2021b) presented a model that uses domain-specific LM and captures commonsense knowledge into a context-aware bidirectional gated recurrent network. Sawhney et al. (2021) presented an ordinal hierarchical attention model for Suicide Risk Assessment where text embeddings obtained by Longformer were fed to BiLSTM with attention and ordinal loss as an objective function. However, there is no PLM trained on health-related text collected from social media that directly benefit the applications related to PHS.

3 Method

PHS-BERT has the same architecture as BERT. Fig. 1 illustrates an overview of pretraining, fine-tuning, and datasets used in this study. We describe BERT and then the pretraining and fine-tuning process employed in PHS-BERT.

3.1 BERT

PHS-BERT has the same architecture as BERT. BERT was trained on 2 tasks: mask language mod-

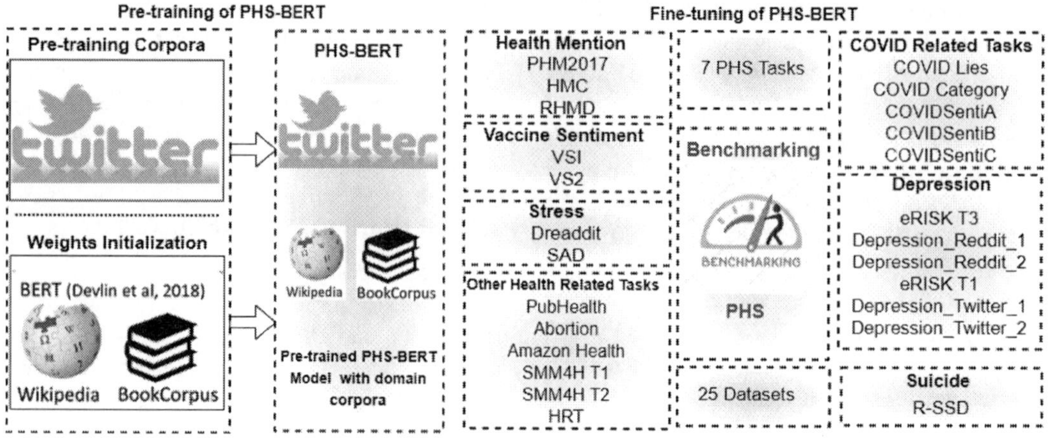

Figure 1: An overview of pretraining, fine-tuning, and the various tasks and datasets used in PHS benchmarking

eling (MLM) (15% of tokens were masked and next sentence prediction (NSP) (Given the first sentence, BERT was trained to predict whether a selected next sentence was likely or not). BERT is pretrained on Wikipedia and BooksCorpus and needs task-specific fine-tuning. Pretrained BERT models include $BERT_{Base}$ (12 layers, 12 attention heads, and 110 million parameters), as well as $BERT_{Large}$ (24 layers, 16 attention heads, and 340 million parameters).

3.2 Pretraining of PHS-BERT

We followed the standard pretraining protocols of BERT and initialized PHS-BERT with weights from BERT during the training phase instead of training from scratch and used the uncased version of the BERT model.

PHS-BERT is the first domain-specific LM for tasks related to PHS and is trained on a corpus of health-related tweets that were crawled via the Twitter API. Focusing on the tasks related to PHS, keywords used to collect pretraining corpus are set to disease, symptom, vaccine, and mental health-related words in English. Pre-processing methods similar to those used in previous works (Müller et al., 2020; Nguyen et al., 2020) were employed prior to training. Retweet tags were deleted from the raw corpus, and URLs and usernames were replaced with HTTP-URL and @USER, respectively. Additionally, the Python emoji[3] library was used to replace all emoticons with their associated meanings. The HuggingFace[4], an open-source python library, was used to segment tweets. Each sequence of BERT LM inputs is converted to 50,265 vocabulary tokens. Twitter posts are restricted to 200 characters, and during the training and evaluation phase, we used a batch size of 8. Distributed training was performed on a TPU v3-8.

3.3 Fine-tuning for downstream tasks

We applied the pretrained PHS-BERT in the binary and multi-class classification of different PHS tasks such as stress, suicide, depression, anorexia, health mention classification, vaccine, and covid related misinformation and sentiment analysis. We fine-tuned the PLMs in downstream tasks. Specifically, we used the `ktrain` library (Maiya, 2020) to fine-tune each model independently for each dataset. We used the embedding of the special token `[CLS]` of the last hidden layer as the final feature of the input text. We adopted the multilayer perceptron (MLP) with the hyperbolic tangent activation function and used Adam optimizer (Kingma and Ba, 2014). The models are trained with a one cycle policy (Smith, 2017) at a maximum learning rate of 2e-05 with momentum cycled between 0.85 and 0.95.

4 Experimental Analysis

4.1 Tasks and Datasets

We evaluated and benchmarked the performance of PHS-BERT on 7 different PHS classification tasks (e.g., stress, suicidal ideation, depression, health mention, vaccine, covid related sentiment analysis, and other health-related tasks) collected from popular social platforms (e.g., Reddit and Twitter). We used 25 datasets (see Table 1) crawled from social media platforms (e.g., Reddit and Twitter). We relied on the datasets that are widely used in the community and described each of these tasks and

[3]https://pypi.org/project/emoji/

[4]https://huggingface.co/

Table 1: Statistics of the datasets used. We used the Stratified 5-Folds cross-validation (CV) strategy for train/test split if original datasets do not have an official train/test split.

Task (Classification)	Dataset	Platform	# of Samples	# of Classes	Training Strategy Used
Suicide	R-SSD (Cao et al., 2019)	Reddit	500 Users	5	Stratified 5-Folds CV
Stress	Dreaddit (Turcan and McKeown, 2019)	Reddit	3553 Posts	2	Official Split
	SAD (Mauriello et al., 2021)	SMS-like	6850 SMS	2	Official Split
Health Mention	PHM (Karisani and Agichtein, 2018)	Twitter	4635 Posts	4	Stratified 5-Folds CV
	PHM (Karisani and Agichtein, 2018)	Twitter	4635 Posts	2	Stratified 5-Folds CV
	HMC2019 (Biddle et al., 2020)	Twitter	15393 Posts	3	Stratified 5-Folds CV
	RHMD (Naseem et al., 2022b)	Reddit	3553 Posts	4	Stratified 5-Folds CV
Vaccine Sentiment	VS1 (Dunn et al., 2020)	Twitter	9261 Posts	3	Stratified 5-Folds CV
	VS2 (Müller and Salathé, 2019)	Twitter	18522 Posts	3	Stratified 5-Folds CV
COVID Related	Covid Lies (Hossain et al., 2020)	Twitter	3204 Posts	3	Stratified 5-Folds CV
	Covid Category (Müller et al., 2020)	Twitter	4328 Posts	2	Stratified 5-Folds CV
	COVIDSentiA (Naseem et al., 2021d)	Twitter	30000 Posts	3	Stratified 5-Folds CV
	COVIDSentiB (Naseem et al., 2021d)	Twitter	30000 Posts	3	Stratified 5-Folds CV
	COVIDSentiC (Naseem et al., 2021d)	Twitter	30000 Posts	3	Stratified 5-Folds CV
Depression	eRISK T3 (Losada and Crestani, 2016)	Reddit	190 Users	4	Stratified 5-Folds CV
	Depression_Reddit_1 (Naseem et al., 2022a)	Reddit	3553 Posts	4	Stratified 5-Folds CV
	eRISK19 T1 (Losada and Crestani, 2016)	Reddit	2810 Users	2	Official Split
	Depression_Reddit_2 (Pirina and Çöltekin, 2018)	Reddit	1841 Posts	2	Stratified 5-Folds CV
	Depression_Twitter_1	Twitter	1793 Posts	3	Stratified 5-Folds CV
	Depression_Twitter_2	Twitter	10314 Posts	2	Stratified 5-Folds CV
Other Health related	PubHealth (Kotonya and Toni, 2020)	News Websites	12251 Posts	4	Official Split
	Abortion (Mohammad et al., 2016)	Twitter	933 Posts	3	Official Split
	Amazon Health (He and McAuley, 2016)	Amazon	2003 Posts	4	Official Split
	SMM4H T1 (Weissenbacher et al., 2018)	Twitter	14954 Posts	2	Official Split
	SMM4H T2 (Weissenbacher et al., 2018)	Twitter	13498 Posts	3	Official Split
	HRT (Paul and Dredze, 2012)	Twitter	2754 Posts	4	Stratified 5-Folds CV

datasets. Below we briefly discussed each task and dataset used in our study (appendix A for details).

1. **Suicide:** The widespread use of social media for expressing personal thoughts and emotions makes it a valuable resource for assessing suicide risk on social media. We used the following dataset to evaluate the performance of our model. We used R-SSD (Cao et al., 2019) dataset to evaluate the performance of our model on suicide risk detection.

2. **Stress**: It is desirable to detect stress early in order to address the growing problem of stress. To evaluate stress detection using social media, we evaluated PHS-BERT on the Dreaddit (Turcan and McKeown, 2019) and SAD (Mauriello et al., 2021) datasets.

3. **Health mention:** In social media platforms, people often use disease or symptom terms in ways other than to describe their health. In data-driven PHS, the health mention classification task aims to identify posts where users discuss health conditions rather than using disease and symptom terms for other reasons. We used PHM (Karisani and Agichtein, 2018), HMC2019 (Biddle et al., 2020) and RHMD[5] health mention-related datasets.

4. **Vaccine sentiment:** Vaccines are a critical component of public health. On the other hand, vaccine hesitancy and refusal can result in clusters of low vaccination coverage, diminishing the effectiveness of vaccination programs. Identifying vaccine-related concerns on social media makes it possible to determine emerging risks to vaccine acceptance. We used VS1 (Dunn et al., 2020) and VS2 (Müller and Salathé, 2019) vaccine-related Twitter datasets to show the effectiveness of our model.

5. **COVID related**: Due to the ongoing pandemic, there is a higher need for tools to identify COVID-19-related misinformation and sentiment on social media. Misinformation can have a negative impact on public opinion and endanger the lives of millions of people if precautions are not taken. We used COVID Lies (Hossain et al., 2020), Covid category (Müller et al., 2020), and COVIDSenti (Naseem et al., 2021d)[6] datasets to test our model.

6. **Depression**: User-generated text on social media has been actively explored for its feasibility in the early identification of depression. We used following eRisk T3 (Losada and Crestani, 2016), eRisk T1 (Losada and Crestani, 2016), Depression_Reddit_1 (Naseem et al.,

[5] https://github.com/usmaann/RHMD-Health-Mention-Dataset

[6] we used 3 subsets (COVIDSentiA, COVIDSentiB and COVIDSentiC)

2022a)[7], Depression_Reddit_2 (Pirina and Çöltekin, 2018), Depression_Twitter_1[8], and Depression_Twitter_2[9] depression-related datasets in our experiments.

7. **Other health related tasks:** We also evaluated the performance of our PHS-BERT on other health-related 6 datasets. We used PUBHEALTH (Kotonya and Toni, 2020), Abortion (Mohammad et al., 2016)[10], Amazon Health dataset (He and McAuley, 2016), SMM4H T1 (Weissenbacher et al., 2018), SMM4H T2 (Weissenbacher et al., 2018) and HRT (Paul and Dredze, 2012).

4.2 Evaluation Metric

To evaluate the performance, we used F1-score and the relative improvement in marginal performance (ΔMP) used in a previous similar study (Müller et al., 2020).

4.3 Baselines

We evaluated the performance of PHS-BERT with various SOTA existing PLMs in different domains. We compared the performance with BERT (Devlin et al., 2019), ALBERT (Lan et al., 2019), and DistilBERT (Sanh et al., 2019) pretrained with general corpus, BioBERT (Lee et al., 2019) pretrained in the biomedical domain, CT-BERT (Müller et al., 2020) and BERTweet (Nguyen et al., 2020) pretrained on covid related tweets and MentalBERT (Ji et al., 2021) pretrained on corpus from Reddit from mental health-related subreddits.

4.4 Results

Table 2 summarizes the results of the presented PHS-BERT in comparison to the baselines. We observe that the performance of PHS-BERT is higher than SOTA PLMs on all tested tasks and datasets. Below we discuss the performance comparison of PHS-BERT with BERT and the results of the second-best PLM.

Suicide Ideation Task: We observed that the marginal increases in performance of PHS-BERT is 18.45% when compared to BERT and 12.79% when compared to second best results.

[7]https://github.com/usmaann/Depression_Severity_Dataset

[8]https://github.com/AshwanthRamji/Depression-Sentiment-Analysis-with-Twitter-Data

[9]https://github.com/viritaromero/Detecting-Depression-in-Tweets

[10]The SemEval 2016 stance detection task has 5 target domains. We used the legalization of abortion.

Stress Detection Task: We showed that PHS-BERT achieved higher performance than the best baseline on both datasets. The average marginal increase in performance of PHS-BERT is 3.80% compared to BERT and 2% when compared to second-best results.

Health Mention Task: PHS-BERT outperformed all the baselines on all health mention classification datasets. The average marginal increase in performance of PHS-BERT is 3.34% compared to BERT and 1.76% when compared to second-best results.

Depression Detection Task: We demonstrated that PHS-BERT outperformed all the baselines on all 6 depression datasets to identify depression on social media. We observed that the average marginal increase in performance of PHS-BERT is 6.03% compared to BERT and 2.76% when compared to second-best results.

Vaccine Sentiment Task: For the vaccine sentiment task, PHS-BERT achieved higher performance compared to all baselines on both datasets. Results showed that the average marginal increase in performance of PHS-BERT is 7.70% than BERT and 0.34% compared to second-best results.

COVID Related Task: PHS-BERT outperformed all baselines on all 5 datasets for COVID-related tasks. On average, the marginal increase in performance is 11.82% compared to BERT and 4.471% compared to the second-best results.

Other Health Related Task: We showed that PHS-BERT outperformed all the baselines on all 6 datasets to identify other health-related tasks on social media. We observed that the average marginal increase in performance of PHS-BERT is 11.82% compared to BERT and 4.71% when compared to second-best results.

4.5 Discussion

We demonstrated the effectiveness of our domain-specific PLM on a downstream classification task related to PHS. Compared to previous SOTA PLMs, PHS-BERT improved the performance on all datasets (7 tasks). Our experimental results showed that BERT, a PLM trained in the general domain, gets competitive results on downstream classification tasks. However, for domain-specific tasks, general domain PLMs (BERT, ALBERT, distilBERT) might need more training on relevant corpora to achieve better performance on the domain-specific downstream classification task. Further, we observed that using a domain-specific PLM trained

Table 2: Comparison of PHS-BERT (Ours) v/s SOTA PLMs. Best results (F1-score) are represented in bold, whereas second-best results are underlined. ΔMP_{BERT} and ΔMP_{SB} represent the marginal increase in performance compared to the BERT and the second-best PLM (under-lined).

Dataset	BERT	ALBERT	distilBERT	CT-BERT	BioBERT	BERTweet	MentalBERT	Ours	ΔMP_{BERT}	ΔMP_{SB}
Suicide Ideation Task										
R-SSD	25.72	23.07	26.96	18.67	23.51	24.82	17.35	**30.28**	18.45↑	12.79↑
Stress Detection Task										
Dreaddit	78.55	79.43	78.22	81.46	78.34	80.03	80.89	**82.89**	5.60↑	1.78↑
SAD	92.66	91.11	91.47	91.11	93.92	94.17	93.23	**94.75**	2.28↑	0.62↑
Average	85.61	85.27	84.85	86.29	86.13	87.10	87.06	**88.82**	3.80↑	2.00↑
Health Mention Task										
PHM (Multi-class)	86.21	80.05	85.06	82.02	82.22	85.59	87.76	**89.38**	3.72↑	1.87↑
PHM (Binary)	91.89	90.53	90.64	92.17	89.62	92.12	92.29	**93.27**	1.52↑	1.07↑
HMC2019	88.99	87.22	88.01	90.82	86.27	90.65	90.17	**91.71**	3.09↑	0.99↑
RHMD	74.20	69.02	73.22	72.87	72.25	74.66	75.28	**77.16**	5.48↑	2.53 ↑
Average	85.07	81.71	84.23	84.47	82.59	85.76	86.38	**87.38**	3.34↑	1.76 ↑
Depression Detection Task										
eRisk T3	64.56	64.78	67.33	63.17	64.86	63.56	67.75	**68.98**	6.95↑	1.84↑
Depression_Reddit_1	22.39	21.09	21.95	24.21	24.00	20.84	21.95	**28.75**	29.73↑	19.56↑
eRisk T1	93.72	93.79	93.34	86.74	91.73	91.92	94.30	**94.52**	0.86↑	0.24↑
Depression_Reddit_2	91.33	90.72	91.01	68.16	90.53	91.75	92.70	**93.36**	2.25↑	0.72↑
Depression_Twitter_1	64.17	51.70	66.71	57.11	64.12	64.24	72.95	**76.18**	19.01↑	4.49↑
Depression_Twitter_2	96.99	96.79	96.70	96.96	96.59	96.87	97.09	**97.12**	0.14↑	0.03↑
Average	72.19	69.81	72.84	66.06	71.97	71.53	74.46	**76.49**	6.03↑	2.76↑
Vaccine Sentiment Task										
VS1	74.14	70.00	73.95	79.92	73.30	76.81	71.56	**79.96**	7.96↑	0.05↑
VS2	76.60	74.82	75.91	81.73	76.77	79.10	77.65	**82.24**	7.46↑	0.63↑
Average	75.37	72.41	74.93	80.84	75.04	77.96	74.61	**81.10**	7.70↑	0.34↑
COVID Related Task										
Covid Lies	92.96	91.53	92.14	92.24	93.79	91.07	94.60	**95.35**	2.60↑	0.80↑
COVID Category	93.98	93.94	94.35	95.29	93.72	93.45	94.97	**95.83**	1.99↑	0.57↑
COVIDSentiA	90.90	90.81	90.90	78.96	90.41	66.30	91.55	**93.97**	3.41↑	2.67↑
COVIDSentiB	91.31	89.88	91.06	86.85	91.02	89.46	92.06	**93.44**	2.36↑	1.52↑
COVIDSentiC	91.24	83.72	90.77	84.83	90.55	61.78	91.66	**93.11**	2.03↑	1.60↑
Average	92.08	89.98	91.84	87.63	91.90	80.41	92.97	**94.34**	2.48↑	1.49↑
Other Health Related Task										
PubHealth	60.30	61.43	60.77	63.97	58.85	60.57	57.30	**64.77**	7.54↑	1.27↑
Abortion	58.79	58.59	68.09	70.39	62.53	62.82	63.03	**72.31**	23.40↑	2.77↑
Amazon Health	63.45	63.18	62.30	54.84	60.27	65.50	65.57	**68.09**	7.43↑	3.90↑
SMM4H T1	33.33	33.86	35.80	45.50	39.45	45.87	39.81	**46.49**	40.71↑	1.38↑
SMM4H T2	75.54	72.76	75.12	79.19	73.43	80.20	77.54	**80.34**	6.44↑	0.18↑
HRT	78.67	76.97	78.35	80.90	76.13	80.48	80.46	**81.12**	3.15↑	0.28↑
Average	61.68	61.13	63.41	65.80	61.78	65.91	63.95	**68.85**	11.82↑	4.71↑

on biomedical corpora (BioBERT) is less effective than pretraining on the target domain. We also observed that using CT-BERT, BERTweet, and MentalBERT, which are trained on social media-based text, performs better compared to PLMs trained in the general and biomedical domain. These results also demonstrated the effectiveness of training in a target domain. In particular, CT-BERT has the second-best performance on 9 datasets, and MentalBERT has the second-best performance on 13 datasets. The results of domain-specific PLMs demonstrated that continued pretraining in the relevant domain improves performance on downstream tasks.

5 Conclusion

We present PHS-BERT, a domain-specific PLM trained on health-related social media data. Our results demonstrate that using domain-specific corpora to train general domain LMs improves performance on PHS tasks. On all 25 datasets related to 7 different PHS tasks, PHS-BERT outperforms previous state-of-the-art PLMs. We expect that the PHS-BERT PLM will benefit the development of new applications based on PHS NLP tasks.

Ethics and Societal Impact

Ethics: No additional ethics approval was sought for the analysis of data in this study because data were drawn from already published studies.

Societal Impact: We train and release a PLM to accelerate the automatic identification of tasks related to PHS on social media. Our work aims to develop a new computational method for screening users in need of early intervention and is not intended to use in clinical settings or as a diagnostic tool.

Reproducibility: For reproducibility and future works, PHS-BERT is publicly released and is available at `https://huggingface.co/publichealthsurveillance/PHS-BERT`.

References

Allison E Aiello, Audrey Renson, and Paul N Zivich. 2020. Social media–and internet-based disease surveillance for public health. *Annual review of public health*, 41:101–118.

Aaron T Beck, Calvin H Ward, Mock Mendelson, Jeremiah Mock, and John Erbaugh. 1961. An inventory for measuring depression. *Archives of general psychiatry*, 4(6):561–571.

Rhys Biddle, Aditya Joshi, Shaowu Liu, Cecile Paris, and Guandong Xu. 2020. Leveraging sentiment distributions to distinguish figurative from literal health reports on twitter. In *Proceedings of The Web Conference 2020*, pages 1217–1227.

Lei Cao, Huijun Zhang, Ling Feng, Zihan Wei, Xin Wang, Ningyun Li, and Xiaohao He. 2019. Latent suicide risk detection on microblog via suicide-oriented word embeddings and layered attention. *arXiv preprint arXiv:1910.12038*.

Lauren E Charles-Smith, Tera L Reynolds, Mark A Cameron, Mike Conway, Eric HY Lau, Jennifer M Olsen, Julie A Pavlin, Mika Shigematsu, Laura C Streichert, Katie J Suda, et al. 2015. Using social media for actionable disease surveillance and outbreak management: a systematic literature review. *PloS one*, 10(10):e0139701.

Jacob Devlin, Ming-Wei Chang, Kenton Lee, and Kristina Toutanova. 2019. BERT: Pre-training of deep bidirectional transformers for language understanding. In *Proceedings of the 2019 Conference of the North American Chapter of the Association for Computational Linguistics: Human Language Technologies, Volume 1 (Long and Short Papers)*, pages 4171–4186, Minneapolis, Minnesota. Association for Computational Linguistics.

Adam G Dunn, Kenneth D Mandl, and Enrico Coiera. 2018. Social media interventions for precision public health: promises and risks. *NPJ digital medicine*, 1(1):1–4.

Adam G Dunn, Didi Surian, Jason Dalmazzo, Dana Rezazadegan, Maryke Steffens, Amalie Dyda, Julie Leask, Enrico Coiera, Aditi Dey, and Kenneth D Mandl. 2020. Limited role of bots in spreading vaccine-critical information among active twitter users in the united states: 2017–2019. *American Journal of Public Health*, 110(S3):S319–S325.

Su Golder, Gill Norman, and Yoon K Loke. 2015. Systematic review on the prevalence, frequency and comparative value of adverse events data in social media. *British journal of clinical pharmacology*, 80(4):878.

Ruining He and Julian McAuley. 2016. Ups and downs: Modeling the visual evolution of fashion trends with one-class collaborative filtering. In *proceedings of the 25th international conference on world wide web*, pages 507–517.

Kirsty Hope, David N Durrheim, Edouard Tursan d'Espaignet, and Craig Dalton. 2006. Syndromic surveillance: is it a useful tool for local outbreak detection?

Tamanna Hossain, Robert L Logan IV, Arjuna Ugarte, Yoshitomo Matsubara, Sean Young, and Sameer Singh. 2020. Covidlies: Detecting covid-19 misinformation on social media. In *Proceedings of the 1st Workshop on NLP for COVID-19 (Part 2) at EMNLP 2020*.

Shaoxiong Ji, Tianlin Zhang, Luna Ansari, Jie Fu, Prayag Tiwari, and Erik Cambria. 2021. Mentalbert: Publicly available pretrained language models for mental healthcare. *arXiv preprint arXiv:2110.15621*.

Payam Karisani and Eugene Agichtein. 2018. Did you really just have a heart attack? towards robust detection of personal health mentions in social media. In *Proceedings of the 2018 World Wide Web Conference*, pages 137–146.

Donna M Kazemi, Brian Borsari, Maureen J Levine, and Beau Dooley. 2017. Systematic review of surveillance by social media platforms for illicit drug use. *Journal of Public Health*, 39(4):763–776.

Diederik Kingma and Jimmy Ba. 2014. Adam: A method for stochastic optimization. *arXiv preprint arXiv:1412.6980*.

Neema Kotonya and Francesca Toni. 2020. Explainable automated fact-checking for public health claims. *CoRR*, abs/2010.09926.

Zhenzhong Lan, Mingda Chen, Sebastian Goodman, Kevin Gimpel, Piyush Sharma, and Radu Soricut. 2019. Albert: A lite bert for self-supervised learning of language representations.

Jinhyuk Lee, Wonjin Yoon, Sungdong Kim, Donghyeon Kim, Sunkyu Kim, Chan Ho So, and Jaewoo Kang. 2019. Biobert: a pre-trained biomedical language representation model for biomedical text mining.

Yinhan Liu, Myle Ott, Naman Goyal, Jingfei Du, Mandar Joshi, Danqi Chen, Omer Levy, Mike Lewis, Luke Zettlemoyer, and Veselin Stoyanov. 2019. Roberta: A robustly optimized bert pretraining approach.

David E Losada and Fabio Crestani. 2016. A test collection for research on depression and language use. In *International Conference of the Cross-Language Evaluation Forum for European Languages*, pages 28–39. Springer.

Arun S. Maiya. 2020. ktrain: A low-code library for augmented machine learning. *arXiv*, arXiv:2004.10703 [cs.LG].

Matthew Louis Mauriello, Thierry Lincoln, Grace Hon, Dorien Simon, Dan Jurafsky, and Pablo Paredes. 2021. Sad: A stress annotated dataset for recognizing everyday stressors in sms-like conversational systems. In *Extended Abstracts of the 2021 CHI Conference on Human Factors in Computing Systems*, pages 1–7.

Saif Mohammad, Svetlana Kiritchenko, Parinaz Sobhani, Xiaodan Zhu, and Colin Cherry. 2016. SemEval-2016 task 6: Detecting stance in tweets. In *Proceedings of the 10th International Workshop on Semantic Evaluation (SemEval-2016)*, pages 31–41, San Diego, California. Association for Computational Linguistics.

Danielle L Mowery, Craig Bryan, and Mike Conway. 2015. Towards developing an annotation scheme for depressive disorder symptoms: A preliminary study using twitter data. In *Proceedings of the 2nd Workshop on Computational Linguistics and Clinical Psychology: From Linguistic Signal to Clinical Reality*, pages 89–98.

Martin Müller, Marcel Salathé, and Per E Kummervold. 2020. Covid-twitter-bert: A natural language processing model to analyse covid-19 content on twitter. *arXiv preprint arXiv:2005.07503*.

Martin M Müller and Marcel Salathé. 2019. Crowdbreaks: Tracking health trends using public social media data and crowdsourcing. *Frontiers in public health*, 7:81.

Usman Naseem, Adam G Dunn, Matloob Khushi, and Jinman Kim. 2021a. Benchmarking for biomedical natural language processing tasks with a domain specific albert. *arXiv preprint arXiv:2107.04374*.

Usman Naseem, Adam G. Dunn, Jinman Kim, and Matloob Khushi. 2022a. Early identification of depression severity levels on reddit using ordinal classification. In *Proceedings of the Web Conference 2022*, pages 1–10.

Usman Naseem, Matloob Khushi, Jinman Kim, and Adam G Dunn. 2021b. Classifying vaccine sentiment tweets by modelling domain-specific representation and commonsense knowledge into context-aware attentive gru. *arXiv preprint arXiv:2106.09589*.

Usman Naseem, Matloob Khushi, Vinay Reddy, Sakthivel Rajendran, Imran Razzak, and Jinman Kim. 2020. Bioalbert: A simple and effective pre-trained language model for biomedical named entity recognition. *arXiv preprint arXiv:2009.09223*.

Usman Naseem, Jinman Kim, Matloob Khushi, and Adam G. Dunn. 2022b. Identification of disease or symptom terms in reddit to improve health mention classification. In *Proceedings of the Web Conference 2022*, pages 11–19.

Usman Naseem, Imran Razzak, Shah Khalid Khan, and Mukesh Prasad. 2021c. A comprehensive survey on word representation models: From classical to state-of-the-art word representation language models. *Transactions on Asian and Low-Resource Language Information Processing*, 20(5):1–35.

Usman Naseem, Imran Razzak, Matloob Khushi, Peter W Eklund, and Jinman Kim. 2021d. Covidsenti: A large-scale benchmark twitter data set for covid-19 sentiment analysis. *IEEE Transactions on Computational Social Systems*, 8(4):1003–1015.

Dat Quoc Nguyen, Thanh Vu, and Anh Tuan Nguyen. 2020. Bertweet: A pre-trained language model for english tweets. *arXiv preprint arXiv:2005.10200*.

Michael J Paul and Mark Dredze. 2012. A model for mining public health topics from twitter. *Health*, 11(16-16):1.

Michael J Paul and Mark Dredze. 2017. Social monitoring for public health. *Synthesis Lectures on Information Concepts, Retrieval, and Services*, 9(5):1–183.

Inna Pirina and Çağrı Çöltekin. 2018. Identifying depression on reddit: The effect of training data. In *Proceedings of the 2018 EMNLP Workshop SMM4H: The 3rd Social Media Mining for Health Applications Workshop & Shared Task*, pages 9–12.

Guozheng Rao, Chengxia Peng, Li Zhang, Xin Wang, and Zhiyong Feng. 2020. A knowledge enhanced ensemble learning model for mental disorder detection on social media. In *International Conference on Knowledge Science, Engineering and Management*, pages 181–192. Springer.

Victor Sanh, Lysandre Debut, Julien Chaumond, and Thomas Wolf. 2019. Distilbert, a distilled version of bert: smaller, faster, cheaper and lighter. *arXiv preprint arXiv:1910.01108*.

Ramit Sawhney, Harshit Joshi, Saumya Gandhi, and Rajiv Ratn Shah. 2021. Towards ordinal suicide ideation detection on social media. In *Proceedings of the 14th ACM International Conference on Web Search and Data Mining*, pages 22–30.

Leslie N Smith. 2017. Cyclical learning rates for training neural networks. In *2017 IEEE winter conference on applications of computer vision (WACV)*, pages 464–472. IEEE.

Elsbeth Turcan and Kathleen McKeown. 2019. Dreaddit: A reddit dataset for stress analysis in social media. *arXiv preprint arXiv:1911.00133*.

Davy Weissenbacher, Abeed Sarker, Michael J. Paul, and Graciela Gonzalez-Hernandez. 2018. Overview of the third social media mining for health (SMM4H) shared tasks at EMNLP 2018. In *Proceedings of the 2018 EMNLP Workshop SMM4H: The 3rd Social Media Mining for Health Applications Workshop & Shared Task*, pages 13–16, Brussels, Belgium. Association for Computational Linguistics.

Li Zhang, Haimeng Fan, Chengxia Peng, Guozheng Rao, and Qing Cong. 2020. Sentiment analysis methods for hpv vaccines related tweets based on transfer learning. In *Healthcare*, volume 8, page 307. Multidisciplinary Digital Publishing Institute.

A Dataset description

1. **Depression**: We used 6 depression-related datasets in our experiments.

    - **eRisk T3**: We used eRISK, a publicly available dataset, released by (Losada and Crestani, 2016) and labeled across 4 depression severity levels using Beck's Depression Inventory (Beck et al., 1961) criteria to detect the existence of depression and identify its severity level in social media posts. eRISK was later used in the CLEF's eRISK challenge Task 3[11] on early identification of depression in social media. Since in each years' challenge author released a small number of user's data (ranging from 70-90 users data), we combined and used the data of the last 3 years, which is equivalent to 190 Reddit users, labeled across 4 depression severity levels.
    - **Depression_Reddit_1**: We used new Reddit depression data released by Naseem et al. (2022a). This dataset consists of 3,553 Reddit posts to identify the depression severity on social media. Annotators manually labeled data into 4 depression severity levels i.,e., (i) minimal depression; (ii) mild depression, (iii) moderate depression; and (iv) severe depression using Depressive Disorder Annotation scheme (Mowery et al., 2015).
    - **eRisk T1**: The third depression data is from eRisk shared task 1 (Losada and Crestani, 2016), which is a public competition for detecting early risk in health-related areas. The eRisk data consists of posts from 2,810 users, with 1,370 expressing depression and 1,440 as a control group without depression.
    - **Depression_Reddit_2**: The fourth depression dataset used is released by Pirina and Çöltekin (Pirina and Çöltekin, 2018). The authors used Reddit to collect additional social data, which they combined with previously collected data to identify depression.
    - **Depression_Twitter_1**: Our fifth depression dataset is a publicly availabl[12]. This data is collected from Twitter and labeled into 3 labels (e.g., Positive, Negative, and Neutral) for depression sentiment analysis.
    - **Depression_Twitter_2**: Our sixth depression dataset is a public dataset[13], collected from Twitter and labeled into 2 labels (e.g., Positive and Negative) for depression detection.

2. **Health Mention:** We used 3 health mention-related datasets in our experiments.

    - **PHM**: Karisani and Agichtein (2018) constructed and released the PHM dataset consisting of 7,192 English tweets across 6 diseases and symptoms. They used the Twitter API to retrieve the data using the colloquial disease names as search keywords. They manually annotated the tweets and categorized them into 4 labels. In addition to 4 labels, similar to Karisani and Agichtein (2018) we also used binary labels for health mention classification.
    - **HMC2019**: HMC2019 is presented by Biddle et al. (2020) by extending the PHM dataset to include 19,558 tweets and included labels related to figurative mentions, and included 4 more different disease or symptom terms (10 in total) for health mention classification.
    - **RHMD**: We also used Reddit health mention dataset (RHMD)(Naseem et al., 2022b) for HMC task. RHMD consists of 10K+ Reddit posts manually annotated with 4 labels (personal health mention, non-personal health mention, figurative health mention, hyperbolic health mention). In our study, we used 3 label versions of data released by authors where they merged figurative health mention and hyperbolic health mention into 1 class.

3. **Suicide:** We used the following dataset to evaluate the performance of our model on suicide risk detection.

    - **R-SSD**: For suicide ideation, we used a dataset released by Cao et al. (2019), which contains 500 individuals' Reddit postings categorized into 5 increasing suicide risk classes from 9 mental health and suicide-related subreddits.

4. **Stress**: To evaluate stress detection using social media, we evaluated PHS-BERT on the following datasets.

    - **Dreaddit**: For stress detection, we used Dreaddit (Turcan and McKeown, 2019) collected from 5 different Reddit forums.

[11] https://erisk.irlab.org/2021/index.html

[12] https://github.com/AshwanthRamji/Depression-Sentiment-Analysis-with-Twitter-Data

[13] https://github.com/viritaromero/Detecting-Depression-in-Tweets

Dreaddit consists of 3,553 posts and focuses on three major stressful topics: interpersonal conflict, mental illness, and financial need. Posts in Dreaddit are collected from 10 subreddits, including some mental health domains such as anxiety and PTSD.

- **SAD**: The SAD (Mauriello et al., 2021) dataset, which contains 6,850 SMS-like sentences, is used to recognize everyday stressors. The SAD dataset is derived from stress management articles, chatbot-based conversation systems, crowdsourcing, and web crawling. Some of the more specific stressors are work-related issues like fatigue or physical pain, financial difficulties like debt or anxiety, school-related decisions like final projects or group projects, and interpersonal relationships like friendships and family relationships.

5. **Vaccine sentiment:** We used two vaccine-related Twitter datasets to show the effectiveness of our model.

    - **VS1**: Our first dataset consists of tweets about vaccine dissemination on Twitter from January 12, 2017, to December 3, 2019. Dunn et al. (2020) crawled and labeled this data. The total tweets count is 9,212, with 6,683 positive, 1,084 negatives, and 1,445 neural tweets.
    - **VS2**: The second dataset[14] includes tweets about measles and vaccinations obtained via the Twitter Streaming API between July 2018 and January 2019 and provided by Müller and Salathé (2019). The total number of tweets is 18,503, with 8,965 pro-vaccine tweets, 1,976 anti-vaccine tweets, and 7,562 neutral tweets.

6. **COVID**: We used 5 covid related datasets to test our model.

    - **COVID Lies**: Hossain et al. (2020) released COVIDLIES, a dataset (6761 tweets) annotated by experts with known COVID-19 misconceptions and tweets that agree, disagree, or express no stance.
    - **Covid category**: Covid category dataset is released by Müller et al. (2020). Amazon Turk annotators were asked to classify a given tweet text as personal narrative or news. Crowdbreaks was used to perform the annotation.
    - **COVIDSenti**: We used a newly released large-scale sentiment dataset, COVIDSenti, which contains 90,000 COVID-19-related tweets obtained during the pandemic's early stages, from February to March 2020. The tweets are labeled into positive, negative, and neutral sentiment classes. In our experiments, we used 3 subsets (COVIDSentiA, COVIDSentiB and COVIDSentiC) released by authors (Naseem et al., 2021d).

7. **Other health related tasks:** We used PUBHEALTH (Kotonya and Toni, 2020), a dataset for automated fact-checking of public health claims that are explainable. PUBHEALTH is labeled with its factuality (true, false, unproven, mixture). (ii) Abortion: In SemEval 2016 stance detection task (Mohammad et al., 2016), 5 target domains are given: legalization of abortion, atheism, climate change, feminism, and Hillary Clinton. We used the legalization of abortion in our experiments. (iii) Amazon Health dataset: The Amazon Health dataset (He and McAuley, 2016) contains reviews of Amazon healthcare products and has 4 classes i.e., strongly positive, positive, negative, and strongly negative. (iv) SMM4H T1: We used Social Media Mining for Health (SMM4H) Shared Task 1 recognizing whether a tweet is reporting an adverse drug reaction (Weissenbacher et al., 2018). (v) SMM4H T2: Drug Intake Classification (SMM4H Task 2) (Weissenbacher et al., 2018) where participants were given tweets manually categorized as definite intake, possible intake, or no intake. (vi) HRT: Health related tweets (HRT) (Paul and Dredze, 2012) were collected using Twitter and manually annotated using Mechanical Turk as related or unrelated to health. Health-related tweets were further labeled as sick (the text implied that the user was suffering from an acute illness, such as a cold or the flu) or health (the text made general comments about the user's or the other's health, such as chronic health conditions, lifestyle, or diet) and unrelated tweets were further labeled as unrelated (texts that were not about a specific person's health, such as news and updates about the swine flu or advertisements for diet pills) and non-English.

[14]https://github.com/digitalepidemiologylab/crowdbreaks-paper

Why only Micro-F_1? Class Weighting of Measures for Relation Classification

David Harbecke[♣], Yuxuan Chen[♣], Leonhard Hennig[♣], Christoph Alt[♠♡]

[♣]German Research Center for Artificial Intelligence (DFKI), Berlin

[♠]Humboldt Universität zu Berlin [♡]Science of Intelligence

[♣]{firstname}.{lastname}@dfki.de

[♠]christoph.alt@posteo.de

Abstract

Relation classification models are conventionally evaluated using only a single measure, e.g., micro-F_1, macro-F_1 or AUC. In this work, we analyze weighting schemes, such as *micro* and *macro*, for imbalanced datasets. We introduce a framework for weighting schemes, where existing schemes are extremes, and two new intermediate schemes. We show that reporting results of different weighting schemes better highlights strengths and weaknesses of a model.

1 Introduction

Relation classification (RC) models are typically compared with either micro-F_1 or macro-F_1, often without discussing the measure's properties (see e.g. Zhang et al., 2017; Yao et al., 2019). Each measure highlights different aspects of model performance (Sun et al., 2009). However, using an inappropriate measure can lead to the preference of an unsuitable model (Branco et al., 2016), e.g., tasks with an imbalanced or long-tailed class distribution. We argue that model evaluation should better reflect this, particularly as rare phenomena become more important in NLP (Rogers, 2021).

For instance, popular datasets for RC, such as TACRED (Zhang et al., 2017), NYT (Riedel et al., 2010), ChemProt (Kringelum et al., 2016), DocRED (Yao et al., 2019), and SemEval-2010 Task 8 (Hendrickx et al., 2010), often exhibit a highly imbalanced label distribution (see Table 1 and, e.g., the TACRED class distribution[1]). The main reasons are the natural data imbalance, i.e. the occurrence frequency of relation mentions in text, as well as the incompleteness of knowledge graphs like Freebase (Bollacker et al., 2008) used in distantly supervised RC. For example, 58% of the relations in the NYT dataset (Riedel et al., 2010) have fewer than 100 training instances (Han et al., 2018), and the most frequent relation *location/contains* is assigned to 48.3% of the positive test instances. However, for applying RC to real-world problems, it is especially important to discover instances of relations that are not yet covered well in a given knowledge base.

Table 1 lists statistics of the aforementioned RC datasets, including their perplexity and common evaluation measures. TACRED and the original version of NYT contain predominantly negative samples[2]. All datasets, except for undirectional SemEval, exhibit a large ratio between most frequent and least frequent positive class in the test set. The perplexity of test set distributions is also much lower than the relation count for all datasets except SemEval. Reporting only a single measure therefore cannot exhaustively capture model performance on these datasets, especially for the long tail of relation types. For example, Alt et al. (2019) show that on the NYT dataset, AUC scores and P-R-Curves of several state-of-the-art models are heavily skewed towards the two most frequent relation types *location/contains* and *person/nationality*. TACRED, ChemProt, DocRED and SemEval results are usually only reported in micro-F_1, which does not consider class membership.

In this paper, we introduce a framework for weighting schemes of measures to address these evaluation deficits. We present and motivate two new weighting schemes that are in between the extremes of micro- and macro-weighting. We demonstrate these, micro-, class-weighted- and macro-F_1 on TACRED and SemEval with two popular models each. We show that more information about models can be inferred from our results and point out what further steps should be taken to improve evaluation in relation classification.

[1]https://nlp.stanford.edu/projects/tacred/#stats

[2]Negative samples in RC means none of the dataset's relations hold. Depending on the dataset, this class is coined *no-relation*, *NA* or *Other*. We use negative class or *NA*.

Proceedings of NLP Power! The First Workshop on Efficient Benchmarking in NLP, pages 32 - 41

Dataset	#Rel	#Samples	%NA	Perplexity w NA	Perplexity w/o NA	Ratio	Evaluation
TACRED	42	106264	79.5	3.31	23.39	250	micro-F_1
NYT	53	694491	79.4	1.27	7.84	2793	precision at k, AUC
	24	66194	0	6.24	6.24	2485	
ChemProt	13	10065	0	7.23	7.23	314	micro-F_1
DocRED	96	50503	0	33.13	33.13	2837	micro-F_1, AUC
SemEval	19	10717	17.4	14.45	14.37	291	macro-F_1 (official),
	10	10717	17.4	9.61	8.80	2.10	micro-F_1 (popular)

Table 1: Statistics for popular RC datasets. The number of relations, samples and percent of negative samples are for the whole dataset. Perplexity of the classes is given for the test set, with and without negative samples. This value would be equal to #Rel for a fully balanced dataset. Ratio is between the counts of the most and least frequent positive class of the test set. We also list the popular evaluation methods. The upper line for NYT indicates the original dataset by Riedel et al. (2010), the lower line is the frequently used version by Hoffmann et al. (2011). The upper SemEval entry considers the direction between the nominals, the lower one does not.

2 Methods

We first give background on the F_1-score and existing F_1 weighting schemes. We present our framework of weighting schemes. We introduce two new weighting schemes. Finally, we outline statistical tests.

2.1 Background

The F_β-score (Rijsbergen, 1979; Lewis and Gale, 1994) calculates a score in the interval $[0, 1]$ through the formula

$$F_\beta = \frac{(1+\beta^2) \cdot TP}{(1+\beta^2) \cdot TP + \beta^2 \cdot FN + FP} \quad (1)$$

with the true positives (TP), false negatives (FN) and false positives (FP) of a confusion matrix. This definition is identical to the weighted harmonic mean of precision and recall. The positive coefficient β is used as a trade-off between the error types FN and FP. If there is no preference known or pre-determined, this coefficient is usually set to 1. In multi-class classification the confusion matrix can either be calculated once for the whole dataset, or separately for each class. The former method yields micro-F_1.

Micro weighting does not consider class membership for any test sample. If the predictions and labels of all classes are considered, micro-F_1 is equal to accuracy, as the denominator in Eq. 1 is twice the dataset. In RC, the TP of the negative class are usually not considered, in which case micro-F_1 is not equal to accuracy. For the F-score, *micro* is the only weighting where the impact of a sample on the score is not conditioned on the model performance on the rest of the class (Forman and Scholz, 2010). If the test set is considered to have a representative data distribution, the micro-weighted score is a frequentist evaluation of model performance.

There exist two other ways to calculate and combine F_1-scores for a multi-class problem. First, multi-class F_1-scores can be calculated for each class and then a weighted average class score is taken. Second, precision and recall scores for each class can be calculated and weighted, then the harmonic mean of weighted precision and weighted recall is taken. Opitz and Burst (2019) show that the first method is more robust and less favorable to biased classifiers. We use this method in our proposed framework.

(Class-)weighted-F_1 is similar to micro-F_1. F_1-scores are calculated for each class individually and then weighted by the class count. Thus, both schemes approximately weigh all samples equally.

Macro weighting gives an equal weight for each class with positive sample count regardless of the specific sample count. This gives information about model performance if class imbalance is not considered.

In general, there is a correspondence between training loss and evaluation measure (Li et al., 2020). One disadvantage of multiple weighting schemes is that each weighting scheme can be optimized for. To achieve a better score for a specific weighting, class weights could be set proportional to the weighting of the class during training. How-

Method	Formula	Focus
Micro	-	calculation over dataset, class membership is not considered
Weighted	n_i	weighting all classes by instance count, similar to micro
Dodrans	${n_i}^{3/4}$	evaluating closer to generalization performance
Entropy	$-n_i \cdot \log_2(n_i/\sum_j n_j)$	reducing impact of data distribution on evaluation
Macro	1	equal weighting of all classes

Table 2: Weighting schemes for evaluation of multi-class classification. n_i indicates the count of elements for class i and the Formula column shows the weight the class is assigned before normalization. The metrics are loosely ordered from top to bottom with the higher entries focusing more on instances and the lower entries focusing more on class membership. This usually corresponds to the model score, it is rare that models are better on classes with fewer samples. Methods in bold are proposed by us.

ever, we argue that model results should always be presented with multiple weightings for one dataset. Especially, when comparing different models all weightings should be reported for each model. This can clarify whether a model is good for all weightings or just *micro* or *macro*. Furthermore, with datasets that are currently evaluated with different weightings, it is easier to identify whether a model is specifically good for a dataset or for a weighting.

2.2 Framework for Weighting Schemes

We discuss a framework that summarizes the rules we give to class-weighting schemes. Then we introduce two new class weighting schemes. All discussed weighting schemes can be found in Table 2. They are independent of the measure that is used to calculate a score for each class.

(Class-)weighted and *macro* weighting are the extremes of "degressive proportionality"[3] or "allocation functions" (Słomczyński and Życzkowski, 2012). These are, e.g., used by the European Parliament to allocate seats to member nations depending on the population of the nation. They state that allocation should be monotonic increasing (see D1) and proportionally decreasing (see D2). To adopt this to a weighting scheme for multi-class evaluation, we add a normalizing desideratum that determines the sum of weights over all classes to be 1 (see D0).

Let $n_i > 0$ be the count of samples of class i and $w_i \geq 0$ the weight assigned to the score of class i.

We have the following desiderata:

$$\sum_i w_i = 1 \tag{D0}$$

$$n_i \geq n_j \Rightarrow w_i \geq w_j \tag{D1}$$

$$n_i \geq n_j \Rightarrow \frac{w_i}{n_i} \leq \frac{w_j}{n_j} \tag{D2}$$

Note that these desiderata do not restrict the scoring function that assigns scores s_i to class i. The weighted evaluation score is then given by $\sum_i w_i s_i$.

2.3 Weighting Schemes

Macro: Macro weighting is one extreme by setting equality on the weights of desideratum D1. It implies that we do not consider the instance counts per class, but treat all classes equally.

(Class-)weighted: Class-weighted is the other extreme by setting equality on the fraction of weights and counts in desideratum D2. It implies that we do not consider class constituency but weight all samples equally.

Dodrans: Cao et al. (2019) demonstrate that their balanced generalization error bound for binary classifiers in the separable case can be optimized by setting margins proportional to ${n_i}^{-1/4}$. They use this derivation from a limited theoretical scenario to improve the performance of several classifiers on imbalanced multi-class datasets. A term proportional to ${n_i}^{-1/4}$ is added in the loss function. While this added term is not directly transferable, we propose adapting this as a multiplicative factor in weighting classes for multi-class evaluation: $w_i \propto {n_i}^{-1/4} n_i = n_i^{3/4}$. We coin this weighting *dodrans* ("three-quarter").

Entropy: We also want to provide a weighting scheme that takes into consideration how hard a

[3]https://eur-lex.europa.eu/legal-content/EN/TXT/HTML/?uri=CELEX:32013D0312&from=EN#d1e114-57-1

class is to predict. To this end, we propose weighting classes proportional to their term in the Shannon entropy formula

$$H(X) = -\sum_i P(x_i)\log(P(x_i)) \tag{2}$$

$$w_i \propto P(x_i)\log(P(x_i)). \tag{3}$$

We interpret $P(x_i)$ for class i to be the probability of it appearing in the dataset, s.t. $P(x_i) = n_i/\sum_j n_j$. Thus, without normalization the model score is now the sum over all classes of the model performance on a class times the difficulty and frequency of the class. Note, that this weighting scheme does not fulfil desideratum D1, since it is decreasing for classes i with $P(x_i) > e^{-1}$. This is related to the fact that classes that are too large become easier to predict for a model, the model can just default to predicting this class. It can also be desirable that a class does not gain relative importance once it contains more than half of the dataset. For RC, this often has little consequence. If we include *NA* in the normalization, it is usually the largest class and other classes are below an e-th of the dataset. Table 2 shows an overview of the mentioned schemes.

Figure 1 displays the weights that these schemes assign to the classes of the TACRED test set. The *weighted* scheme is proportional to class counts and produces the most imbalanced weights. *Dodrans* and *entropy* produce slightly more balanced weights and differ from *weighted* for the most frequent classes. *Macro* considers all classes equally, regardless of class count.

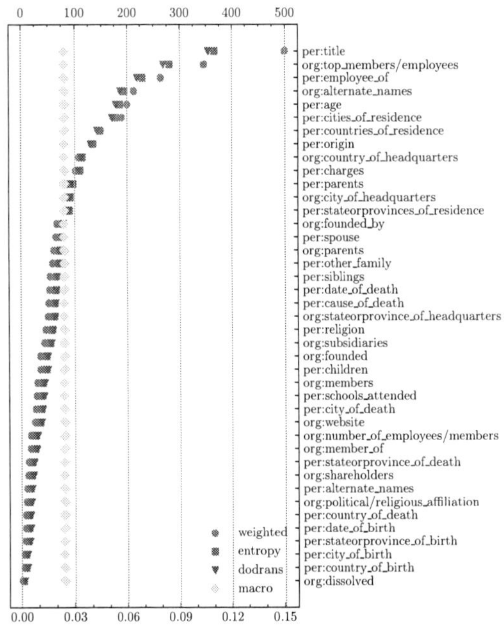

Figure 1: TACRED relations and their respective weights under different weighting schemes. The lower x-axis denotes the normalized weight given to a relation for a scheme. The upper x-axis corresponds to the counts of the relations in the test set for the class-weighted scheme. The y-axis denotes all positive relations. The negative *NA* class is not listed and has 12184 samples. The entropy and dodrans weighting scheme produce similar weights and are between weighted and macro weighting.

2.4 Statistical Testing

Currently, most RC works report a single score for each dataset. This can be the result from a single run or the median score from multiple runs. However, this does not allow to measure how large the difference between models is. Recently, analysis papers in NLP have recorded mean and standard deviation over multiple runs (Madhyastha and Jain, 2019; Zhou et al., 2020), as this allows for statistical tests.

We first test for significance and report p-values. We employ Welch's t-test to test the hypothesis that the models have equal mean. Following Zhu et al. (2020), we also report Cohen's d effect size to determine how large the difference between models is for a specific measure. For two models with the same number $n > 1$ of runs, Cohen's d is given by

$$d = \sqrt{2}\frac{\mu_1 - \mu_2}{\sqrt{\sigma_1^2 + \sigma_2^2}} \tag{4}$$

with μ_i and σ_i^2 being mean and variance of model i's scores. We do this, as two different models never perform exactly the same, i.e. significance just depends on the number of runs and we also want to score the difference between the models.

3 Experiments

We evaluate and compare three RC methods with our proposed measures on two datasets. We choose these methods, as RECENT (Lyu and Chen, 2021) and BERT_{EM} (Baldini Soares et al., 2019) are based on vanilla fine-tuning of a pre-trained language model, with a classification head on top. PTR (Han et al., 2021) is based on prompt-tuning. RECENT and PTR report similar micro-F_1 performance on TACRED, as do BERT_{EM} and PTR on SemEval. In

Method	Micro	Weighted	Dodrans	Entropy	Macro
RECENT	71.5±0.4	67.8±0.4	62.5±0.4	63.6±0.4	43.1±0.6
PTR	72.5±0.3	72.1±0.5	69.8±0.5	70.3±0.5	60.3±0.8
p-value	$3 \cdot 10^{-3}$	$3 \cdot 10^{-6}$	10^{-8}	$2 \cdot 10^{-8}$	$2 \cdot 10^{-10}$
Cohen's d	2.8	8.7	14.8	13.5	24.2

Table 3: TACRED F_1-scores with different weighting schemes. Positive scores indicate PTR performs better than RECENT for all weighting schemes. The difference is smallest for the micro and largest for the macro weighting scheme. All p-values are smaller than $\alpha = 0.05$. All effect sizes are huge (> 2.0) under Sawilowsky (2009)'s rules of thumb.

Method	Micro	Weighted	Dodrans	Entropy	Macro
BERT_{EM}	89.1±0.3	89.1±0.3	88.7±0.3	88.6±0.3	82.7±0.4
PTR	88.4±0.3	88.3±0.3	88.1±0.3	88.0±0.3	87.8±0.5
p-value	0.005	0.006	0.023	0.023	$7 \cdot 10^{-8}$
Cohen's d	-2.5	-2.4	-1.8	-1.8	11.5

Table 4: SemEval F_1-scores with different weighting schemes. The directionality is of the relations is considered, s.t. there are 19 classes, the negative class is not included in evaluation. Negative scores indicate BERT_{EM} performs better, positive scores indicate PTR performs better. All p-values are smaller than $\alpha = 0.05$. All absolute effect sizes are very large (> 1.2) or huge (> 2.0).

this way we can compare performance of the two paradigms for other weightings.

RECENT proposes a model-agnostic paradigm that exploits entity types to narrow down the candidate relations. Given an entity-type combination, a separate classifier is trained on the restricted classes. Baldini Soares et al. (2019) compare various strategies that extract relation representation from Transformers and claim ENTITY START (i.e. insert entity markers at the start of two entity mentions) yields the best performance. PTR also takes entity types into consideration and constructs prompts composed of three subprompts, two corresponding to the fill-in of the entity types and one predicting the relation.

In our experiments we use $\text{RECENT}_{\text{GCN}}$ for RECENT, BERT_{EM} with ENTITY START, and unreversed prompts for PTR. We use the official repositories for RECENT and PTR, we reimplement BERT_{EM}[4]. We use the hyperparameters proposed in the original papers and conduct five runs for each model. Additional implementation and training details can be found in Appendices A and B.

The main focus is unearthing performance information about these methods that was previously obscured by single score measures. The number of weighting schemes does not influence the computational cost, as each score is determined through the predictions in a run and does not require specific tuning.[5] We acknowledge that each weighting scheme could be optimized for during training which gives additional importance to reporting multiple measures for each model.

3.1 Results

Table 3 shows results for TACRED. PTR significantly outperforms RECENT across all weighting schemes. The difference between the models is smallest for micro-F_1 and increases for all schemes that weigh classes more equally. For macro-F_1 the difference is starkest with effect size 24.2.

Table 4 displays results for SemEval. BERT_{EM} significantly outperforms PTR in the micro-F_1 measure and all other weightings except for macro-F_1. All effect sizes are either large or huge, by far the largest effect size is between PTR and BERT_{EM} regarding macro-F_1 though. The SemEval test set contains a single sample of the *Entity-*

[4]Our reimplementation is available at https://github.com/dfki-nlp/mtb-bert-em.

[5]We provide a package to add these scores to a Scikit-learn (Pedregosa et al., 2011) classification report at https://github.com/DFKI-NLP/weighting-schemes-report.

Destination(e2,e1) class which is quite impactful for the macro-F_1 of the models but has negligible impact on all other weighting schemes. The scores from *dodrans* and *entropy* indicate that only if all classes are considered equally important the PTR model should be preferred. This indicates that either the PTR model learns almost regardless of class frequency or BERT_{EM} has a class preference that is only discoverable with macro-F_1.

We demonstrate that evaluation on micro-F_1 does not give adequate information about model performance on long-tail classes. In Tables 3 and 4 we see that the model which performs better under micro-F_1 can either be significantly better or worse for classes with few samples. The weighted-F_1 produces similar results to micro-F_1 except for RECENT. Macro-F_1 on the other hand is very sensitive to model performance on single samples, e.g. the *Entity-Destination(e2,e1)* class in SemEval.

The scores of our proposed schemes are in between the existing measures and might be the best indicators for robust generalization performance. For all experiments, they produce similar results to each other. This could just be a coincidence of the datasets, and is also indicated by Figure 1. Overall, it might be fair to say that one of the former and latter measures is enough. It would mean one measure that does weigh proportional to sample count (micro- or weighted-F_1), an intermediary measure (dodrans-F_1 or entropy-F_1) and macro-F_1.

PTR performs better for macro-F_1 on both datasets. Its scores decrease less when classes are weighted more equally. This suggests that it is a better model for classes with low sample counts. Le Scao and Rush (2021) show that prompts can be worth hundreds of data points which would explain why the macro- and micro-F_1 scores are much closer together than for RECENT and BERT_{EM}.

4 Related Work

Chauhan et al. (2019) do a thorough evaluation of their model and notice the significantly different performance measured by *micro* and *macro* statistics due to the class imbalance, suggesting that the choice of evaluation measure is crucial. Huang and Wong (2020) further use the closeness between micro- and macro-F_1 scores to claim the stable performance of their model.

Mille et al. (2021) point out that evaluating with a single score favors overfitting. They show different evaluation suites that can be created for a dataset. Bragg et al. (2021) address the disjoint evaluation settings across recent research threads in (few-shot) NLP and propose a unified evaluation benchmark which regulates dataset, sample size etc., but fail to take the evaluation measure into consideration, reporting only mean accuracy instead. Post (2018) criticises the inconsistency and under-specification in reporting scores. This problem is also prevalent in RC where the F_1 weighting scheme is often not specified.

Zhang et al. (2020) show that bias from corpora persists for fine-tuned pre-trained language models. These models struggle with rare phenomena. For better performance debiasing with weighting is performed. Søgaard et al. (2021) argue against using random splits. They show that evaluating models with random splits is not a realistic setting but makes tasks easier by fixing the test data distribution to the train data distribution.

Long-tail evaluation is becoming more prominent in NLP research. Models in deep learning tend to show a gap in performance between frequent and infrequent phenomena (Rogers, 2021). Models in NLP have been shown to perform badly on specific subsets of data (Zhang et al., 2020).

Sokolova and Lapalme (2009) analyze measures for multi-class classification and present invariances regarding the confusion matrix. Gösgens et al. (2021) also determine which class measures (including F_1) fulfil specific assumptions. Further evaluation can be based on this. Our weighting schemes for F_1 can be transferred to other measures that calculate a score for each class.

5 Outlook

We suggest creating and using a bidimensional leaderboard like Kasai et al. (2021) where measures and models can be contributed. To this end, benchmarking of RC models could be done on a centralized site where a model or test set predictions are submitted and measures are calculated automatically through a script. For measures that modify weighting of classes and intra-class scoring, this does not require additional training computation.

Due to the reproducibility crisis (Baker, 2016), not all state-of-the-art scores can be replicated. Possible future work includes a comprehensive evaluation study of papers on leaderboards of RC tasks. This would enable an in-depth discussion of strength and weaknesses (including reproducibility) of these models.

The analysis we present can also be extended to other NLP tasks with imbalanced datasets, such as named entity recognition (Tjong Kim Sang and De Meulder, 2003), part-of-speech tagging (Pradhan et al., 2013) and coreference resolution (Pradhan et al., 2012).

6 Conclusion

We criticise the current practice of reporting a single score when evaluating imbalanced RC datasets. We propose a new framework to weight scores for multi-class evaluation of imbalanced datasets. We provide two new weighting schemes, *dodrans* and *entropy*, which are positioned between *class-weighted* and *macro*. In our experiments, we show that model performance on both TACRED and SemEval, especially on the long-tail relations, is not adequately captured by a single score. Thus, we advocate the use of multiple weighing schemes when reporting model performance on imbalanced datasets.

Acknowledgments

We would like to thank Nils Feldhus, Sebastian Möller, Lisa Raithel, Robert Schwarzenberg and the anonymous reviewers for their feedback on the paper. This work was partially supported by the German Federal Ministry of Education and Research as part of the project CORA4NLP (01IW20010) and by the German Federal Ministry for Economic Affairs and Climate Action as part of the project PLASS (01MD19003E). Christoph Alt is supported by the Deutsche Forschungsgemeinschaft (DFG, German Research Foundation) under Germany's Excellence Strategy – EXC 2002/1 "Science of Intelligence" – project number 390523135.

References

Christoph Alt, Marc Hübner, and Leonhard Hennig. 2019. Fine-tuning pre-trained transformer language models to distantly supervised relation extraction. In *Proceedings of the 57th Annual Meeting of the Association for Computational Linguistics*, pages 1388–1398, Florence, Italy. Association for Computational Linguistics.

Monya Baker. 2016. Reproducibility crisis. *Nature*, 533(26):353–66.

Livio Baldini Soares, Nicholas FitzGerald, Jeffrey Ling, and Tom Kwiatkowski. 2019. Matching the blanks: Distributional similarity for relation learning. In *Proceedings of the 57th Annual Meeting of the Association for Computational Linguistics*, pages 2895–2905, Florence, Italy. Association for Computational Linguistics.

Kurt Bollacker, Colin Evans, Praveen Paritosh, Tim Sturge, and Jamie Taylor. 2008. Freebase: a collaboratively created graph database for structuring human knowledge. In *Proceedings of the 2008 ACM SIGMOD international conference on Management of data*, pages 1247–1250.

Jonathan Bragg, Arman Cohan, Kyle Lo, and Iz Beltagy. 2021. Flex: Unifying evaluation for few-shot nlp. *Advances in Neural Information Processing Systems*, 34.

Paula Branco, Luís Torgo, and Rita P. Ribeiro. 2016. A survey of predictive modeling on imbalanced domains. *ACM Computing Surveys (CSUR)*, 49(2):1–50.

Kaidi Cao, Colin Wei, Adrien Gaidon, Nikos Arechiga, and Tengyu Ma. 2019. Learning imbalanced datasets with label-distribution-aware margin loss. *Advances in Neural Information Processing Systems*, 32:1567–1578.

Geeticka Chauhan, Matthew B.A. McDermott, and Peter Szolovits. 2019. REflex: Flexible framework for relation extraction in multiple domains. In *Proceedings of the 18th BioNLP Workshop and Shared Task*, pages 30–47, Florence, Italy. Association for Computational Linguistics.

George Forman and Martin Scholz. 2010. Apples-to-apples in cross-validation studies: pitfalls in classifier performance measurement. *Acm Sigkdd Explorations Newsletter*, 12(1):49–57.

Martijn Gösgens, Anton Zhiyanov, Aleksey Tikhonov, and Liudmila Prokhorenkova. 2021. Good classification measures and how to find them. *Advances in Neural Information Processing Systems*, 34.

Xu Han, Weilin Zhao, Ning Ding, Zhiyuan Liu, and Maosong Sun. 2021. Ptr: Prompt tuning with rules for text classification. *CoRR*, arXiv:2105.11259.

Xu Han, Hao Zhu, Pengfei Yu, Ziyun Wang, Yuan Yao, Zhiyuan Liu, and Maosong Sun. 2018. FewRel: A large-scale supervised few-shot relation classification dataset with state-of-the-art evaluation. In *Proceedings of the 2018 Conference on Empirical Methods in Natural Language Processing*, pages 4803–4809, Brussels, Belgium. Association for Computational Linguistics.

Iris Hendrickx, Su Nam Kim, Zornitsa Kozareva, Preslav Nakov, Diarmuid Ó Séaghdha, Sebastian Padó, Marco Pennacchiotti, Lorenza Romano, and Stan Szpakowicz. 2010. SemEval-2010 task 8: Multi-way classification of semantic relations between pairs of nominals. In *Proceedings of the 5th International Workshop on Semantic Evaluation*, pages 33–38. Association for Computational Linguistics.

Raphael Hoffmann, Congle Zhang, Xiao Ling, Luke Zettlemoyer, and Daniel S. Weld. 2011. Knowledge-based weak supervision for information extraction of overlapping relations. In *Proceedings of the 49th Annual Meeting of the Association for Computational Linguistics: Human Language Technologies*, pages 541–550, Portland, Oregon, USA. Association for Computational Linguistics.

Haojie Huang and Raymond Wong. 2020. Deep embedding for relation extraction on insufficient labelled data. In *2020 International Joint Conference on Neural Networks (IJCNN)*, pages 1–8.

Jungo Kasai, Keisuke Sakaguchi, Ronan Le Bras, Lavinia Dunagan, Jacob Morrison, Alexander R Fabbri, Yejin Choi, and Noah A Smith. 2021. Bidimensional leaderboards: Generate and evaluate language hand in hand. *CoRR*, arXiv:2112.04139.

Jens Kringelum, Sonny Kjaerulff, Søren Brunak, Ole Lund, Tudor Oprea, and Olivier Taboureau. 2016. Chemprot-3.0: A global chemical biology diseases mapping. *Database*, 2016:bav123.

Teven Le Scao and Alexander Rush. 2021. How many data points is a prompt worth? In *Proceedings of the 2021 Conference of the North American Chapter of the Association for Computational Linguistics: Human Language Technologies*, pages 2627–2636, Online. Association for Computational Linguistics.

David D. Lewis and William A. Gale. 1994. A sequential algorithm for training text classifiers. In *Proceedings of the 17th annual international ACM SIGIR conference on Research and development in information retrieval*, pages 3–12.

Xiaoya Li, Xiaofei Sun, Yuxian Meng, Junjun Liang, Fei Wu, and Jiwei Li. 2020. Dice loss for data-imbalanced NLP tasks. In *Proceedings of the 58th Annual Meeting of the Association for Computational Linguistics*, pages 465–476, Online. Association for Computational Linguistics.

Shengfei Lyu and Huanhuan Chen. 2021. Relation classification with entity type restriction. In *Findings of the Association for Computational Linguistics: ACL-IJCNLP 2021*, pages 390–395, Online. Association for Computational Linguistics.

Pranava Madhyastha and Rishabh Jain. 2019. On model stability as a function of random seed. In *Proceedings of the 23rd Conference on Computational Natural Language Learning (CoNLL)*, pages 929–939, Hong Kong, China. Association for Computational Linguistics.

Simon Mille, Kaustubh Dhole, Saad Mahamood, Laura Perez-Beltrachini, Varun Gangal, Mihir Kale, Emiel van Miltenburg, and Sebastian Gehrmann. 2021. Automatic construction of evaluation suites for natural language generation datasets. In *Thirty-fifth Conference on Neural Information Processing Systems Datasets and Benchmarks Track (Round 1)*.

Juri Opitz and Sebastian Burst. 2019. Macro f1 and macro f1. *CoRR*, arXiv:1911.03347.

Adam Paszke, Sam Gross, Francisco Massa, Adam Lerer, James Bradbury, Gregory Chanan, Trevor Killeen, Zeming Lin, Natalia Gimelshein, Luca Antiga, Alban Desmaison, Andreas Kopf, Edward Yang, Zachary DeVito, Martin Raison, Alykhan Tejani, Sasank Chilamkurthy, Benoit Steiner, Lu Fang, Junjie Bai, and Soumith Chintala. 2019. Pytorch: An imperative style, high-performance deep learning library. In H. Wallach, H. Larochelle, A. Beygelzimer, F. d'Alché-Buc, E. Fox, and R. Garnett, editors, *Advances in Neural Information Processing Systems 32*, pages 8024–8035. Curran Associates, Inc.

Fabian Pedregosa, Gaël Varoquaux, Alexandre Gramfort, Vincent Michel, Bertrand Thirion, Olivier Grisel, Mathieu Blondel, Peter Prettenhofer, Ron Weiss, Vincent Dubourg, Jake Vanderplas, Alexandre Passos, David Cournapeau, Matthieu Brucher, Matthieu Perrot, and Édouard Duchesnay. 2011. Scikit-learn: Machine learning in python. *Journal of Machine Learning Research*, 12(85):2825–2830.

Matt Post. 2018. A call for clarity in reporting BLEU scores. In *Proceedings of the Third Conference on Machine Translation: Research Papers*, pages 186–191, Brussels, Belgium. Association for Computational Linguistics.

Sameer Pradhan, Alessandro Moschitti, Nianwen Xue, Hwee Tou Ng, Anders Björkelund, Olga Uryupina, Yuchen Zhang, and Zhi Zhong. 2013. Towards robust linguistic analysis using OntoNotes. In *Proceedings of the Seventeenth Conference on Computational Natural Language Learning*, pages 143–152, Sofia, Bulgaria. Association for Computational Linguistics.

Sameer Pradhan, Alessandro Moschitti, Nianwen Xue, Olga Uryupina, and Yuchen Zhang. 2012. CoNLL-2012 shared task: Modeling multilingual unrestricted coreference in OntoNotes. In *Joint Conference on EMNLP and CoNLL - Shared Task*, pages 1–40, Jeju Island, Korea. Association for Computational Linguistics.

Sebastian Riedel, Limin Yao, and Andrew McCallum. 2010. Modeling relations and their mentions without labeled text. In *Joint European Conference on Machine Learning and Knowledge Discovery in Databases*, pages 148–163. Springer.

C. J. Van Rijsbergen. 1979. *Information Retrieval*, 2nd edition. Butterworth-Heinemann.

Anna Rogers. 2021. Changing the world by changing the data. In *Proceedings of the 59th Annual Meeting of the Association for Computational Linguistics and the 11th International Joint Conference on Natural Language Processing (Volume 1: Long Papers)*, pages 2182–2194, Online. Association for Computational Linguistics.

Shlomo S. Sawilowsky. 2009. New effect size rules of thumb. *Journal of modern applied statistical methods*, 8(2):26.

Wojciech Słomczyński and Karol Życzkowski. 2012. Mathematical aspects of degressive proportionality. *Mathematical Social Sciences*, 63(2):94–101.

Anders Søgaard, Sebastian Ebert, Jasmijn Bastings, and Katja Filippova. 2021. We need to talk about random splits. In *Proceedings of the 16th Conference of the European Chapter of the Association for Computational Linguistics: Main Volume*, pages 1823–1832.

Marina Sokolova and Guy Lapalme. 2009. A systematic analysis of performance measures for classification tasks. *Information processing & management*, 45(4):427–437.

Yanmin Sun, Andrew K. C. Wong, and Mohamed S. Kamel. 2009. Classification of imbalanced data: a review. *International Journal of Pattern Recognition and Artificial Intelligence*, 23(04):687–719.

Erik F. Tjong Kim Sang and Fien De Meulder. 2003. Introduction to the CoNLL-2003 shared task: Language-independent named entity recognition. In *Proceedings of the Seventh Conference on Natural Language Learning at HLT-NAACL 2003*, pages 142–147.

Thomas Wolf, Lysandre Debut, Victor Sanh, Julien Chaumond, Clement Delangue, Anthony Moi, Pierric Cistac, Tim Rault, Remi Louf, Morgan Funtowicz, Joe Davison, Sam Shleifer, Patrick von Platen, Clara Ma, Yacine Jernite, Julien Plu, Canwen Xu, Teven Le Scao, Sylvain Gugger, Mariama Drame, Quentin Lhoest, and Alexander Rush. 2020. Transformers: State-of-the-art natural language processing. In *Proceedings of the 2020 Conference on Empirical Methods in Natural Language Processing: System Demonstrations*, pages 38–45, Online. Association for Computational Linguistics.

Yuan Yao, Deming Ye, Peng Li, Xu Han, Yankai Lin, Zhenghao Liu, Zhiyuan Liu, Lixin Huang, Jie Zhou, and Maosong Sun. 2019. DocRED: A large-scale document-level relation extraction dataset. In *Proceedings of the 57th Annual Meeting of the Association for Computational Linguistics*, pages 764–777, Florence, Italy. Association for Computational Linguistics.

Guanhua Zhang, Bing Bai, Junqi Zhang, Kun Bai, Conghui Zhu, and Tiejun Zhao. 2020. Demographics should not be the reason of toxicity: Mitigating discrimination in text classifications with instance weighting. In *Proceedings of the 58th Annual Meeting of the Association for Computational Linguistics*, pages 4134–4145, Online. Association for Computational Linguistics.

Yuhao Zhang, Victor Zhong, Danqi Chen, Gabor Angeli, and Christopher D. Manning. 2017. Position-aware attention and supervised data improve slot filling. In *Proceedings of the 2017 Conference on Empirical Methods in Natural Language Processing*, pages 35–45. Association for Computational Linguistics.

Xiang Zhou, Yixin Nie, Hao Tan, and Mohit Bansal. 2020. The curse of performance instability in analysis datasets: Consequences, source, and suggestions. In *Proceedings of the 2020 Conference on Empirical Methods in Natural Language Processing (EMNLP)*, pages 8215–8228, Online. Association for Computational Linguistics.

Haotian Zhu, Denise Mak, Jesse Gioannini, and Fei Xia. 2020. NLPStatTest: A toolkit for comparing NLP system performance. In *Proceedings of the 1st Conference of the Asia-Pacific Chapter of the Association for Computational Linguistics and the 10th International Joint Conference on Natural Language Processing: System Demonstrations*, pages 40–46, Suzhou, China. Association for Computational Linguistics.

A Implementation Details

To evaluate RECENT and PTR, we use the official code at `https://github.com//Saintfe/RECENT` (last updated on 01.10.2021) and `https://github.com/thunlp/PTR` (last updated on 20.11.2021). Since the official code of BERT_{EM} is not available, we implement this method using the HuggingFace Transformers library (Wolf et al., 2020) and PyTorch (Paszke et al., 2019), and make our code base available at `https://github.com/dfki-nlp/mtb-bert-em`. To make our results reproducible, we randomly generated seeds {9, 148, 378, 459, 687} and employed these for all models in their 5 runs.

B Training Details

B.1 RECENT

We consider GCN as the base model. Following the paper and the official code, we set the batch size to be 50, the optimizer to be SGD with learning rate 0.3, and the number of epochs to be 100. It takes a single RTX-A6000 GPU approximately 10 hours to complete all 5 runs on TACRED.

B.2 BERT_{EM}

We use the pre-trained language model (PLM) `bert-large-uncased` from the HuggingFace model hub and directly fine-tune the model for the RC task, without matching-the-blank pre-training. As the paper suggests, we set the batch size to be 64, the optimizer to be Adam with learning rate $3 \cdot 10^{-5}$, and the number of epochs to be 5. Additionally, we use the max sequence length of 512.

It takes a single RTX-A6000 GPU 30 minutes to complete all 5 runs on SemEval.

B.3 PTR

According to the paper and the official code base, we apply the same settings to evaluate both TACRED and SemEval: We use the PLM `roberta-large` and set the max sequence length to be 512, the batch size to be 64, the optimizer to be Adam with learning rate $3 \cdot 10^{-5}$, the weight decay to be 10^{-2}, and the number of epochs to be 5. It takes 4 Quadro-P5000 GPUs 84 hours to complete 5 runs on TACRED, and it takes 8 Titan-V GPUs 9 hours on SemEval.

Automatically Discarding Straplines to Improve Data Quality for Abstractive News Summarization

Amr Keleg*, **Matthias Lindemann***, **Danyang Liu***, **Wanqiu Long***, **Bonnie L. Webber**
Institute for Language, Cognition and Computation, University of Edinburgh
{a.keleg,m.m.lindemann}@sms.ed.ac.uk,
{dyliu,wanqiu.long,bonnie.webber}@ed.ac.uk

Abstract

Recent improvements in automatic news summarization fundamentally rely on large corpora of news articles and their summaries. These corpora are often constructed by scraping news websites, which results in including not only summaries but also other kinds of texts. Apart from more generic noise, we identify straplines as a form of text scraped from news websites that commonly turn out not to be summaries. The presence of these non-summaries threatens the validity of scraped corpora as benchmarks for news summarization. We have annotated extracts from two news sources that form part of the Newsroom corpus (Grusky et al., 2018), labeling those which were straplines, those which were summaries, and those which were both. We present a rule-based strapline detection method that achieves good performance on a manually annotated test set[1]. Automatic evaluation indicates that removing straplines and noise from the training data of a news summarizer results in higher quality summaries, with improvements as high as 7 points ROUGE score.

1 Introduction

Automatic text summarization is a challenging task. Recent progress has been driven by benchmarks that were collected by scraping a large collection of web-pages, including Gigaword (Rush et al., 2015), CNN/DailyMail (Nallapati et al., 2016), Newsroom (Grusky et al., 2018), and XSum (Narayan-Chen et al., 2019). Due to the way they are collected, these datasets contain a substantial portion of articles that are paired with texts that are not summaries. This flaw in data quality negatively impacts research in two ways: (i) models trained on these benchmarks tend to reproduce flaws in the data, making them less useful for summarization, and (ii) any evaluation against a reference text is meaningless if the reference is not actually a summary.

Figure 1: A **strapline** ("Don't expect ...") that is mistaken for a summary in the Newsroom corpus.

In this work, we present methods for improving the data quality in scraped news summarization corpora, focusing on the Newsroom benchmark (Grusky et al., 2018). We identify two main issues with the data quality: (i) noise in the extraction process (the wrong field being scraped, markup, ...), which was previously also identified to be an issue by Kryscinski et al. (2019), and (ii) *straplines*. According to the writing guidelines used by CERN[2], "[t]he strap[line] gives added "teaser information not included in the headline, providing a succinct summary of the most important points of the article. It tells the reader what to expect, and invites them to find out more."

Figure 1 shows an example of a strapline ("Don't expect to be riding one by 2020") below the regular headline. While the CERN guidelines emphasize the function of straplines to provide a summary, we find that most straplines in the Newsroom corpus are not summaries of their associated articles. Therefore, in order to obtain high quality data, it is necessary to distinguish a strapline aimed at piquing a reader's interest from an abstractive summary. To the best of our knowledge, no work has tried to distinguish straplines from summaries before, and even the word "strapline" does not appear in the ACL anthology in a research paper.

In our work, one pair of us designed a strapline

*Equal contribution

[1]We release our code at https://github.com/namednil/straplines

[2]https://writing-guidelines.web.cern.ch/entries/strapline-strap.html

Proceedings of NLP Power! The First Workshop on Efficient Benchmarking in NLP, pages 42 - 51
May 26, 2022

annotation guideline through discussions and manual pre-annotations (§3.1) and then annotated a development and test set for evaluating strapline classifiers. Based on the guideline, a separate pair created heuristics for a rule-based classifier that distinguishes straplines from summaries (§3.2). We empirically verify the usefulness of these heuristics for strapline detection (§4.2). Automatic evaluation indicates that removing straplines and noise from the training data with our heuristics results in higher quality summaries, with improvements as high as 7 points ROUGE score when compared to reference summaries (§4.3).

2 Related work

Several works have analyzed existing summarization datasets from different aspects but none have identified straplines as an issue. Kryscinski et al. (2019) quantified HTML artifacts in two large scraped summarization datasets which are CNN/DM (Nallapati et al., 2016), and Newsroom (Grusky et al., 2018). They found that "summaries" containing such artifacts were found in $\approx 3.2\%$ of the Newsroom data. They also argued that many of these artifacts could be detected using simple regular expressions and heuristics. Jung et al. (2019) define three sub-aspects of text summarization and analyze how different domains of summarization dataset are biased to these aspects. Bommasani and Cardie (2020) evaluate the quality of ten summarization datasets, and their results show that in most summarization datasets there are a sizable number of low quality examples and that their metrics can detect generically low quality examples. Tejaswin et al. (2021) analyzed 600 samples from three popular datasets, studying the data quality issues and varying degrees of sample complexity, and their analysis of summarization models demonstrate that performance is heavily dependent on the data and that better quality summarization datasets are necessary.

Given that research has shown that the training data of summarization models are noisy, researchers have proposed methods for training summarization models based on noisy data. For example, Kano et al. (2021) propose a model that can quantify noise to train summarization models from noisy data. The improvement of the models indicates that the noisy data has noticeable impacts for the training of the models.

3 Methodology

The Newsroom corpus contains articles from 38 news sources that vary in style and topics. News articles were scraped from HTML pages, where the page's title tag is parsed as the article's headline, while the page's body tag is parsed as the article's body. Since there was no consistent metadata tag indicating the summary of an article, Grusky et al. (2018) used different metadata tags to extract summaries. These tags are generally added to be used by social media platforms, and search engines. News publishers do not share a single format for organizing metadata. Nevertheless, all (or most) use the metadata label *description*, albeit for different things. Since the creators of Newsroom take as the summary of each article, the first tag in its metadata having the keyword *description*, this might be one reason that a strapline appears in the extract for an article in place of the real summary. Knowing that the "summaries" in the Newsroom corpus are of mixed quality, we call what Grusky et al. (2018) scraped from the web *extracts*, which may or may not be a genuine summary.

Grusky et al. (2018) classify extracts according to how much text they repeat verbatim from the article into three categories: extractive (nearly everything appears verbatim in the article), abstractive (summarize in different words) and mixed.

We have focused on extracts classified as "abstractive". We have also limited our study to two of the 38 news sources – ones with different styles and covering different topics, specifically the New York Times (NYT) and time.com.

3.1 Annotation

The extracts in the Newsroom corpus do not all fall neatly into the categories straplines and summaries and noise; in particular, straplines and summaries are not mutually exclusive, and can be seen to form a continuum.

Even in this continuum, what one would definitively classify as a summary depends on multiple factors like its purpose and audience (Spärck Jones, 1999). Therefore, we only identify *common characteristics* of straplines and summaries, restricted to the context of news articles, such as those in the Newsroom corpus. Regarding purpose and audience, we generally assume the audience consists of people who read news on a somewhat regular basis, and that this is the same audience as for the summaries. The purpose is to provide a brief overview of the news of the day, and we assume this overview includes the headline. This means that the headline plays a central role in our annotation procedure. A practical implication of this is that annotation decisions can sometimes be made very swiftly without reading the actual article.

We identify the following main characteristics of **straplines** that we want to exclude (ordered by importance):

Clickbait A strapline can be designed to attract a reader's attention, rather than being informative.

Little or redundant information A strapline does not add much information to the headline.

General A strapline can make a very general statement, i.e. it would fit for a number of very different articles.

Comment A strapline can be a comment on the event described in the article. This does not apply if the article itself is an opinion piece.

Joke A strapline can be a joke.

Informal A strapline may use informal language.

An extract need not have all the stated properties to be considered a strapline. The characteristics are illustrated in Table 1.

The characteristics of summaries are partially complementary to those of straplines. Again, an extract need not have all the characteristics to be considered a **summary**:

Adds information A summary adds information to the headline.

Relevance A summary contains no irrelevant information and little background information.

Focus The summary of an article describing an event (entity) focuses on that event (entity).

Proposition A summary tends to be one or more propositions.

The following example illustrates that some extracts have characteristics of both a summary and a strapline:

> Jan. 18 Internet Blackout to Protest SOPA: Reddit Says Yes
>
> Following speculation, Reddit has confirmed plans to go dark on Jan. 18 to protest the Stop Online Piracy Act. Wikipedia may follow suit, but what about Google, Facebook and other big-name tech companies?

While the extract adds relevant information to the headline, it also uses a question to attract the reader's attention instead of giving away that "[...] Google and Twitter declined to comment on their support for an Internet blackout", as can be found in the main article.

Labels Because of this overlap in the categories, we annotate each article with one of the following labels: "summary", "strapline", "strapline and summary", "neither" and "paraphrase". We use the category "neither" for noise or when the headline or the extract are difficult to understand before reading the article. We sometimes observe that the extract is a close paraphrase of the headline. By definition, a paraphrase does not add information and therefore would not qualify as a summary. In another use case however, where we assume that a user does not have access to the headline, the extract may provide valuable information. In order to make our annotation more robust to this use case, we include the category of paraphrase, so that those extracts can be included or excluded accordingly.

3.2 Strapline detection pipeline

Before detecting straplines, we preprocess the data to exclude *noisy* extracts (e.g., extracts with HTML tags). Afterwards, the strapline detection method is used to split the remaining extracts into straplines and summaries. The following subsections describe the main heuristics used for noise filtration and strapline detection, with implementation details included in Appendix A.

3.2.1 Noise filtration

Kryscinski et al. (2019) mention that noisy samples represent about 3.2% of Newsroom, hinting that such samples can be detected with simple patterns, but without explicitly describing these patterns. Consequently, we start by looking for patterns of noise in the Newsroom dataset as a first preprocessing step, and identify five clear patterns

Headline	Extract	Characteristic	Heuristic
Awesome! Interactive Internet health map checks your states connection	Check to see if you're part of a bigger problem	Clickbait	Imperative, pronouns
Sochi Olympics: USA Canada Hockey Game Sparks "Loser Keeps Bieber" Ad	USA! USA! USA!	Little information	Too short, exclamation mark
Bill OReilly: More trouble overseas for President Obama and America	The OReilly Factor on FoxNews.com with Bill OReilly, Weeknights at 8 PM and 11 PM EST	General statement	Repeated extract
Sofia Vergara and fiance split, read (and love) the charming statement	At least we know Sofia is probably writing this herself!	Comment	Pronouns
£Quieres seguir viendo noticias en Facebook? Aquí te decimos qué hacer	Facebook cambió su algoritmo para priorizar [...]	N/A	Non-English article

Table 1: Examples of straplines from the Newsroom along with a salient characteristic and the relevant automatic heuristics for strapline detection.

of noise:

Web formatting syntax An extract containing remnants of web formatting syntax. The formatting attributes are inconsistent and not sufficiently relevant for summarization.

Truncation An extract ending abruptly, forming an incomplete sentence. This might be attributed to the fact that news providers tend to have a truncated version of the summary that ended up being scraped in place of the long version of the summary.

Dateline An extract that is just a date, which is most probably the dateline field of an article instead of its summary.

Shortness An extract that is trivially short.

Non-English An extract that isn't written in English.

3.2.2 Strapline detection heuristics

As mentioned in §3.1, one can distinguish straplines from summaries based on the common features that characterize each of them. As a way to automatically detect a range of straplines in the dataset, we present the following set of six rule-based heuristics:

Beginning with imperative speech One way to capture the reader's attention is to start a strapline with an imperative to read the article ("Check out ...").

Strapline characteristics: Clickbait, Little or redundant information.

Having high quotes coverage A common feature of a strapline is to quote a statement said by a person that is mentioned in the corresponding article or a quote that is related to the article's topic.

Strapline characteristics: Little or redundant information, Comment.

Using 1st or 2nd person pronouns Straplines may refer to the readers. This is done typically using 1st and 2nd person pronouns such as *you* and *we*.

Strapline characteristics: Clickbait, Joke, Informal.

Using question/exclamation marks Straplines are sometimes used to pose questions that stimulate the interest of the readers. On the contrary, summaries use objective sentences focusing on the main events of the articles, which makes it unlikely to find interrogative phrases in a summary.

Strapline characteristics: Little or redundant information, Joke.

Using a repeated extract Journalists tend to use the same strapline for an article that is being published on a regular basis (e.g.: a daily/weekly column or a message to the editor section). Consequently, an article with a non-unique extract indicates that the extract is a general statement, making it a strapline.

Strapline characteristics: Little or redundant information, General.

Using a clickbait Classifying an extract as a clickbait, as described in §4.2, can be employed to detect some of the extracts that are originally straplines.

Strapline characteristics: Clickbait.

Source	Summary	Strapline	Both	Neither	Paraphrase
NYT	87%	5%	3%	2%	3%
Time.com	48%	33%	6%	8%	5%
Combined	67.5%	19%	4.5%	5%	4%

Table 2: Distribution of extract annotations among labels on the annotated portion of the test set. Annotations were collected for 100 random samples from each source (NYT, and Time.com) resulting in a total of 200 annotated samples.

Round	Straplines		Summaries	
	Raw	κ	Raw	κ
1	0.70	0.36	0.72	0.37
2	0.82	0.55	0.80	0.49

Table 3: Inter-annotator agreement for strapline and summary annotations.

Source	Accuracy	Precision	Recall	Strapline%
NYT	90%	43%	75%	8%
Time.com	73%	68%	64%	39%

Table 4: Results of the rule-based strapline classification as a binary classification problem (Strapline/ Not Strapline).

Source		Noise	Strapline	Total
NYT	Training Set	899 (1.89%)	9,537 (20.07%)	47,529
	Test Set	101 (2.00%)	1,002 (19.86%)	5,045
Time.com	Training Set	937 (4.35%)	8,102 (37.61%)	21,541
	Test Set	108 (4.60%)	893 (38.03%)	2,348

Table 5: Number and % of noise and straplines our rule-based heuristics detected in NYT or Time.com data sections of Newsroom.

4 Experiments

4.1 Annotation

Two annotators[3] annotated 50 articles each from the NYT and time.com sections of the test set of Newsroom. We performed two rounds, resulting in a total of 200 articles with double annotation. In order to provide a single ground truth for the test set, the two annotators discussed their annotations and agreed on a single label for each article. For tuning the strapline detection method, we further annotated 50 articles each from the development sets of NYT and time.com sections.

Results Table 2 shows how often the annotators chose a particular label for the different news sources. Proper summaries are the largest class for both news sources, but Time.com has a considerably higher proportion of undesired straplines, and also a higher proportion of extracts that are both summaries as well as straplines.

In order to see how reliable the extracts can be annotated, we compute inter-annotator agreement between the two annotators. Table 3 shows the results for two annotation rounds. We compute the agreement by splitting our annotation into two binary labels, namely straplines vs. non-straplines, and summaries vs. non-summaries, excluding paraphrases. We report the proportion of labels that are the same for both annotators ("Raw" in the table), and Cohen's κ (Cohen, 1960), which accounts for agreement that is expected by chance. The results in Table 3 show that the agreement is high, but due to the class imbalance a sizable part of that high agreement might be due to chance (low κ value). However, the results show improvements in the consistency between the two annotators in the second round.

[3]The annotators are authors of this paper who were not involved in the development of the heuristics and the person responsible for the heuristics did not look at the annotations.

4.2 Strapline detection

Given the lack of annotated data for training a supervised strapline classification model, we implement a rule-based classifier by marking an extract as a strapline if any of the heuristics described in §3.2.2 apply to it. For the clickbait detector, we fine-tune the distilled BERT (Sanh et al., 2019) on the Webis-Clickbait-17 (Potthast et al., 2018) dataset and incorporate it into our strapline detector.

Results Table 4 shows the evaluation result of the strapline detector on the human annotated test set. We can observe that NYT test set is unbalanced where only 8 out of 100 samples are annotated as straplines, which also explains the difference between the accuracy and precision/recall. Time.com set is more balanced, and we can see that our model achieves a good performance with a precision of 68% and recall of 64%.

We apply the strapline detector on the training set to exclude the noisy samples and straplines. The result is shown in Table 5. We can observe that 20.07% samples of NYT and 37.61% of Time.com are classified as straplines, which shows that the strapline is an issue that cannot be ignored in the summarization dataset.

Training set		Original Test Set			Cleaned Test Set		
		R-1	R-2	R-L	R-1	R-2	R-L
NYT	original	13.57	3.03	11.60	12.25	1.09	10.16
	w/o straplines	**20.83**	**4.69**	**16.29**	**22.39**	**5.31**	**17.30**
Time.com	original	**15.96**	3.28	**13.39**	19.09	4.28	**15.83**
	w/o straplines	15.87	**3.34**	13.27	**19.12**	**4.32**	15.81
Combined	original	**19.16**	**4.89**	**15.58**	20.24	4.50	16.03
	w/o straplines	19.06	4.13	15.25	**21.29**	**4.94**	**16.82**

Table 6: ROUGE-1, ROUGE-2, and ROUGE-L scores for the abstractive summarizer (T5-base version) trained on the dataset with and without the straplines. The best results are in **bold**.

4.3 Summarization with cleaner data

We employ the most popular pre-trained sequence-to-sequence model, T5 (Raffel et al., 2019), as the basic summarizer in our experiments. We exclude the noisy samples and straplines by our proposed strapline detector (§4.2) from the NYT and Time.com dataset, forming a cleaner training set. We use T5-base and T5-large model in our experiments. We fine-tune them on the original and the cleaned dataset to see the influence of excluding noise and straplines. We use ROUGE (Lin, 2004a,b) to automatically evaluate the performance of the summarizers.

Results Table 6 shows the ROUGE-1, ROUGE-2, and ROUGE-L scores for the (T5-base) summarizer trained on the original training set and the cleaned training set[4]. We can observe that the impact of straplines on NYT is more significant than Time.com. For Time.com dataset, most ROUGE scores increase slightly by excluding the straplines. However, performance on NYT is greatly improved by up to 7 points. In part this is due to a repetition problem that we observe specifically on NYT: the model trained on the original data re-uses some summaries multiple times, with a single re-occurring sentence accounting for 10% of generated outputs whereas all summaries of the model trained on the cleaned data are unique. That is, the model seems to perpetuate the property of repeating extracts in the training data (see §3.2.2).

Case study For each news source, we manually compare the output of two T5-base models fine-tuned on the articles of the news source in the original dataset $M_{original}$ and the cleaned one M_{clean} in order to investigate the effect of excluding noise and straplines from Newsroom. Table 7 demonstrates the differences between the generated summaries by T5-base models that are fine-tuned on articles of each news source. The "Output of Original Model" $M_{original}$ column refers to the summaries generated by a model fine-tuned on the articles of Newsroom from the news source specified in the first column. On the other hand, the "Output of Cleaned Model" M_{clean} column refers to the summaries generated by a model fine-tuned on the articles of Newsroom from the news source after discarding the articles whose extracts are flagged as noisy or as straplines. We found two main improvements in the quality of the generated summaries: (i) M_{clean} tend to be more informative in compared to $M_{original}$ and (ii) M_{clean} do not exhibit as much undesired characteristics of straplines like: using a repeated summary, using a question mark, and using the 1st person pronouns, while $M_{original}$ tend to have such properties. The fact that these improvements do not have huge impact on the automatic evaluation metric (ROUGE) for Time.com implies that human evaluation is needed to accompany the automatic evaluation metrics in order to quantify such qualitative improvements.

5 Conclusion

We present methods for improving the data quality in scraped news summarization corpora, focusing on the New York Times and Time magazine sections of Newsroom (Grusky et al., 2018). We identify two main issues with the data quality that make Newsroom less appropriate as a summarization benchmark: (i) noise in the extraction process and (ii) presence of straplines in place of genuine summaries. After identifying common characteristics of straplines, we develop a set of effective heuristics for detecting straplines and noise.

Our work shows that when straplines and noisy data are excluded from the training data, the result-

[4]The corresponding scores for the T5-large summarizer are reported in Table 1 in the Appendix.

News source	Output of Original Model ($M_{original}$)	Output of Cleaned Model (M_{clean})
NYT	**A day in the life of** a Olympic athlete.	The Australian swimmer Mack Horton was booed by Chinese swimmers after his victory in the 200-meter freestyle, and Russian swimmer Irina Efimova was booed.
NYT	**A day in the life of** a Yankees fan.	The Yankees victory parade on Friday was a celebration of the teamâs success, but not everyone was there.
NYT	**A New York Times blog about** comic book publishing and design.	Kevin Conroys performances as Batman in the comic books, movies and television series stand out.
NYT	**New York Times reporters and editors are reporting from Washington, D.C.**	A New Hampshire biologist turned to film school to learn how to communicate scientific information.
NYT	**Reading, watching, discussing and blogging the day's local, national, and international news at The New York Times.**	The University of Illinois, Chicago, has a bright spot in its diversity.
NYT	**To the Editor:.**	Readers respond to an Op-Ed article about climate talks.
NYT	**To the Editor:.**	Readers responded to a recent editorial about the dangers of concealed carry.
Time.com	TIME 100 poll: **Who is the world's most influential leader?**	The Russian president has risen to second place in the TIME 100 poll, beating out world leaders like Pope Francis and Barack Obama
Time.com	California is cutting back on its water use, but **where is it going?**	California is cutting back on water usage by 25%, but the state isn't out of water
Time.com	A new survey shows that Millennials are becoming more entrepreneurial, but **we** need to do more to prepare them	A new survey finds that 82 percent of Millennials are interested in starting their own businesses
Time.com	A new report finds that more and more counties aren't affordable. Here's what **you** need to know	A new report finds that 9% of U.S. counties aren't affordable

Table 7: Example summaries selected from the outputs of the model fine-tuned on the original dataset and the cleaned dataset. Spans showing characteristics of straplines are **underlined and shown in bold text**.

ing summarizer produces better summaries based on comparison to reference texts. Although we found noise and straplines to be more prevalent in the Time magazine data, the impact of removing noise and straplines is bigger for the model trained on the NYT data, which avoids reusing the same summary multiple times. We plan to investigate this further in future work.

Because of our focus on two specific news sources in Newsroom, we suspect that our heuristics might not work quite as well on other news sources having different styles, or on other datasets that were collected differently.

Acknowledgments

This work was supported in part by the UKRI Centre for Doctoral Training in Natural Language Processing, funded by the UKRI (grant EP/S022481/1) and the University of Edinburgh, School of Informatics and School of Philosophy, Psychology & Language Sciences.

References

Rishi Bommasani and Claire Cardie. 2020. Intrinsic evaluation of summarization datasets. In *EMNLP*.

Jacob Cohen. 1960. A coefficient of agreement for nominal scales. *Educational and psychological measurement*, 20(1):37–46.

Martin Ester, Hans-Peter Kriegel, Jörg Sander, Xiaowei Xu, et al. 1996. A density-based algorithm for discovering clusters in large spatial databases with noise. In *kdd*, volume 96, pages 226–231.

Max Grusky, Mor Naaman, and Yoav Artzi. 2018. Newsroom: A dataset of 1.3 million summaries with diverse extractive strategies. In *Proceedings of the 2018 Conference of the North American Chapter of* the Association for Computational Linguistics: Human Language Technologies, Volume 1 (Long Papers), pages 708–719, New Orleans, Louisiana. Association for Computational Linguistics.

Matthew Honnibal and Ines Montani. 2017. spaCy 2: Natural language understanding with Bloom embeddings, convolutional neural networks and incremental parsing. To appear.

Taehee Jung, Dongyeop Kang, Lucas Mentch, and Eduard H. Hovy. 2019. Earlier isnt always better: Subaspect analysis on corpus and system biases in summarization. *ArXiv*, abs/1908.11723.

Ryuji Kano, Takumi Takahashi, Toru Nishino, Motoki Taniguchi, Tomoki Taniguchi, and Tomoko Ohkuma. 2021. Quantifying appropriateness of summarization data for curriculum learning. In *Proceedings of the 16th Conference of the European Chapter of the Association for Computational Linguistics: Main Volume*, pages 1395–1405, Online. Association for Computational Linguistics.

Wojciech Kryscinski, Nitish Shirish Keskar, Bryan McCann, Caiming Xiong, and Richard Socher. 2019. Neural text summarization: A critical evaluation. In *Proceedings of the 2019 Conference on Empirical Methods in Natural Language Processing and the 9th International Joint Conference on Natural Language Processing (EMNLP-IJCNLP)*, pages 540–551, Hong Kong, China. Association for Computational Linguistics.

Chin-Yew Lin. 2004a. Looking for a few good metrics: Automatic summarization evaluation-how many samples are enough? In *NTCIR*.

Chin-Yew Lin. 2004b. Rouge: A package for automatic evaluation of summaries. In *Text summarization branches out*, pages 74–81.

Ilya Loshchilov and Frank Hutter. 2018. Fixing weight decay regularization in adam.

Ramesh Nallapati, Bowen Zhou, Cicero dos Santos, Çağlar Gulçehre, and Bing Xiang. 2016. Abstractive text summarization using sequence-to-sequence RNNs and beyond. In *Proceedings of The 20th SIGNLL Conference on Computational Natural Language Learning*, pages 280–290, Berlin, Germany. Association for Computational Linguistics.

Anjali Narayan-Chen, Prashant Jayannavar, and Julia Hockenmaier. 2019. Collaborative dialogue in Minecraft. In *Proceedings of the 57th Annual Meeting of the Association for Computational Linguistics*, pages 5405–5415, Florence, Italy. Association for Computational Linguistics.

Martin Potthast, Tim Gollub, Kristof Komlossy, Sebastian Schuster, Matti Wiegmann, Erika Patricia Garces Fernandez, Matthias Hagen, and Benno Stein. 2018. Crowdsourcing a large corpus of clickbait on twitter. In *Proceedings of the 27th international conference on computational linguistics*, pages 1498–1507.

Colin Raffel, Noam Shazeer, Adam Roberts, Katherine Lee, Sharan Narang, Michael Matena, Yanqi Zhou, Wei Li, and Peter J Liu. 2019. Exploring the limits of transfer learning with a unified text-to-text transformer. *arXiv preprint arXiv:1910.10683*.

Alexander M. Rush, Sumit Chopra, and Jason Weston. 2015. A neural attention model for abstractive sentence summarization. In *Proceedings of the 2015 Conference on Empirical Methods in Natural Language Processing*, pages 379–389, Lisbon, Portugal. Association for Computational Linguistics.

Victor Sanh, Lysandre Debut, Julien Chaumond, and Thomas Wolf. 2019. Distilbert, a distilled version of bert: smaller, faster, cheaper and lighter. *ArXiv*, abs/1910.01108.

Nakatani Shuyo. 2010. Language detection library for java.

Karen Spärck Jones. 1999. Automatic summarising: factors and directions. In *Advances in automatic text summarisation*. MIT Press.

Priyam Tejaswin, Dhruv Naik, and Pengfei Liu. 2021. How well do you know your summarization datasets? In *FINDINGS*.

A Implementation details of noise filtration and strapline detection heuristics

Before applying the noise filtration and the strapline detection heuristics, Spacy's model (namely `en_core_web_sm`) (Honnibal and Montani, 2017) was used to tokenize the extracts, and determine the pos tags of the tokens.

A.1 Noise filtration

Web formatting syntax The following regular expressions `<[a-zA-Z0-9_]+[/]?>`, and `[a-z]+="` were used to determine the presence of HTML tags and key/value pairs as part of the extract. The first one looks for opening HTML tags in the form `<ALPHA_NUMERIC_SYBMBOL>`, and closing HTML tags in the form `<ALPHA_NUMERIC_SYBMBOL/>`. The second regular expression looks for alphabetic symbols followed by an equal sign and a double quotation.

Truncation An extract is considered to be truncated if it ends with a comma or ends with a word whose part of speech (pos) tag is a determiner, a coordinating conjunction, a subordinating conjunction, or an unknown pos tag.

Dateline Since dates might have different formats, a python package called *dateutil* [5] was used to parse the extract. An extract is considered as a dateline if the package manages to parse it according to any of the package's formats for dates.

Shortness Extracts having three or less tokens (after excluding punctuation marks) are considered to be trivially short and thus removed from the dataset.

Non-English On looking at the unique characters of the Newsroom dataset, we noticed that it contains characters from other scripts such as: Arabic, and Chinese. Consequently, a python package called *langdetect* [6] which is ported from one of Google's projects (Shuyo, 2010) was used in order to filter-out articles that aren't written in English. The article's text was used instead of the extract to detect the language, since the *langdetect* package has higher precision when supplied with longer spans of text (i.e. when given the whole article text instead of just the extract). This implies that we are assuming that the language of the article's body and its extract will be the same, and that having a non-English body is enough to discard the article-extract pair from the dataset.

A.2 Strapline detection

Beginning with imperative speech If the pos tag of the first token in the extract is VB (base form of verb), then the extract is considered to be beginning with an imperative.

Having high quotes coverage A simple pattern matching function is used to compute the percentage of the tokens found between quotes in the extract. An extract is considered as a strapline if its quotes coverage is higher than a preset threshold (a hyperparameter set to 0.35 based on manual investigations of the dataset).

Using 1st or 2nd person pronouns If any of the extracts' tokens is part of the following list (i, me, mine, myself, we, our, ours, ourselves, you, your, yours, yourself, yourselves), then it's said to use a 1st or 2nd person pronouns.

Using question/exclamation marks The presence of a question or an exclamation mark is used to simplify the detection of interrogative/ exclamation phrases.

[5] https://dateutil.readthedocs.io/en/stable/

[6] https://pypi.org/project/langdetect/

Using a repeated extract If an extract is repeated more than once in the training dataset then it's discarded. Using a clustering method such as Density-Based Spatial Clustering of Applications with Noise (DBSCAN) (Ester et al., 1996) on top of sparse term frequency vectors representing the extracts achieves better performance at the expense of running time. Therefore, we opted to use the simple method of having exact matches as a method to detect repeated extracts.

B Hyperparameters in the experiments

Clickbait Detector We fine-tune distilled BERT using AdamW optimizer (Loshchilov and Hutter, 2018), the early stopping mechanism with patience of 5, a batch size of 128, and a learning rate of 10^{-4}. The max input length is set to 512.

T5-based Summarizer The max length of input and output are set to 512 and 128, respectively. We fine-tune T5 using AdamW optimizer (Loshchilov and Hutter, 2018), the early stopping mechanism with patience of 5, a batch size of 32, and a learning rate of 10^{-4}.

C Results of fine-tuning T5-large

Looking at the ROUGE scores in Table 1, one can notice that similar trends are achieved on fine-tuning a T5-large summarizer to these found on fine-tuning a T5-base summarizer (as discussed in the main paper). While T5-large achieves higher absolute ROUGE scores, the effect of removing noise, and straplines from the training corpus is nearly the same for both the T5-base, and the T5-large models, which demonstrates that more attention needs to be given to the quality of the dataset rather than using larger models.

D Distribution of Heuristics

Table 2 shows the distribution within the NYT and Time.com datasets, including both noisy samples and straplines. Note that there might be overlap between different heuristics.

Training Set		Original Test Set			Cleaned Test Set		
		R-1	R-2	R-L	R-1	R-2	R-L
NYT	original	16.62	4.35	13.63	15.87	2.59	12.56
	w/o straplines	**21.80**	**5.30**	**17.19**	**23.43**	**6.03**	**18.34**
Time.com	original	**16.47**	**3.44**	**13.64**	**19.36**	4.32	15.82
	w/o straplines	16.07	3.38	13.43	19.28	**4.46**	**15.96**
Combined	original	**20.19**	**5.50**	**16.41**	21.54	5.25	17.05
	w/o straplines	19.61	4.60	15.79	**22.07**	**5.55**	**17.60**

Table 1: ROUGE-1, ROUGE-2, and ROUGE-L scores for the abstractive summarizer (T5-large version) trained on the dataset with and without the straplines. The best results are in bold.

Heuristic		NYT		Time.com	
		Training Set	Test Set	Training Set	Test Set
Noise	too_short	**1.42%**	**1.55%**	**3.61%**	**3.92%**
	is_a_date	0%	0%	0.32%	0.43%
	has_HTML	0.09%	0.06%	0.55%	0.55%
	strange_ending	0.09%	0.12%	0.26%	0.21%
	is_non_english	0.31%	0.34%	0.01%	0%
Strapline	mostly_quotes	0.03%	0.06%	0.15%	0.22%
	has_1st_or_2nd_person_pronoun	**6.80%**	**7.54%**	14.11%	14.60%
	has_question_exclamation_marks	5.69%	6.05%	6.08%	5.67%
	imperative_speech	1.07%	1.01%	4.12%	4.68%
	is_repeated	5.78%	4.43%	0%	0%
	is_clickbait	6.34%	6.53%	**29.03%**	**28.75%**

Table 2: The distribution of the heuristics (both noises and straplines) within the datasets.

A global analysis of metrics used for measuring performance in natural language processing

Kathrin Blagec and **Georg Dorffner** and **Milad Moradi** and
Simon Ott and **Matthias Samwald**
Institute of Artificial Intelligence;
Center for Medical Statistics, Informatics, and Intelligent Systems;
Medical University of Vienna, Vienna, Austria.

Abstract

Measuring the performance of natural language processing models is challenging. Traditionally used metrics, such as BLEU and ROUGE, originally devised for machine translation and summarization, have been shown to suffer from low correlation with human judgment and a lack of transferability to other tasks and languages. In the past 15 years, a wide range of alternative metrics have been proposed. However, it is unclear to what extent this has had an impact on NLP benchmarking efforts. Here we provide the first large-scale cross-sectional analysis of metrics used for measuring performance in natural language processing. We curated, mapped and systematized more than 3500 machine learning model performance results from the open repository 'Papers with Code' to enable a global and comprehensive analysis. Our results suggest that the large majority of natural language processing metrics currently used have properties that may result in an inadequate reflection of a models' performance. Furthermore, we found that ambiguities and inconsistencies in the reporting of metrics may lead to difficulties in interpreting and comparing model performances, impairing transparency and reproducibility in NLP research.

1 Introduction

Benchmarking, i.e., the process of measuring and comparing model performance on a specific task or set of tasks, is an important driver of progress in natural language processing (NLP). Benchmark datasets are conceptualized as fixed sets of data that are manually, semi-automatically or automatically generated to form a representative sample for these specific tasks to be solved by a model. A model's performance on such a benchmark is then assessed based on a single or a small set of performance metrics. While this enables quick comparisons, it may entail the risk of conveying an incomplete picture of model performance since metrics inherently condense performance to a single number, omitting certain performance aspects completely or balancing trade-offs between different aspects (e.g. accuracy vs. fluency). Additionally the capacity of metrics to capture performance may differ strongly between tasks and languages.

Capturing model performance in a single metric is an inherently difficult task, and this is further aggravated in the NLP domain by the structural and semantic complexity of human language. Traditionally used NLP metrics such as BLEU or ROUGE, originally devised for machine translation and summarization, were shown to suffer from low correlation with human judgment and poor transferability to other tasks (Lin, 2004; Liu and Liu, 2008; Ng and Abrecht, 2015; Novikova et al., 2017; Chen et al., 2019). These fundamental problems are increasingly recognized by the NLP community—e.g., metric evaluation was even introduced as an independent task at the annual Machine Translation conference (Ma et al., 2019).

In the past 15 years, a wide variety of superior metrics for evaluating models on NLP tasks have been proposed, including task-agnostic, AI-based metrics such as BERTscore (Zhang et al., 2019; Peters et al., 2018; Clark et al., 2019). However, it is unknown to what extent this had an impact on metrics used in NLP research.

We aim to address this question by providing a global analysis of performance measures used in NLP benchmarking. Our contributions are threefold: (1) We curated, mapped and systematized performance metrics covering more than 3500 performance results from the open repository 'Papers with Code' to enable a global and comprehensive analysis. (2) Based on this dataset, we provide a cross-sectional analysis of the prevalence of performance measures in the subset of natural language processing benchmarks. (3) We describe inconsistencies and ambiguities in the reporting and usage of metrics, which may lead to difficulties in interpreting and comparing model performances.

Proceedings of NLP Power! The First Workshop on Efficient Benchmarking in NLP, pages 52 - 63
May 26, 2022

2 Methods

2.1 Dataset

Our analyses are based on data available from Papers with Code (PWC), a large, web-based open platform that collects Machine learning papers and summarizes evaluation results on benchmark datasets. PWC is built on automatically extracted data from arXiv submissions and manual crowd-sourced annotation.

The Intelligence Task Ontology (ITO) aims to provide a comprehensive map of artificial intelligence tasks using a richly structured hierarchy of processes, algorithms, data and performance metrics.[1] ITO is based on data from PWC and the EDAM ontology [2]. The development process of ITO is detailed in (Blagec et al., 2021). We built on ITO for further curation and on of a hierarchical mapping of the raw performance metric data from PWC.

2.2 Hierarchical mapping and further curation of metric names

The raw dataset exported from PWC contained a total number of 812 different strings representing metric names that appeared as distinct data property instances in ITO. These metric names were used by human annotators on the PWC platform to add results for a given model to the evaluation table of the relevant benchmark dataset's leaderboard on PWC. This list of raw metrics in the PWC database was manually curated into a canonical hierarchy by our team. This entailed some complexities and required extensive manual curation which was conducted based on the mapping proceduce described below.

In many cases, the same metric was reported under multiple different synonyms and abbreviations. Furthermore, many results were reported in specialized sub-variants of established metrics. For each metric a canonical property denoting its general form (e.g., 'BLEU score') was created, and synonyms and sub-variants were mapped to it. For example, the reported performance metrics 'BLEU-1', 'BLEU-2' and 'B-3' were made sub-metrics of 'BLEU score'. Throughout the paper, we will refer to canonical properties and mapped metrics as 'top-level metrics' and 'sub-metrics', respectively.

In case a library that implemented a metric was used as the metric name (e.g., SacreBLEU, which is a reference implementation of the BLEU score available as a Python package), this property was made sub-metric of the more general metric name, in this case 'BLEU score'.

271 entries from the original list could not be assigned a metric and were subsumed under a separate category 'Undetermined'. After this extensive manual curation, the resulting list covered by our dataset could be reduced from 812 to 187 distinct performance metrics. Where possible, we used the respective preferred Wikipedia article titles as canonical names for the metrics. For an excerpt of the resulting property hierarchy, see Figure A.1 in Appendix A.

2.3 Grouping of top-level metrics

Top-level metrics were further grouped into categories based on the task type they are usually applied to: Classification, Computer vision, Natural language processing, Regression, Game playing, Ranking, Clustering and 'Other'. We limited our main analysis to the category 'Natural language processing', which only contains metrics that are specific to NLP, such as ROUGE, BLEU or METEOR. We provide additional statistics on general classification metrics, such as Accuracy or F1 score that are also often used in NLP benchmarks but are not specific to NLP tasks in Table B.1 in Appendix B.

2.4 Analysis

Analyses were performed based on the ITO release of 13.7.2020. Raw statistics were generated based on the ITO ontology using SPARQL queries and further processed and analyzed using Jupyter Notebooks and the Python 'pandas' library. Data, code and notebooks to generate these statistics are available on Github (see section 'Data and code availability').

3 Results

3.1 Data basis

32,209 benchmark results across 2,298 distinct benchmark datasets reported in a total number of 3,867 papers were included in this analysis. Included papers consist of papers in the PWC database that were annotated with at least one performance metric as of July 2020. A single paper can thus contribute results to more than one benchmark and to one or more performance metrics.

[1] https://github.com/OpenBioLink/ITO

[2] http://edamontology.org/

	Total dataset	NLP subset
Number of benchmark datasets	2,298	491
Number of benchmark results	32,209	4,812
Time span covered	2000-2020	2000-2020

Table 1: General descriptives of the analyzed dataset (as of July 2020).

The publication period of the analyzed papers covers twenty years, from 2000 until 2020, with the majority having been published in the past ten years (see Figure B.2 in Appendix B).

The subset of NLP benchmark datasets considered in our analysis included 4,812 benchmark results across 491 benchmark datasets (see Table 1).

3.2 Which performance metrics are most frequently reported in NLP benchmarking?

Table 2 lists the top 10 most frequently reported performance metrics. Considering submetrics, ROUGE-1, ROUGE-2 and ROUGE-L were the most commonly annotated ROUGE variants, and BLEU-4 and BLEU-1 were the most frequently annotated BLEU variants. For a large fraction of BLEU and ROUGE annotations, the subvariant was not specified in the annotation.

The BLEU score was used across a wide range of NLP benchmark tasks, such as machine translation, question answering, summarization and text generation. ROUGE metrics were mostly used for text generation, video captioning and summarization tasks while METEOR was mainly used for image and video captioning, text generation and question answering tasks.

3.3 Are metrics reported together with other metrics or do they stand alone?

The BLEU score was reported without any other metrics in 80.2% of the cases, whereas the ROUGE metrics more often appeared together with other metrics and stood alone in only nine out of 24 occurrences. METEOR was, in all cases, reported together with at least one other metric. Figure B.1 in Appendix B shows the co-occurrence matrix for the top 10 most frequently used NLP-specific metrics. BLEU was most often reported together with the ROUGE metrics (n=12) and METEOR (n=12). ROUGE likewise frequently appeared together with METEOR (n=10). We additionally provide statistics on the number of distinct metrics per benchmark for the total dataset in Figure B.3 in Appendix B.

3.4 Inconsistencies and ambiguities in the reporting of performance metrics

During the mapping process it became evident that performance metrics are often reported in an inconsistent or ambiguous manner. One example for this are the ROUGE metrics, which have originally been proposed in different variants (e.g., ROUGE-1, ROUGE-L) but are often simply referred to as 'ROUGE'. Furthermore, ROUGE metrics have originally been proposed in a 'recall' and 'precision' sub-variant, such as 'ROUGE-1 precision' and 'ROUGE-1 recall'. Further, the harmonic mean between these two scores (ROUGE-1 F1 score) can be calculated. However, results are often reported as, e.g., 'ROUGE-1' without specifying the variant, which may lead to ambiguities when comparing results between different publications.

4 Discussion

NLP covers a wide range of different tasks and thus shows a large diversity of utilized metrics. We limited our analysis to more complex NLP tasks beyond simple classification, such as machine translation, question answering, and summarization. Metrics designed for these tasks generally aim to assess the similarity between a machine-generated text and a reference text or set of reference texts that are human-generated.

We found that, despite their known shortcomings, the BLEU score and ROUGE metrics continue to be the most frequently used metrics for such tasks.

Several weaknesses of BLEU have been pointed out by the research community, such as its sole focus on n-gram precision without considering recall and its reliance on exact n-gram matchings. Zhang et al. have discussed properties of the BLEU score and NIST, a variant of the BLEU score that gives more weight to rarer n-grams than to more frequent ones, and came to the conclusion that neither of the

Performance metric	Number of benchmark datasets	Percent
BLEU score	300	61.1
ROUGE metric	114	23.2
Perplexity	48	9.8
METEOR	39	7.9
Word error rate	36	7.3
Exact match	33	6.7
CIDEr	24	4.9
Unlabeled attachment score	18	3.7
Labeled attachment score	15	3.1
Bit per character	12	2.4

Table 2: Top 10 reported NLP metrics and percent of NLP benchmark datasets (n=491) that use the respective metric. BLEU: Bilingual Evaluation Understudy, CIDEr: Consensus-based Image Description Evaluation, ROUGE: Recall-Oriented Understudy for Gisting Evaluation, METEOR: Metric for Evaluation of Translation with Explicit ORdering.

two metrics necessarily show high correlation with human judgments of machine translation quality (Doddington, 2002; Zhang et al., 2004).

The ROUGE (Recall-Oriented Understudy for Gisting Evaluation) metrics family was the second most used NLP-specific metric in our dataset after the BLEU score. While originally proposed for summarization tasks, a subset of the ROUGE metrics (i.e., ROUGE-L, ROUGE-W and ROUGE-S) has also been shown to perform well in machine translation evaluation tasks (Lin, 2004; Och, 2004). However, the ROUGE metrics set has also been shown to not adequately cover multi-document summarization, tasks that rely on extensive paraphrasing, such as abstractive summarization, and extractive summarization of multi-logue text types (i.e., transcripts with many different speakers), such as meeting transcripts (Lin, 2004; Liu and Liu, 2008; Ng and Abrecht, 2015). Several new variants have been proposed in recent years, which make use of the incorporation of word embeddings (ROUGE-WE), graph-based approaches (ROUGE-G), or the extension with additional lexical features (ROUGE 2.0) (Ng and Abrecht, 2015; ShafieiBavani et al., 2018; Ganesan, 2018). ROUGE-1, ROUGE-2 and ROUGE-L were the most common ROUGE metrics in our analyzed dataset, while newer proposed ROUGE variants were not represented.

METEOR (Metric for Evaluation of Translation with Explicit Ordering) was proposed in 2005 to address weaknesses of previous metrics (Banerjee and Lavie, 2005). METEOR is an F-measure derived metric that has repeatedly been shown to yield higher correlation with human judgment across several tasks as compared to BLEU and NIST (Lavie et al., 2004; Graham et al., 2015; Chen et al., 2019). Matchings are scored based on their unigram precision, unigram recall (given higher weight than precision), and a comparison of the word ordering of the translation compared to the reference text. This is in contrast to the BLEU score, which does not take into account n-gram recall. Furthermore, while BLEU only considers exact word matches in its scoring, METEOR also takes into account words that are morphologically related or synonymous to each other by using stemming, lexical resources and a paraphrase table. Additionally, METEOR was designed to provide informative scores at sentence-level and not only at corpus-level. An adapted version of METEOR, called METEOR++ 2.0, was proposed in 2019 (Guo and Hu, 2019). This variant extends METEOR's paraphrasing table with a large external paraphrase database and has been shown to correlate better with human judgement across many machine translation tasks.

Compared to BLEU and ROUGE, METEOR was rarely used as a performance metric (8%) across the NLP benchmark datasets included in our dataset.

The GLEU score was proposed as an evaluation metric for NLP applications, such as machine translation, summarization and natural language generation, in 2007 (Mutton et al., 2007). It is a Support Vector Machine-based metric that uses a combination of individual parser-derived metrics as features. GLEU aims to assess how well the generated text conforms to 'normal' use of human

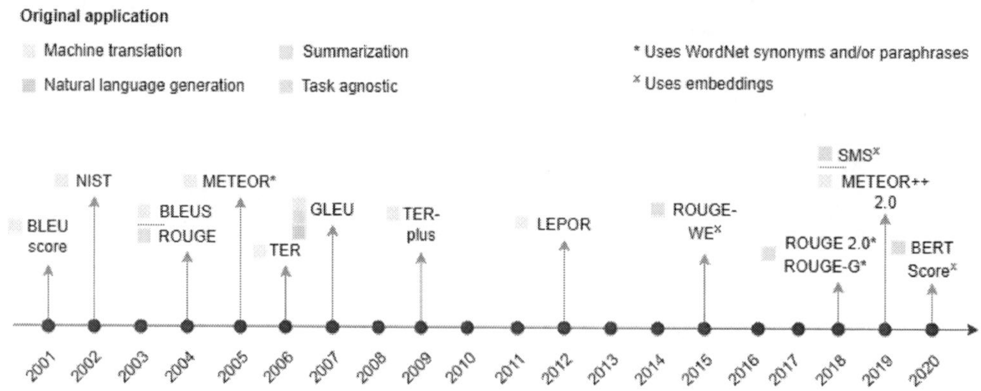

Figure 1: Timeline of the introduction of NLP metrics and their original application. SMS: Sentence Mover's Similarity.

language, i.e., its 'fluency'. This is in contrast to other commonly used metrics that focus on how well a generated text reflects a reference text or vice versa. GLEU was reported only in 1.8% of NLP benchmark datasets.

Additional alternative metrics that have been proposed by the NLP research community but do not appear as performance metrics in the analyzed dataset include Translation error rate (TER), TER-Plus, "Length Penalty, Precision, n-gram Position difference Penalty and Recall" (LEPOR), Sentence Mover's Similarity, and BERTScore. Figure 1 depicts the timeline of introduction of NLP metrics and their original application.

TER was proposed as a metric for evaluating machine translation quality. TER measures quality by the number of edits that are needed to change the machine-generated text into the reference text(s), with lower TER scores indicating higher translation quality (Snover et al., 2006). TER considers five edit operations to change the output into the reference text: Matches, insertions, deletions, substitutions and shifts. An adaptation of TER, TER-Plus, was proposed in 2009. Ter-Plus extends TER with three additional edit operations, i.e., stem matches, synonym matches and phrase substitution (Snover et al., 2009). TER-Plus was shown to have higher correlations with human judgements in machine translation tasks than BLEU, METEOR and TERp (Snover et al., 2009). LEPOR and its variants hLEPOR and nLEPOR were proposed as a language-independent model that aims to address the issue that several previous metrics tend to perform worse on languages other than those it was originally designed for. It has been shown to yield higher correlations with human judgement than METEOR, BLEU, or TER (Han et al., 2012).

Sentence Mover's Similarity (SMS) is a metric based on ELMo word embeddings and Earth mover's distance, which measures the minimum cost of turning a set of machine generated sentences into a reference text's sentences (Peters et al., 2018; Clark et al., 2019). It was proposed in 2019 and was shown to yield better results as compared to ROUGE-L in terms of correlation with human judgment in summarization tasks.

BERTScore was proposed as a task-agnostic performance metric in 2019 (Zhang et al., 2019). It computes the similarity of two sentences based on the sum of cosine similarities between their token's contextual embeddings (BERT), and optionally weighs them by inverse document frequency scores (Devlin et al., 2018). BERTScore was shown to outperform established metrics, such as BLEU, METEOR and ROUGE-L in machine translation and image captioning tasks. It was also more robust than other metrics when applied to an adversarial paraphrase detection task. However, the authors also state that BERTScore's configuration should be adapted to task-specific needs since no single configuration consistently outperforms all others across tasks.

Difficulties associated with automatic evaluation of machine generated texts include poor correlation with human judgement, language bias (i.e., the metric shows better correlation with human judgment for certain languages than others), and worse suitability for language generation tasks other than the one it was proposed for (Novikova et al., 2017). In fact, most NLP metrics have originally been conceptualized for a very specific application, such as BLEU and METEOR for machine translation, or ROUGE for the evaluation of machine generated text summaries, but have since then been introduced as metrics for several other NLP tasks, such as question-answering, where all three of the above mentioned scores are regularly used. Non-transferability to other tasks has recently been shown by Chen et al. who have compared several metrics (i.e., ROUGE-L, METEOR, BERTScore, BLEU-1, BLEU-4, Conditional BERTScore and Sentence Mover's Similarity) for evaluating generative Question-Answering (QA) tasks based on three QA datasets. They recommend that from the evaluated metrics, METEOR should preferably be used and point out that metrics originally introduced for evaluating machine translation and summarization do not necessarily perform well in the evaluation of question answering tasks (Chen et al., 2019).

Many NLP metrics use very specific sets of features, such as specific word embeddings or linguistic elements, which may complicate comparability and replicability. To address the issue of replicability, reference open source implementations have been published for some metrics, such as, ROUGE, sentBleu-moses as part of the Moses toolkit and sacreBLEU (Lin, 2004).

In summary, we found that the large majority of metrics currently used to report NLP research results have properties that may result in an inadequate reflection of a models' performance. While several alternative metrics that address problematic properties have been proposed, they are currently rarely used in NLP benchmarking. Our findings are in line with a recent, focused meta-analysis on machine translation conducted by Marie et al. who found that 82.1% of papers report BLEU as the only performance metric despite its well-known shortcomings (Marie et al., 2021). Our analysis extends these findings by providing a global overview of metrics used in the entire NLP domain.

4.1 Recommendations for reporting performance results and future considerations

In the following, we provide recommendations on the reporting of performance metrics and discuss potential future avenues for improving measuring performance using benchmarks in NLP.

4.1.1 Increasing transparency and consistency in the reporting of performance metrics

Performance metrics should be reported in a clear and unambiguous way to improve transparency, avoid misinterpretation and enable reproducibility.

- For performance metrics that have various sub-variants, it should be clearly stated which variant is reported (e.g., ROUGE-1 F1 score instead of ROUGE-1). If multiple metrics are averaged, it should be stated what kind of mean is used (e.g., arithmetic mean, geometric mean, harmonic mean) if this is not clear from the definition of the metric itself (e.g., F1 score).
- If a metric is used that allows for adaptations, such as weighting, these should be explicitly stated and be marked clearly in the result tables. Ideally, when using abbreviations, the variant should be included in the abbreviation or e.g., marked by a subscript.
- To increase transparency and allow reproducibility, the formula for calculating the metric should be included in the manuscript or in the Appendix.
- For more complex metrics, if available, a reference implementation should be used and cited. If such a reference implementation is not available, or a custom implementation or adaptation is used, the code should be made available.

In the future, a taxonomic hierarchy of performance metrics that captures definitions, systematizes metrics together with all existing variants and lists recommended applications based on comparative evaluation studies. In this work, we have created a starting point for creating such a taxonomy using a bottom-up approach as part of ITO (Blagec et al., 2021).

4.1.2 Maximizing the informative value in the reporting of performance results

Developing metrics for NLP tasks is an ongoing research area, new metrics outperforming previous ones are proposed on a regular basis, and suitability is strongly task- and dataset-dependent, therefore general advice on which metric to use cannot be given.

Instead, it should be critically evaluated whether a metric is suitable for a given dataset, task or language, especially if the metric was originally proposed for a different application. Comparative evaluation studies, such as in (Chen et al., 2019) can provide an indication for the suitability.

If a metric is used that has been shown to have limited informative value (in general, or in specific use cases) and no alternative is available, the limitations and their relevance for the task and/or dataset should be discussed.

If more than one suitable metric is available, consider reporting all of them, especially if there is a discrepancy in performance results.

Even if a benchmark is historically evaluated based on a certain metric, consider additionally reporting newer proposed metrics if they are suitable and have been evaluated to be useful for the task.

4.2 Future considerations on performance metrics in the context of benchmarking

Comparative evaluation studies investigating performance metrics, their properties and their correlation across multiple tasks, datasets and languages could help to better understand metrics and their suitability for different applications. While studies focusing on a small set of metrics exist, such as in (Chen et al., 2019), larger studies are, to the best of our knowledge, yet to be undertaken.

Recent work introduced the notions of dynamic benchmarks that allow users to weigh different performance metrics of interest. An example of this is 'Dynascore' which allows customizable aggregation of performance across different aspects including non-traditionally assessed performance dimensions, such as memory, robustness, and "fairness (Ma et al., 2021). Further, bidimensional leaderboards based on linear ensembles of metrics have been proposed (Gehrmann et al., 2021; Ruder, 2021; Kasai et al., 2021). These approaches could further improve the practical utility of benchmark results.

4.3 Limitations

Our analyses are based on ITO v0.21 which encompasses data until mid 2020. To ensure that our results are still relevant given the fast pace of research, we checked whether considering data from the recently released ITO v1.01 which includes data until mid 2021 leads to any significant time-dependent changes of our results [3]. Including this more recent data did, however, not alter the described usage patterns of NLP metrics.

The results presented in this paper are based on a large set of machine learning papers available from the PWC database, which is the largest annotated dataset of benchmark results currently available. The database comprises both preprints of papers published on arXiv and papers published in peer-reviewed journals. While it could be argued that arXiv preprints are not representative of scientific journal articles, it has recently been shown that a large fraction of arXiv preprints (77%) are subsequently published in peer-reviewed venues (Lin et al., 2020).

5 Conclusions

The reporting of metrics was partly inconsistent and partly unspecific, which may lead to ambiguities when comparing model performances, thus negatively impacting the transparency and reproducibility of NLP research. Large comparative evaluation studies of different NLP-specific metrics across multiple benchmarking tasks are needed.

Data and code availability

The OWL (Web Ontology Language) file of the ITO model is made available on Github [4] and BioPortal [5]. The ontology file is distributed under a CC-BY-SA license. ITO includes data from the Papers With Code project [6]. Papers With Code is licensed under the CC-BY-SA license. Data from Papers With Code are partially altered (manual curation to improve ontological structure and data quality). ITO includes data from the EDAM ontology. The EDAM ontology is licensed under a CC-BY-SA license.

Notebooks containing the queries and code for data analysis are also accessible via GitHub.

Acknowledgements

We thank the team from 'Papers With Code' for making their database available and all annotators who contributed to it.

References

Satanjeev Banerjee and Alon Lavie. 2005. METEOR: An automatic metric for MT evaluation with im-

[3]Data curation in ITO v1.01 is still incomplete. Therefore, results are based on the fully curated ITO v0.21.

[4]https://github.com/OpenBioLink/ITO

[5]https://bioportal.bioontology.org/ontologies/ITO

[6]https://paperswithcode.com/

proved correlation with human judgments. *Proceedings of the ACL Workshop on Intrinsic and Extrinsic Evaluation Measures for Machine Translation and/or Summarization*.

Kathrin Blagec, Adriano Barbosa-Silva, Simon Ott, and Matthias Samwald. 2021. A curated, ontology-based, large-scale knowledge graph of artificial intelligence tasks and benchmarks.

Anthony Chen, Gabriel Stanovsky, Sameer Singh, and Matt Gardner. 2019. Evaluating question answering evaluation. In *Proceedings of the 2nd Workshop on Machine Reading for Question Answering*, pages 119–124, Stroudsburg, PA, USA. Association for Computational Linguistics.

Elizabeth Clark, Asli Celikyilmaz, and Noah A. Smith. 2019. Sentence mover's similarity: Automatic evaluation for multi-sentence texts. In *Proceedings of the 57th Annual Meeting of the Association for Computational Linguistics*, pages 2748–2760, Stroudsburg, PA, USA. Association for Computational Linguistics.

Jacob Devlin, Ming-Wei Chang, Kenton Lee, and Kristina Toutanova. 2018. BERT: Pre-training of deep bidirectional transformers for language understanding. *arXiv*.

George Doddington. 2002. Automatic evaluation of machine translation quality using n-gram co-occurrence statistics |proceedings of the second international conference on human language technology research.

Kavita Ganesan. 2018. ROUGE 2.0: Updated and improved measures for evaluation of summarization tasks. *arXiv*.

Sebastian Gehrmann, Tosin Adewumi, Karmanya Aggarwal, Pawan Sasanka Ammanamanchi, Aremu Anuoluwapo, Antoine Bosselut, Khyathi Raghavi Chandu, Miruna Clinciu, Dipanjan Das, Kaustubh D. Dhole, Wanyu Du, Esin Durmus, Ondřej Dušek, Chris Emezue, Varun Gangal, Cristina Garbacea, Tatsunori Hashimoto, Yufang Hou, Yacine Jernite, Harsh Jhamtani, Yangfeng Ji, Shailza Jolly, Mihir Kale, Dhruv Kumar, Faisal Ladhak, Aman Madaan, Mounica Maddela, Khyati Mahajan, Saad Mahamood, Bodhisattwa Prasad Majumder, Pedro Henrique Martins, Angelina McMillan-Major, Simon Mille, Emiel van Miltenburg, Moin Nadeem, Shashi Narayan, Vitaly Nikolaev, Rubungo Andre Niyongabo, Salomey Osei, Ankur Parikh, Laura Perez-Beltrachini, Niranjan Ramesh Rao, Vikas Raunak, Juan Diego Rodriguez, Sashank Santhanam, João Sedoc, Thibault Sellam, Samira Shaikh, Anastasia Shimorina, Marco Antonio Sobrevilla Cabezudo, Hendrik Strobelt, Nishant Subramani, Wei Xu, Diyi Yang, Akhila Yerukola, and Jiawei Zhou. 2021. The GEM benchmark: Natural language generation, its evaluation and metrics. *arXiv*.

Yvette Graham, Timothy Baldwin, and Nitika Mathur. 2015. Accurate evaluation of segment-level machine translation metrics. In *Proceedings of the 2015 Conference of the North American Chapter of the Association for Computational Linguistics: Human Language Technologies*, pages 1183–1191, Stroudsburg, PA, USA. Association for Computational Linguistics.

Yinuo Guo and Junfeng Hu. 2019. Meteor++ 2.0: Adopt syntactic level paraphrase knowledge into machine translation evaluation. In *Proceedings of the Fourth Conference on Machine Translation (Volume 2: Shared Task Papers, Day 1)*, pages 501–506, Stroudsburg, PA, USA. Association for Computational Linguistics.

Aaron L. F. Han, Derek F. Wong, and Lidia S. Chao. 2012. LEPOR: A robust evaluation metric for machine translation with augmented factors. *Proceedings of COLING 2012*.

Jungo Kasai, Keisuke Sakaguchi, Ronan Le Bras, Lavinia Dunagan, Jacob Morrison, Alexander R. Fabbri, Yejin Choi, and Noah A. Smith. 2021. Bidimensional leaderboards: Generate and evaluate language hand in hand. *arXiv*.

Alon Lavie, Kenji Sagae, and Shyamsundar Jayaraman. 2004. The significance of recall in automatic metrics for MT evaluation. In Robert E. Frederking, Kathryn B. Taylor, David Hutchison, Takeo Kanade, Josef Kittler, Jon M. Kleinberg, Friedemann Mattern, John C. Mitchell, Moni Naor, Oscar Nierstrasz, C. Pandu Rangan, Bernhard Steffen, Madhu Sudan, Demetri Terzopoulos, Dough Tygar, Moshe Y. Vardi, and Gerhard Weikum, editors, *Machine translation: from real users to research*, volume 3265 of *Lecture notes in computer science*, pages 134–143. Springer Berlin Heidelberg, Berlin, Heidelberg.

Chin-Yew Lin. 2004. ROUGE: A package for automatic evaluation of summaries. *Text Summarization Branches Out*.

Jialiang Lin, Yao Yu, Yu Zhou, Zhiyang Zhou, and Xiaodong Shi. 2020. How many preprints have actually been printed and why: a case study of computer science preprints on arXiv. *Scientometrics*.

Feifan Liu and Yang Liu. 2008. Correlation between ROUGE and human evaluation of extractive meeting summaries. In *Proceedings of the 46th Annual Meeting of the Association for Computational Linguistics on Human Language Technologies Short Papers - HLT '08*, page 201, Morristown, NJ, USA. Association for Computational Linguistics.

Qingsong Ma, Johnny Wei, Ondřej Bojar, and Yvette Graham. 2019. Results of the WMT19 metrics shared task: Segment-level and strong MT systems pose big challenges. In *Proceedings of the Fourth Conference on Machine Translation (Volume 2: Shared Task Papers, Day 1)*, pages 62–90, Stroudsburg, PA, USA. Association for Computational Linguistics.

Zhiyi Ma, Kawin Ethayarajh, Tristan Thrush, Somya Jain, Ledell Wu, Robin Jia, Christopher Potts, Adina Williams, and Douwe Kiela. 2021. Dynaboard: An evaluation-as-a-service platform for holistic next-generation benchmarking. *arXiv*.

Benjamin Marie, Atsushi Fujita, and Raphael Rubino. 2021. Scientific credibility of machine translation research: A meta-evaluation of 769 papers. In *Proceedings of the 59th Annual Meeting of the Association for Computational Linguistics and the 11th International Joint Conference on Natural Language Processing (Volume 1: Long Papers)*, pages 7297–7306, Stroudsburg, PA, USA. Association for Computational Linguistics.

Andrew Mutton, Mark Dras, Stephen Wan, and Robert Dale. 2007. [PDF] GLEU: Automatic evaluation of sentence-level fluency |semantic scholar. *undefined*.

Jun-Ping Ng and Viktoria Abrecht. 2015. Better summarization evaluation with word embeddings for ROUGE. In *Proceedings of the 2015 Conference on Empirical Methods in Natural Language Processing*, pages 1925–1930, Stroudsburg, PA, USA. Association for Computational Linguistics.

Jekaterina Novikova, Ondřej Dušek, Amanda Cercas Curry, and Verena Rieser. 2017. Why we need new evaluation metrics for NLG. In *Proceedings of the 2017 Conference on Empirical Methods in Natural Language Processing*, pages 2241–2252, Stroudsburg, PA, USA. Association for Computational Linguistics.

Franz Josef Och. 2004. Automatic evaluation of machine translation quality using longest common subsequence and skip-bigram statistics. *Proceedings of the 42nd annual meeting of the association for computational linguistics*, pages 606–613.

Matthew Peters, Mark Neumann, Mohit Iyyer, Matt Gardner, Christopher Clark, Kenton Lee, and Luke Zettlemoyer. 2018. Deep contextualized word representations. In *Proceedings of the 2018 Conference of the North American Chapter of the Association for Computational Linguistics: Human Language Technologies, Volume 1 (Long Papers)*, pages 2227–2237, Stroudsburg, PA, USA. Association for Computational Linguistics.

Sebastian Ruder. 2021. Challenges and Opportunities in NLP Benchmarking. `http://ruder.io/nlp-benchmarking`.

Elaheh ShafieiBavani, Mohammad Ebrahimi, Raymond Wong, and Fang Chen. 2018. A graph-theoretic summary evaluation for ROUGE. In *Proceedings of the 2018 Conference on Empirical Methods in Natural Language Processing*, pages 762–767, Stroudsburg, PA, USA. Association for Computational Linguistics.

Matthew Snover, Bonnie Dorr, Richard Schwartz, Linnea Micciulla, and John Makhoul. 2006. A study of translation edit rate with targeted human annotation. *In Proceedings of Association for Machine Translation in the Americas*, pages 223–231.

Matthew G. Snover, Nitin Madnani, Bonnie Dorr, and Richard Schwartz. 2009. TER-plus: paraphrase, semantic, and alignment enhancements to translation edit rate. *Machine Translation*, 23(2-3):117–127.

Tianyi Zhang, Varsha Kishore, Felix Wu, Kilian Q. Weinberger, and Yoav Artzi. 2019. BERTScore: Evaluating text generation with BERT. *arXiv*.

Ying Zhang, Stephan Vogel, and Alex Waibel. 2004. Interpreting BLEU/NIST scores: How much improvement do we need to have a better system? *Proceedings of the Fourth International Conference on Language Resources and Evaluation (LREC'04)*.

A Appendix: Performance metric property hierarchy

B Appendix: Additional statistics on the dataset

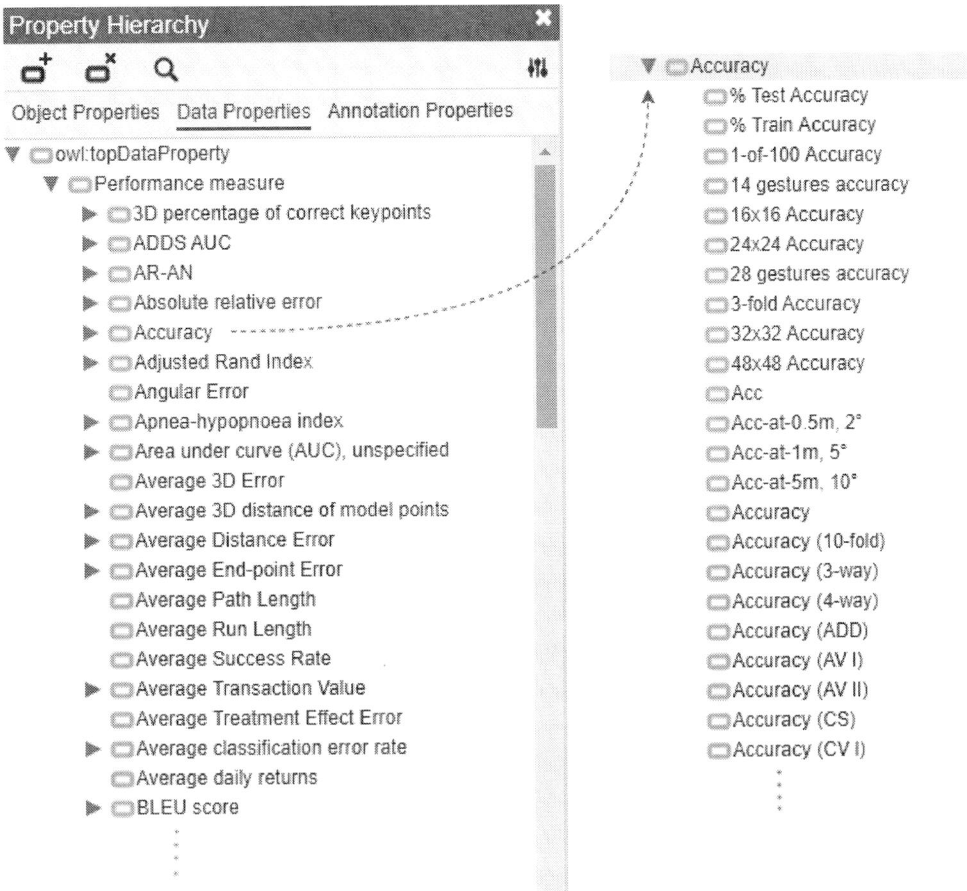

Figure A.1: Property hierarchy after manual curation of the raw list of metrics. The left side of the image shows an excerpt of the list of top-level performance metrics; the right side shows an excerpt of the list of submetrics for the top-level metric 'Accuracy'.

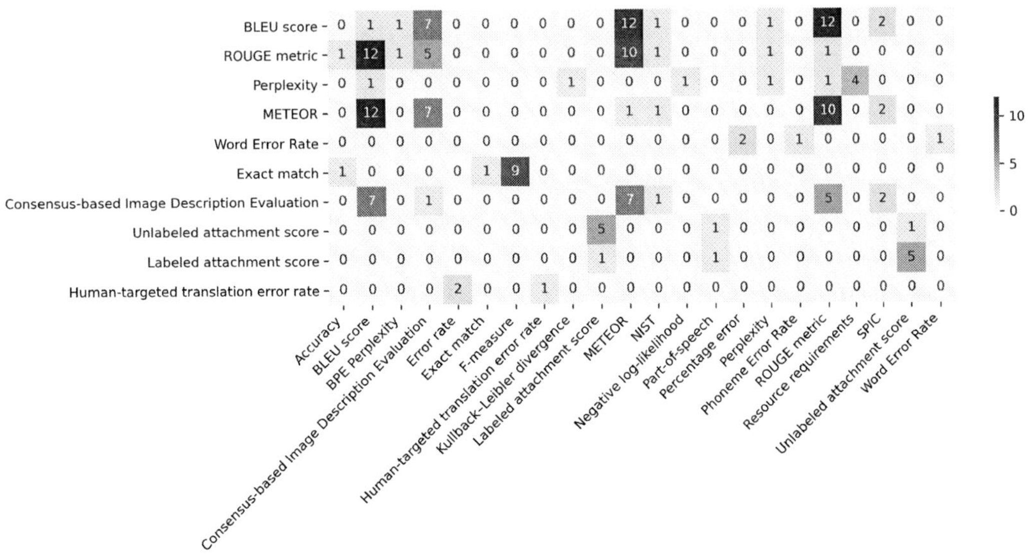

Figure B.1: Co-occurrence matrix for the top 10 most frequently used NLP metrics (y-axis). Only metrics that were reported at least one time together with either one of the selected metrics are shown (x-axis).

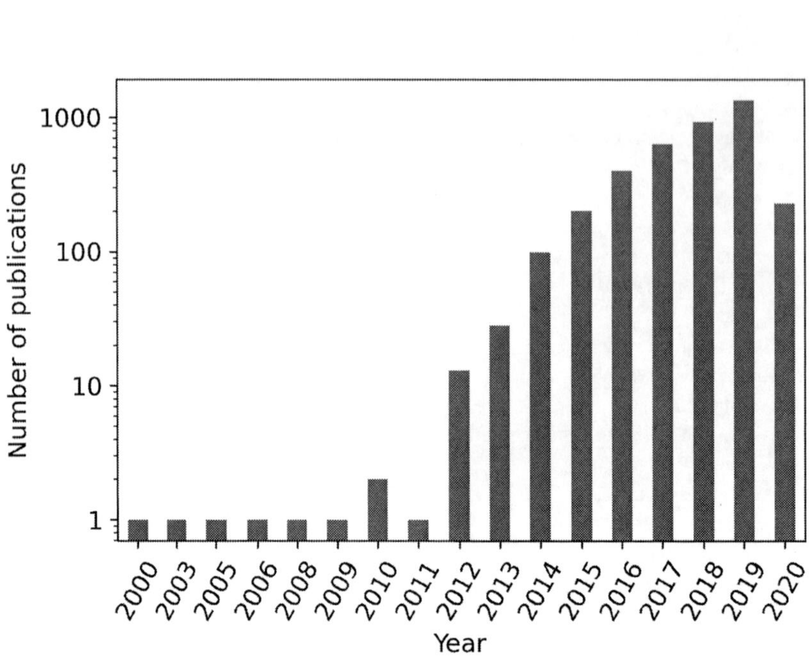

Figure B.2: Number of publications covered by the total dataset per year. The y-axis is scaled logarithmically.

Performance metric	Number of benchmark datasets	Percent
Accuracy	871	37.9
F-measure	393	17.1
Precision	374	16.3
R@k	143	6.2
AUC	123	5.4
IoU	115	5.0
Recall	79	3.4
Hits@k	69	3.0
P@k	33	1.4
Error rate	30	1.3

Table B.1: Top 10 reported simple classification metrics and percent of benchmark datasets that use the respective metric. R@k: Recall at k, AUC: Area under the curve, IoU: Intersection over union, P@k: Precision at k. AUC contains both ROC-AUC and PR-AUC.

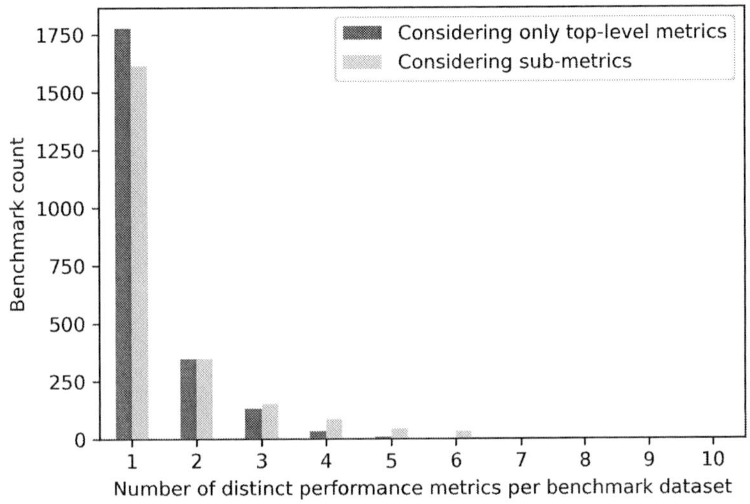

Figure B.3: Count of distinct metrics per benchmark dataset when considering only top-level metrics as distinct metrics (blue bars), and when considering sub-metrics as distinct metrics (grey bars). Median number of distinct metrics per benchmark: 1. Data is shown for the complete dataset (n=2,298).

Beyond Static Models and Test Sets: Benchmarking the Potential of Pre-trained Models Across Tasks and Languages

Kabir Ahuja[1] **Sandipan Dandapat**[2] **Sunayana Sitaram**[1] **Monojit Choudhury**[2]
[1] Microsoft Research, India
[2] Microsoft R&D, India
{t-kabirahuja,sadandap,sunayana.sitaram,monojitc}@microsoft.com

Abstract

Although recent Massively Multilingual Language Models (MMLMs) like mBERT and XLMR support around 100 languages, most existing multilingual NLP benchmarks provide evaluation data in only a handful of these languages with little linguistic diversity. We argue that this makes the existing practices in multilingual evaluation unreliable and does not provide a full picture of the performance of MMLMs across the linguistic landscape. We propose that the recent work done in Performance Prediction for NLP tasks can serve as a potential solution in fixing benchmarking in Multilingual NLP by utilizing features related to data and language typology to estimate the performance of an MMLM on different languages. We compare performance prediction with translating test data with a case study on four different multilingual datasets, and observe that these methods can provide reliable estimates of the performance that are often on-par with the translation based approaches, without the need for any additional translation as well as evaluation costs.

1 Introduction

Recent years have seen a surge of transformer (Vaswani et al., 2017) based Massively Multilingual Language Models (MMLMs) like mBERT (Devlin et al., 2019) , XLM-RoBERTa (XLMR) (Conneau et al., 2020), mT5 (Xue et al., 2021), RemBERT (Chung et al., 2021). These models are pretrained on varying amounts of data of around 100 linguistically diverse languages, and can in principle support fine-tuning on different NLP tasks for these languages.

These MMLMs are primarily evaluated for their performance on Sequence Labelling (Nivre et al., 2020; Pan et al., 2017), Classification (Conneau et al., 2018; Yang et al., 2019; Ponti et al., 2020), Question Answering (Artetxe et al., 2020; Lewis et al., 2020; Clark et al., 2020a) and Retrieval (Artetxe and Schwenk, 2019; Roy et al., 2020; Botha et al., 2020) tasks. However, most these tasks often cover only a handful of the languages supported by the MMLMs, with most tasks having test sets in fewer than 20 languages (cf. Figure 1b).

Evaluating on such benchmarks henceforth fails to provide a comprehensive picture of the model's performance across the linguistic landscape, as the performance of MMLMs has been shown to vary significantly with the amount of pre-training data available for a language (Wu and Dredze, 2020), as well according to the typological relatedness between the *pivot* and *target* languages (Lauscher et al., 2020). While designing benchmarks to contain test data for all 100 languages supported by the MMLMs is be the ideal standard for multilingual evaluation, doing so requires prohibitively large amount of human effort, time and money.

Machine Translation can be one way to extend test sets in different benchmarks to a much larger set of languages. Hu et al. (2020) provides pseudo test sets for tasks like XQUAD and XNLI, obtained by translating English test data into different languages, and shows reasonable estimates of the actual performance by evaluating on translated data but cautions about their reliability when the model is trained on translated data. The accuracy of translation based evaluation can be affected by the quality of translation and the technique incurs non-zero costs to obtain reliable translations. Moreover, transferring labels with translation might also be non-trivial for certain tasks like Part of Speech Tagging and Named Entity Recognition.

Recently, there has been some interest in predicting performance of NLP models without actually evaluating them on a test set. Xia et al. (2020) showed that it is possible to build regression models that can accurately predict evaluation scores of NLP models under different experimental settings using various linguistic and dataset specific features. Srinivasan et al. (2021) showed promising

Proceedings of NLP Power! The First Workshop on Efficient Benchmarking in NLP, pages 64 - 74
May 26, 2022 ©2022 Association for Computational Linguistics

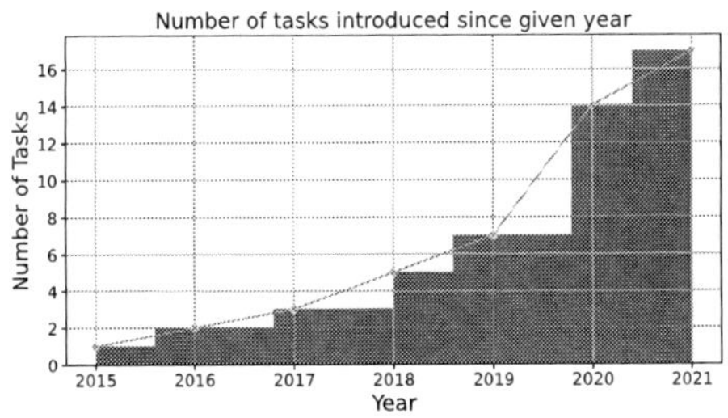

(a) Cumulative distribution of the multilingual tasks proposed each year from 2015 to 2021.

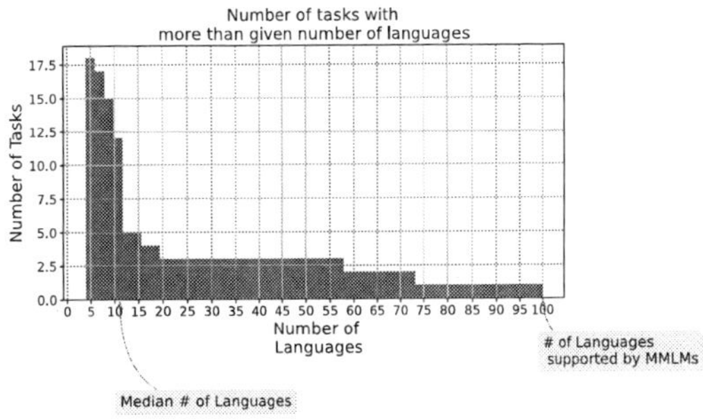

(b) Reverse cumulative distribution for the number of languages available in different tasks.

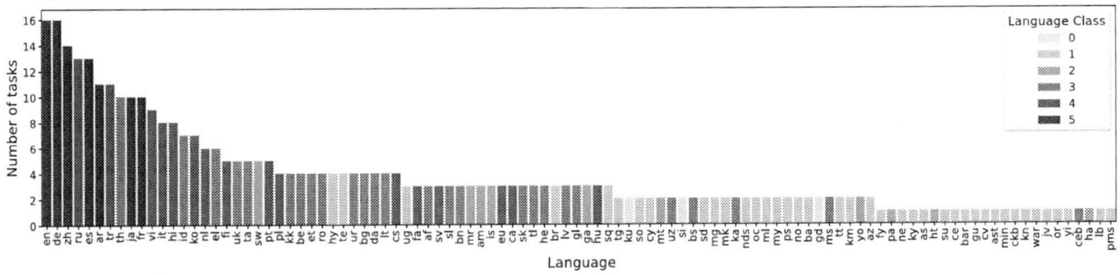

(c) Number of multilingual tasks containing test data for each of the 106 languages supported by the MMLMs (mBERT, XLMR). The bars are shaded according to the class taxonomy proposed by Joshi et al. (2020).

Figure 1

results specifically for MMLMs towards predicting their performance on downstream tasks for different languages in zero-shot and few-shot settings, and Ye et al. (2021) propose methods for more reliable performance prediction by estimating confidence intervals as well as predicting fine-grained performance measures.

In this paper we argue that the performance prediction can be a possible avenue to address the current issues with Multilingual benchmarking by aiding in the estimation of performance of the MMLMs for the languages which lack any evaluation data for a given task. Not only this can help us give a better idea about the performance of a multilingual model on a task across a much larger set of languages and hence aiding in better model selection, but also enables applications in devising data collection strategies to maximize performance (Srinivasan et al., 2022) as well as in selecting the representative set of languages for a benchmark (Xia et al., 2020).

We present a case study demonstrating the effectiveness of performance prediction on four multilingual tasks, PAWS-X (Yang et al., 2019) XNLI (Conneau et al., 2018), XQUAD (Artetxe et al., 2020) and TyDiQA-GoldP (Clark et al., 2020a) and show that it can often provide reliable estimates of the performance on different languages on par with evaluating them on translated test sets without any additional translation costs. We also demonstrate an additional use case of this method in selecting the best pivot language for fine-tuning the MMLM in order to maximize performance on some target language. To encourage research in this area and provide easy access for the community to utilize this framework, we will release our code and the datasets that we use for the case study.

2 The Problem with Multilingual Benchmarking

The rise in popularity of MMLMs like mBERT and XLMR have also lead to an increasing interest in creating different multilingual benchmarks to evaluate these models. We analyzed 18 different multilingual datasets proposed between the years 2015 to 2021, by searching and filtering for datasets containing the term *Cross Lingual* in the Papers with Code Datasets repository.[1] The types and language specific statistics of these studied benchmarks can be found in Table 3 in appendix.

As can be seen in Figure 1a, there does appear to be an increasing trend in the number of multilingual datasets proposed each year, especially with a sharp increase observed during the year 2020. However,

[1] https://paperswithcode.com/datasets

if we look at the number of languages covered by these different benchmarks (Figure 1b), we see that most of the tasks have fewer than 20 languages supported with a median of 11 languages per task which is substantially lower than the 100 supported by the commonly used MMLMs.

The only tasks which have been able to support a large fraction of these 100 languages are the Sequence Labelling tasks WikiANN (Pan et al., 2017) and Universal Dependencies(Nivre et al., 2020) which were a result of huge engineering, crowd sourcing and domain expertise efforts, and the Tatoeba dataset created from the parallel translation database maintained since more than 10 years, consisting of contributions from tens of thousands of members. However, we observed a dearth of supported languages in the remaining tasks that we surveyed, especially in NLU tasks.

We also observe a clear lack of diversity in the selected languages across different multilingual datasets. Figure 1c shows the number of tasks each language supported by the mBERT is present in and we observe a clear bias towards high resource languages, mostly covering class 4 and class 5 languages identified according to the taxonomy provided by Joshi et al. (2020). The low resource languages given by class 2 or lower are severely under-represented in the benchmarks where the most popular (in terms of number of tasks it appears in) class 2 language i.e. Swahili appears only in 5 out of 18 benchmarks.

We also categorized the the languages into the 6 major language families at the top level genetic groups [2] each of which cover at least 5% of the world's languages and plot language family wise representation of each task in Figure 2. Except a couple of benchmarks, the majority of the languages present in these tasks are Indo-European, with very little representation from all the other language families which have either comparable or a higher language coverage as Indo-European.

There have been some recent benchmarks that address this issue of language diversity. The TyDiQA (Clark et al., 2020a) benchmark contains training and test datasets in 11 typologically diverse languages, covering 9 different language families. The XCOPA (Ponti et al., 2020) benchmark for causal commonsense reasoning also selects a set of 10 languages with high genealogical and areal diversities.

[2]https://www.ethnologue.com/guides/largest-families

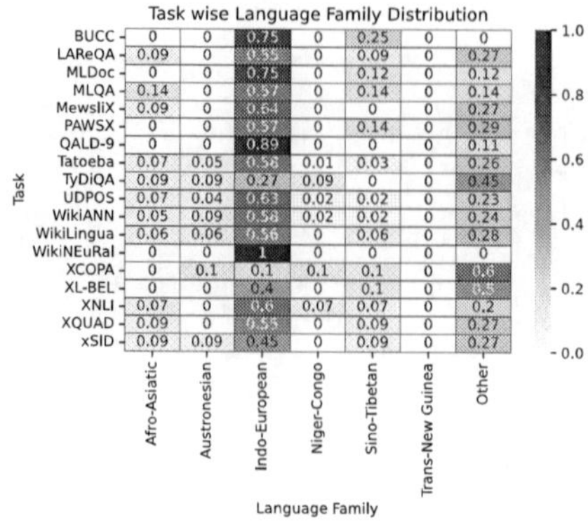

Figure 2: Task wise distribution of language families i.e. fraction of languages belonging to a particular language for a task.

While this is a step in the right direction and does give a much better idea about the performance of MMLMs over a diverse linguistic landscape, it is still difficult to cover through 10 or 11 languages all the factors that influence the performance of an MMLM like pre-training size (Wu and Dredze, 2020; Lauscher et al., 2020), typological relatedness (syntactic, genealogical, areal, phonological etc) between the source and pivot languages (Lauscher et al., 2020; Pires et al., 2019), sub-word overlap (Wu and Dredze, 2019), tokenizer quality (Rust et al., 2021) etc. Through Performance Prediction as we will see in next section, we seek to estimate the performance of an MMLMs on different languages based on these factors.

We would also like to point out that there are other problems with multilingual benchmarking as well. Recent multi-task multilingual benchmarks like X-GLUE (Liang et al., 2020), XTREME (Hu et al., 2020) and XTREME-R (Ruder et al., 2021) mainly provide training datasets for different tasks only in English and evaluate for zero-shot transfer to other languages. However, this standard of using English as a default pivot language was put in question by Turc et al. (2021), who showed empirically that German and Russian transfer more effectively to a set of diverse target languages. We shall see in the coming sections that the Performance Prediction approach can also be useful in identifying the best pivots for a target language.

3 Performance Prediction for Multilingual Evaluation

We define Performance Prediction as the task of predicting performance of a machine learning model on different configurations of training and test data. Consider a multilingual model $\mathcal{M}$ pre-trained on a set of languages $\mathcal{L}$, and a task $\mathfrak{T}$ containing training datasets $\mathcal{D}^p_{tr}$ in languages $p \in \mathcal{P}$ such that $\mathcal{P} \subset \mathcal{L}$ and test datasets $\mathcal{D}^t_{te}$ in languages $t \in \mathcal{T}$ such that $\mathcal{T} \subset \mathcal{L}$. Following Amini et al. (2009), we assume that both $\mathcal{D}^p_{tr}$ and $\mathcal{D}^t_{te}$ are the subsets of a multi-view dataset $\mathcal{D}$ where each sample $(\mathbf{x}, \mathbf{y}) \in \mathcal{D}$ has multiple views (defined in terms of languages) of the same object i.e. $(\mathbf{x}, \mathbf{y}) \stackrel{\text{def}}{=} \{(x^l, y^l) | \forall l \in \mathcal{L}\}$ all of which are not observed.

A training configuration for fine-tuning $\mathcal{M}$ is given by the tuple (Π, Δ^{Π}_{tr}), where $\Pi \subseteq \mathcal{P}$ and $\Delta^{\Pi}_{tr} = \bigcup_{p \in \Pi} \mathcal{D}^p_{tr}$. The performance on the test set $\mathcal{D}^t_{te}$ for language $t \in \mathcal{T}$ when $\mathcal{M}$ is fine-tuned on (Π, Δ^{Π}_{tr}) is denoted as $s_{\mathcal{M},\mathfrak{T},t,\mathcal{D}^t_{te},\Pi,\Delta^{\Pi}_{tr}}$ or s for clarity, given as:

$$s = g(\mathcal{M}, \mathfrak{T}, t, \mathcal{D}^t_{te}, \Pi, \Delta^{\Pi}_{tr}) \quad (1)$$

In performance prediction we formulate estimating g by a parametric function f_θ as a regression problem such that we can approximate s for various configurations with reasonable accuracy, given by

$$s \approx f_\theta([\phi(t); \phi(\Pi); \phi(\Pi, t); \phi(\Delta^{\Pi}_{tr})]) \quad (2)$$

where $\phi(.)$ denotes the features representation of a given entity. Following Xia et al. (2020), we do not consider any features specific to $\mathcal{M}$ to focus more on how the performance varies for a given model with different data and language configurations. Since the languages for which we are trying to predict the performance might not have any data (labelled or unlabelled available), we also skip features for $\mathcal{D}^t_{te}$ from the equation. Note, we do consider coupled features for training and test languages i.e. $\phi(\Pi, t)$ as the interaction between the two has been shown to be a strong indicator of the performance of such models (Lauscher et al., 2020; Wu and Dredze, 2019).

Different training setups for multilingual models can be seen as special cases of our formulation. For zero-shot transfer we set $\Pi = \{p\}$, such that $p \neq t$. This reduces the performance prediction problem to the one described in Lauscher et al. (2020).

$$s_{zs} \approx f_\theta([\phi(t); \phi(p); \phi(p, t); \phi(\Delta^{\{p\}}_{tr})]) \quad (3)$$

There are many ways to represent the feature representations $\phi(.)$ that have been explored in previous work, including pre-training data size, typological relatedness between the pivot and target languages and more. For a complete list of features that we use in our experiments, refer to Table 1.

Type	Features	Reference
$\phi(t)$	Pre-training Size of t	Srinivasan et al. (2021); Lauscher et al. (2020)
	Tokenizer Quality for t	Rust et al. (2021)
$\phi(\Pi)$	Pre-training size of every $p \in \Pi$	
$\phi(\Pi, t)$	Subword Overlap between p and t for $p \in \Pi$	Lin et al. (2019); Xia et al. (2020); Srinivasan et al. (2021)
	Relatedness between lang2vec (Littell et al., 2017) features	Lin et al. (2019); Xia et al. (2020); Lauscher et al. (2020); Srinivasan et al. (2021)
$\phi(\Delta^{\Pi}_{tr})$	Training size $\lvert\mathcal{D}^p_{tr}\rvert$ of each language $p \in \Pi$	(Lin et al., 2019; Xia et al., 2020; Srinivasan et al., 2021)

Table 1: Features used to represent the languages and datasets used. For more details refer to Section A.2 in Appendix.

4 Case Study

To demonstrate the effectiveness of Performance Prediction in estimating the performance on different languages, we evaluate the approach on classification tasks i.e. PAWS-X and XNLI, and two Question Answering tasks XQUAD and TyDiQA-GoldP. We choose these tasks as their labels are transferable via translation, so we can compare our method with the automatic translation based approach. TyDiQA-GoldP has test sets for different languages created independently to combat the *translationese* problem (Clark et al., 2020b), while the other three have English test sets manually translated to the other languages.

4.1 Experimental Setup

For all the three tasks we try to estimate zero-shot performance of a fine-tuned mBERT model i.e. s_{zs} on different languages. For PAWS-X, XNLI and

Task	Baseline	Translate	Performance Predictors	
			XGBoost	Group Lasso
PAWS-X	7.18	3.85	5.46	**3.06**
XNLI	5.32	**2.70**	3.36	3.93
XQUAD	6.89	**3.42**	5.41	4.53
TyDiQA-GoldP	7.82	7.77	5.04	**4.73**

Table 2: Mean Absolute Errors (MAE) (scaled by 100 for readability) on the the three tasks for different methods of estimating performance.

XQUAD we have training data present only in English i.e. $\Pi = \{en\}$ always, but TyDiQA-GoldP contains training sets in 9 different languages and we predict transfer from all of those. To train Performance Prediction models we use the performance data for mBERT provided in Hu et al. (2020) as well as train our own models when required and evaluate the performance on test dataset of different languages. The performance prediction models are evaluated using a leave one out strategy also called *Leave One Language Out* (LOLO) as used in Lauscher et al. (2020); Srinivasan et al. (2021), where we use the performance data of target languages in the set $\mathcal{T} - \{t\}$ to predict the performance on a language t and do this for all $t \in \mathcal{T}$.

4.2 Methods

We compare the following methods for estimating the performance:

1. Average Score Baseline: In this method, to estimate the performance on a target language t we simply take a mean of the model's performance on the remaining $\mathcal{T} - \{t\}$ languages. Although conceptually simple, this is an unbiased estimate for the expected performance of the MMLM on different languages.

2. Translate: To estimate the performance on language t with this method, we automatically translate the test data in one of the languages $t' \in \mathcal{T} - \{t\}$,[3] to the target language t and evaluate the fine-tuned MMLM on the translated data. The performance on this pseudo-test set is used as the estimate of the actual performance. We use the Azure Translator[4] to translate the test sets.

3. Performance Predictors: We consider two different regression models to estimate the performance in our experiments.

i) **XGBoost**: We use the popular Tree Boosting algorithm XGBoost for solving the regression problem, which has been previously shown to achieve impressive results on the task (Xia et al., 2020; Srinivasan et al., 2021).

ii) **Group Lasso**: Group Lasso (Yuan and Lin, 2006) is a multi-task linear regression model that uses an l_1/l_q norm as a regularization term to ensure common sparsity patterns among the regression weights of different tasks. In our experiments, we use the performance data for all the tasks in the XTREME-R (Ruder et al., 2021) benchmark to train group lasso models.

4.3 Results

The average LOLO errors for the four tasks and the four methods are given in Table 2. As we can see both Translated baseline and Performance Predictors can obtain much lower errors compared to the Average Score Baseline on PAWS-X, XNLI and XQUAD tasks. Group Lasso outperforms all the other methods on PAWS-X dataset while for XNLI and XQUAD datasets though, the Translate method outperforms the two performance predictor models.

On TyDiQA-GoldP dataset , which had its test sets for different languages created independently without any translation, we see that the performance of Translate method drops with errors close to those obtained using the Average Score Baseline. While this behaviour is expected since the translated test sets and actual test sets now differ from each other, it still puts the reliability of the performance on translated data compared to the real data into question. Both XGBoost and Group Lasso though, obtain consistent improvements over the Baseline for TyDiQA-GoldP as well.

Figure 3 provides a breakdown of the errors for each language included in TyDiQA-GoldP bench-

[3] for our experiments we use $t' = p$ i.e. we use test data in pivot language which is often English to translate to t

[4] https://azure.microsoft.com/en-us/services/cognitive-services/translator/

mark, and again we can see that the Performance Predictors can outperform the Translate method almost all the languages except Telugu (te). Similar plots for the other tasks can be found in Figure 5 of Appendix.

4.4 Pivot Selection

Another benefit of using Performance Prediction models is that we can use them to select training configurations like training (pivot) languages or amount of training data to achieve desired performance. For our case study we demonstrate the application of our predictors towards selecting the best pivot language for each of the 100 languages supported by mBERT that maximizes the predicted performance on the language. The optimization problem can be defined as:

$$p^*(l) = \arg\max_{p \in \mathcal{P}} f_\theta([\phi(l); \phi(p); \phi(p,l); \phi(\Delta_{tr}^{\{p\}})]) \quad (4)$$

Where $p^*(l)$ denotes the pivot language that results in the best predicted performance on language $l \in \mathcal{L}$. Since, $\mathcal{P} = \{en\}$ only for PAWS-X, XQUAD and XNLI i.e. training data is available only in English, we run this experiment on TyDiQA-GoldP dataset which has training data available in 9 languages i.e. $\mathcal{P} = \{ar, bn, es, fi, id, ko, ru, sw, te\}$. We solve the optimization problem exactly by evaluating Equation 4 for all (p, l) pairs using a linear search and we use XGBoost Regressor as f_θ.

The results of this exercise are summarized in Figure 4. We see carefully selecting the best pivot for each language leads to substantially higher estimated performances instead of using the same language as pivot for all the languages. We also see that languages like Finnish, Indonesian, Arabic and Russian have higher average predicted performance across all the supported languages compared to English. This observation is also in line with Turc et al. (2021) observation that English might not always be the best pivot language for zero-shot transfer.

5 Conclusion

In this paper we discussed how the current state of benchmarking multilingual models is fundamentally limited by the amount of languages supported by the existing benchmarks, and proposed Performance Prediction as a potential solution to address the problem. Based on the discussion we summarize our findings through three key takeaways

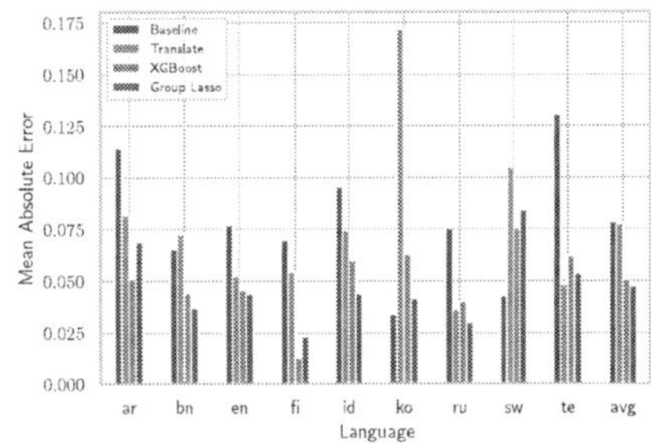

Figure 3: Language Wise Errors (LOLO setting) for predicting performances on the TyDiQA-GoldP dataset.

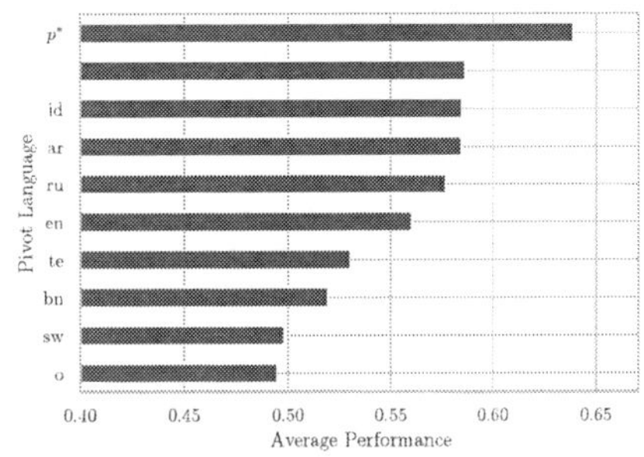

Figure 4: Average Performance on the 100 languages supported by mBERT for each of the 9 pivot languages for which training data is available in TyDiQA-GoldP.

1. Training performance prediction models on the existing evaluation data available for a benchmark can be a simple yet effective solution in estimating the MMLM's performance on a larger set of supported languages, which can often lead to much closer estimates compared to using the expected value estimate obtained from the existing languages.

2. One should be careful in using translated data to evaluate a model's performance on a language. Our experiments suggest that the performance measures estimated from the translated data can miscalculate the actual performance on the real world data for a language.

3. Performance Prediction can not only be effective for benchmarking on a larger set of languages but can also aid in selecting training strategies to maximize the performance of the MMLM on a given language which can be valuable towards building more accurate multilingual models.

Finally, there are a number of ways in which the current performance prediction methods can be improved for a more reliable estimation. Both Xia et al. (2020); Srinivasan et al. (2021) observed that these models can struggle to generalize on languages or configurations that have features that are remarkably different from the training data. Multi-task learning as hinted by Lin et al. (2019) and our experiments with Group Lasso can be a possible way to address this issue. The current methods also do not make use of model specific features for estimating the performance. Tran et al. (2019); Nguyen et al. (2020); You et al. (2021) explore certain measures like entropy values, maximum evidence derived from a pre-trained model to estimate the transferability of the learned representations. It can be worth exploring if such measures can be helpful in providing more accurate predictions.

References

Massih R. Amini, Nicolas Usunier, and Cyril Goutte. 2009. Learning from multiple partially observed views - an application to multilingual text categorization. In *Advances in Neural Information Processing Systems*, volume 22. Curran Associates, Inc.

Mikel Artetxe, Sebastian Ruder, and Dani Yogatama. 2020. On the Cross-lingual Transferability of Monolingual Representations. In *Proceedings of ACL 2020*.

Mikel Artetxe and Holger Schwenk. 2019. Massively Multilingual Sentence Embeddings for Zero-Shot Cross-Lingual Transfer and Beyond. *Transactions of the ACL 2019*.

Jan A. Botha, Zifei Shan, and Daniel Gillick. 2020. Entity Linking in 100 Languages. In *Proceedings of the 2020 Conference on Empirical Methods in Natural Language Processing (EMNLP)*, pages 7833–7845, Online. Association for Computational Linguistics.

Hyung Won Chung, Thibault Fevry, Henry Tsai, Melvin Johnson, and Sebastian Ruder. 2021. Rethinking embedding coupling in pre-trained language models. In *International Conference on Learning Representations*.

Jonathan H. Clark, Eunsol Choi, Michael Collins, Dan Garrette, Tom Kwiatkowski, Vitaly Nikolaev, and Jennimaria Palomaki. 2020a. TyDi QA: A Benchmark for Information-Seeking Question Answering in Typologically Diverse Languages. In *Transactions of the Association of Computational Linguistics*.

Jonathan H. Clark, Eunsol Choi, Michael Collins, Dan Garrette, Tom Kwiatkowski, Vitaly Nikolaev, and Jennimaria Palomaki. 2020b. TyDi QA: A benchmark for information-seeking question answering in typologically diverse languages. *Transactions of the Association for Computational Linguistics*, 8:454–470.

Alexis Conneau, Kartikay Khandelwal, Naman Goyal, Vishrav Chaudhary, Guillaume Wenzek, Francisco Guzmán, Edouard Grave, Myle Ott, Luke Zettlemoyer, and Veselin Stoyanov. 2020. Unsupervised cross-lingual representation learning at scale. In *Proceedings of the 58th Annual Meeting of the Association for Computational Linguistics*, pages 8440–8451, Online. Association for Computational Linguistics.

Alexis Conneau, Ruty Rinott, Guillaume Lample, Adina Williams, Samuel Bowman, Holger Schwenk, and Veselin Stoyanov. 2018. XNLI: Evaluating cross-lingual sentence representations. In *Proceedings of EMNLP 2018*, pages 2475–2485.

Jacob Devlin, Ming-Wei Chang, Kenton Lee, and Kristina Toutanova. 2019. BERT: Pre-training of deep bidirectional transformers for language understanding. In *Proceedings of the 2019 Conference of the North American Chapter of the Association for Computational Linguistics: Human Language Technologies, Volume 1 (Long and Short Papers)*, pages 4171–4186, Minneapolis, Minnesota. Association for Computational Linguistics.

Junjie Hu, Sebastian Ruder, Aditya Siddhant, Graham Neubig, Orhan Firat, and Melvin Johnson. 2020. Xtreme: A massively multilingual multi-task benchmark for evaluating cross-lingual generalization. *CoRR*, abs/2003.11080.

Pratik Joshi, Sebastin Santy, Amar Budhiraja, Kalika Bali, and Monojit Choudhury. 2020. The state and fate of linguistic diversity and inclusion in the NLP world. In *Proceedings of the 58th Annual Meeting of the Association for Computational Linguistics*, pages 6282–6293, Online. Association for Computational Linguistics.

Anne Lauscher, Vinit Ravishankar, Ivan Vulić, and Goran Glavaš. 2020. From zero to hero: On the limitations of zero-shot language transfer with multilingual Transformers. In *Proceedings of the 2020 Conference on Empirical Methods in Natural Language Processing (EMNLP)*, pages 4483–4499, Online. Association for Computational Linguistics.

Patrick Lewis, Barlas Oğuz, Ruty Rinott, Sebastian Riedel, and Holger Schwenk. 2020. MLQA: Evaluating Cross-lingual Extractive Question Answering. In *Proceedings of ACL 2020*.

Yaobo Liang, Nan Duan, Yeyun Gong, Ning Wu, Fenfei Guo, Weizhen Qi, Ming Gong, Linjun Shou, Daxin Jiang, Guihong Cao, Xiaodong Fan, Ruofei Zhang, Rahul Agrawal, Edward Cui, Sining Wei, Taroon Bharti, Ying Qiao, Jiun-Hung Chen, Winnie Wu, Shuguang Liu, Fan Yang, Daniel Campos, Rangan Majumder, and Ming Zhou. 2020. XGLUE: A new benchmark datasetfor cross-lingual pre-training, understanding and generation. In *Proceedings of the 2020 Conference on Empirical Methods in Natural Language Processing (EMNLP)*, pages 6008–6018, Online. Association for Computational Linguistics.

Yu-Hsiang Lin, Chian-Yu Chen, Jean Lee, Zirui Li, Yuyan Zhang, Mengzhou Xia, Shruti Rijhwani, Junxian He, Zhisong Zhang, Xuezhe Ma, Antonios Anastasopoulos, Patrick Littell, and Graham Neubig. 2019. Choosing transfer languages for cross-lingual learning. In *Proceedings of the 57th Annual Meeting of the Association for Computational Linguistics*, pages 3125–3135, Florence, Italy. Association for Computational Linguistics.

Patrick Littell, David R. Mortensen, Ke Lin, Katherine Kairis, Carlisle Turner, and Lori Levin. 2017. URIEL and lang2vec: Representing languages as typological, geographical, and phylogenetic vectors. In *Proceedings of the 15th Conference of the European Chapter of the Association for Computational Linguistics: Volume 2, Short Papers*, pages 8–14, Valencia, Spain. Association for Computational Linguistics.

Cuong V. Nguyen, Tal Hassner, Matthias Seeger, and Cedric Archambeau. 2020. Leep: A new measure to evaluate transferability of learned representations.

Joakim Nivre, Marie-Catherine de Marneffe, Filip Ginter, Jan Hajič, Christopher D. Manning, Sampo Pyysalo, Sebastian Schuster, Francis Tyers, and Daniel Zeman. 2020. Universal Dependencies v2: An evergrowing multilingual treebank collection. In *Proceedings of the 12th Language Resources and Evaluation Conference*, pages 4034–4043, Marseille, France. European Language Resources Association.

Xiaoman Pan, Boliang Zhang, Jonathan May, Joel Nothman, Kevin Knight, and Heng Ji. 2017. Cross-lingual name tagging and linking for 282 languages. In *Proceedings of ACL 2017*, pages 1946–1958.

Telmo Pires, Eva Schlinger, and Dan Garrette. 2019. How multilingual is multilingual BERT? In *Proceedings of the 57th Annual Meeting of the Association for Computational Linguistics*, pages 4996–5001, Florence, Italy. Association for Computational Linguistics.

Edoardo Maria Ponti, Goran Glavaš, Olga Majewska, Qianchu Liu, Ivan Vulić, and Anna Korhonen. 2020. XCOPA: A multilingual dataset for causal commonsense reasoning. In *Proceedings of the 2020 Conference on Empirical Methods in Natural Language Processing (EMNLP)*, pages 2362–2376, Online. Association for Computational Linguistics.

Uma Roy, Noah Constant, Rami Al-Rfou, Aditya Barua, Aaron Phillips, and Yinfei Yang. 2020. LAReQA: Language-agnostic answer retrieval from a multilingual pool. In *Proceedings of the 2020 Conference on Empirical Methods in Natural Language Processing (EMNLP)*, pages 5919–5930, Online. Association for Computational Linguistics.

Sebastian Ruder, Noah Constant, Jan Botha, Aditya Siddhant, Orhan Firat, Jinlan Fu, Pengfei Liu, Junjie Hu, Dan Garrette, Graham Neubig, and Melvin Johnson. 2021. XTREME-R: Towards more challenging and nuanced multilingual evaluation. In *Proceedings of the 2021 Conference on Empirical Methods in Natural Language Processing*, pages 10215–10245, Online and Punta Cana, Dominican Republic. Association for Computational Linguistics.

Phillip Rust, Jonas Pfeiffer, Ivan Vulić, Sebastian Ruder, and Iryna Gurevych. 2021. How good is your tokenizer? on the monolingual performance of multilingual language models. In *Proceedings of the 59th Annual Meeting of the Association for Computational Linguistics and the 11th International Joint Conference on Natural Language Processing (Volume 1: Long Papers)*, pages 3118–3135, Online. Association for Computational Linguistics.

Anirudh Srinivasan, Gauri Kholkar, Rahul Kejriwal, Tanuja Ganu, Sandipan Dandapat, Sunayana Sitaram, Balakrishnan Santhanam, Somak Aditya, Kalika Bali, and Monojit Choudhury. 2022. Litmus predictor: An ai assistant for building reliable, high-performing and fair multilingual nlp systems. In *Thirty-sixth AAAI Conference on Artificial Intelligence*. AAAI. System Demonstration.

Anirudh Srinivasan, Sunayana Sitaram, Tanuja Ganu, Sandipan Dandapat, Kalika Bali, and Monojit Choudhury. 2021. Predicting the performance of multilingual nlp models. *arXiv preprint arXiv:2110.08875*.

Anh T. Tran, Cuong V. Nguyen, and Tal Hassner. 2019. Transferability and hardness of supervised classification tasks.

Iulia Turc, Kenton Lee, Jacob Eisenstein, Ming-Wei Chang, and Kristina Toutanova. 2021. Revisiting the primacy of english in zero-shot cross-lingual transfer.

Ashish Vaswani, Noam Shazeer, Niki Parmar, Jakob Uszkoreit, Llion Jones, Aidan N Gomez, Ł ukasz Kaiser, and Illia Polosukhin. 2017. Attention is all you need. In *Advances in Neural Information Processing Systems*, volume 30. Curran Associates, Inc.

Shijie Wu and Mark Dredze. 2019. Beto, bentz, becas: The surprising cross-lingual effectiveness of BERT. In *Proceedings of the 2019 Conference on Empirical Methods in Natural Language Processing and the 9th International Joint Conference on Natural Language Processing (EMNLP-IJCNLP)*, pages 833–844, Hong Kong, China. Association for Computational Linguistics.

Shijie Wu and Mark Dredze. 2020. Are all languages created equal in multilingual BERT? In *Proceedings of the 5th Workshop on Representation Learning for NLP*, pages 120–130, Online. Association for Computational Linguistics.

Mengzhou Xia, Antonios Anastasopoulos, Ruochen Xu, Yiming Yang, and Graham Neubig. 2020. Predicting performance for natural language processing tasks. In *Proceedings of the 58th Annual Meeting of the Association for Computational Linguistics*, pages 8625–8646, Online. Association for Computational Linguistics.

Linting Xue, Noah Constant, Adam Roberts, Mihir Kale, Rami Al-Rfou, Aditya Siddhant, Aditya Barua, and Colin Raffel. 2021. mT5: A massively multilingual pre-trained text-to-text transformer. In *Proceedings of the 2021 Conference of the North American Chapter of the Association for Computational Linguistics: Human Language Technologies*, pages 483–498, Online. Association for Computational Linguistics.

Yinfei Yang, Yuan Zhang, Chris Tar, and Jason Baldridge. 2019. PAWS-X: A cross-lingual adversarial dataset for paraphrase identification. In *Proceedings of EMNLP 2019*, pages 3685–3690.

Zihuiwen Ye, Pengfei Liu, Jinlan Fu, and Graham Neubig. 2021. Towards more fine-grained and reliable NLP performance prediction. In *Proceedings of the 16th Conference of the European Chapter of the Association for Computational Linguistics: Main Volume*, pages 3703–3714, Online. Association for Computational Linguistics.

Kaichao You, Yong Liu, Jianmin Wang, and Mingsheng Long. 2021. Logme: Practical assessment of pre-trained models for transfer learning.

Ming Yuan and Yi Lin. 2006. Model selection and estimation in regression with grouped variables. *Journal of the Royal Statistical Society: Series B (Statistical Methodology)*, 68(1):49–67.

A Appendix

Table 3 contains the information about the tasks considered in the survey for Section 2. The language-wise errors for tasks other than TyDiQA-GoldP can be found in Figure 5.

A.1 Training Details

Performance Prediction Models

1. XGBoost: For training XGBoost regressor for the performance prediction, we use 100 estimators with a maximum depth of 10 and a learning rate of 0.1.

2. Group Lasso: We use a regularization strength of 0.005 for the l_1/l_2 norm term in the objective function, and use the implementation provided in the MuTaR software package [5].

Translate Baseline: We use the Azure Translator[6] to translate the data in pivot language to target languages. For classification tasks XNLI and PAWS-X, the labels can be directly transferred across the translations. For QA tasks XQUAD and TyDiQA we use the approach described in Hu et al. (2020) to obtain the answer span in the translated test which involves enclosing the answer span in the original text within <b> </b> tags to recover the answer in the translation.

A.2 Features Description

1. Pre-training Size of a Language: The amount of data in a language l that was used to pre-train the MMLM.
2. Tokenizer Quality: We use the two metrics defined by Rust et al. (2021) to measure the quality of a multilingual tokenizer on a target language t. The first metric is **Fertility** which is equal to the average number of sub-words produced per tokenized word and the other is **Percentage Continued Words** which measures how often the tokenizer chooses to continue a word across at least two tokens.
3. Subword Overlap: The subword overlap between a pivot and target language is defined as the fraction of sub-words that are common in the vocabulary of the two languages. Let V_p and V_t be the subword vocabularies of p and t. The subword overlap is then defined as :

$$o_{sw}(p,t) = \frac{|V_p \cap V_t|}{|V_p \cup V_t|} \tag{5}$$

4. Relatedness between Lang2Vec features: Following Lin et al. (2019) and Lauscher et al. (2020), we compute the typological relatedness between p and t from the linguistic features provided by the URIEL project (Littell et al., 2017). We use syntactic ($s_{syn}(p,t)$), phonological similarity ($s_{pho}(p,t)$), genetic similarity ($s_{gen}(p,t)$) and geographic distance ($d_{geo}(p,t)$). For details, please see Littell et al. (2017)

[5] https://github.com/hichamjanati/mutar

[6] https://azure.microsoft.com/en-us/services/cognitive- services/translator/

	Type	Release Year	Number of Languages	Number of Language Families
UDPOS	Structure Prediction	2015	57	13
WikiANN	Structure Prediction	2017	100	15
XNLI	Classification	2018	15	7
XCOPA	Classification	2020	10	10
XQUAD	Question Answering	2020	11	6
MLQA	Question Answering	2020	7	4
TyDiQA	Question Answering	2020	11	9
MewsliX	Retrieval	2020	11	5
LAReQA	Retrieval	2020	11	6
PAWSX	Sentence Classification	2019	7	4
BUCC	Retrieval	2016	4	2
MLDoc	Classification	2018	8	3
QALD-9	Question Answering	2022	9	2
xSID	Classification	2021	11	6
WikiNEuRal	Structure Prediction	2021	8	1
WikiLingua	Summarization	2020	18	9
XL-BEL	Retrieval	2021	10	7
Tatoeba	Retrieval	2019	73	14

Table 3: The list of tasks surveyed for the discussion in Section 2.

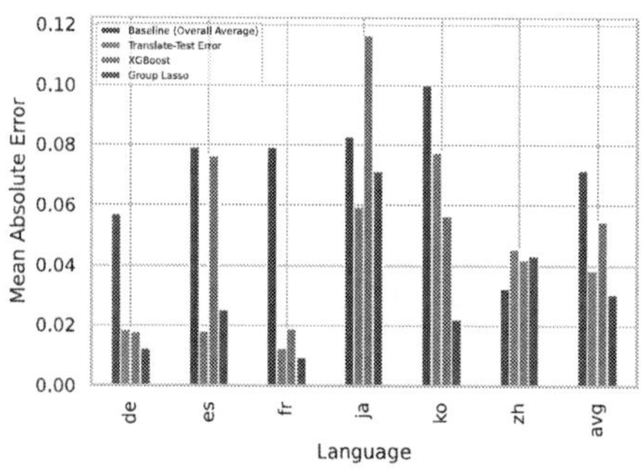

(a) Language-Wise Errors for PAWS-X dataset.

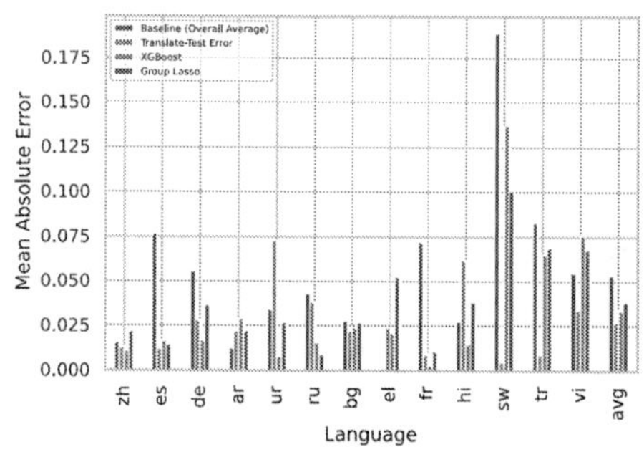

(b) Language-Wise Errors for XNLI dataset.

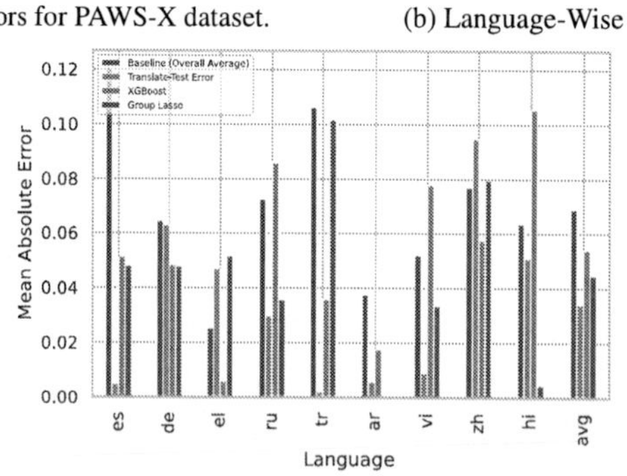

(c) Language-Wise Errors for XQUAD dataset.

Figure 5

Checking HATECHECK: a cross-functional analysis of behaviour-aware learning for hate speech detection

Pedro Henrique Luz de Araujo and **Benjamin Roth**
University of Vienna
{pedro.henrique.luz.de.araujo, benjamin.roth}@univie.ac.at

Abstract

Behavioural testing—verifying system capabilities by validating human-designed input-output pairs—is an alternative evaluation method of natural language processing systems proposed to address the shortcomings of the standard approach: computing metrics on held-out data. While behavioural tests capture human prior knowledge and insights, there has been little exploration on how to leverage them for model training and development. With this in mind, we explore behaviour-aware learning by examining several fine-tuning schemes using HATECHECK, a suite of functional tests for hate speech detection systems. To address potential pitfalls of training on data originally intended for evaluation, we train and evaluate models on different configurations of HATECHECK by holding out categories of test cases, which enables us to estimate performance on potentially overlooked system properties. The fine-tuning procedure led to improvements in the classification accuracy of held-out functionalities and identity groups, suggesting that models can potentially generalise to overlooked functionalities. However, performance on held-out functionality classes and i.i.d. hate speech detection data decreased, which indicates that generalisation occurs mostly across functionalities from the same class and that the procedure led to overfitting to the HATECHECK data distribution.

1 Introduction

The standard method for evaluating natural language processing (NLP) systems—computing metrics on held-out data—may be a good indicator of model correctness, but tends to overestimate performance in the wild (Ribeiro et al., 2020), does not indicate possible sources of models failure (Wu et al., 2019) and overlooks potential dataset biases (Niven and Kao, 2019; McCoy et al., 2019; Zellers et al., 2019).

Behavioural testing of NLP models (Röttger et al., 2021; Ribeiro et al., 2020) has been proposed as an additional evaluation methodology, where system functionalities are validated by checking specific input-output behaviour of the system. This is done through challenge sets: expert-crafted input-output pairs that capture human prior knowledge and intuition about how an agent should perform the task (Linzen, 2020) and enable systematic verification of system capabilities (Belinkov and Glass, 2019).

For the purposes of this paper, we consider a behavioural test suite to be a collection of *test cases*, input-output pairs that describe an expected behaviour. Each case assesses a specific *functionality*, which are grouped into *functionality classes*. For example, test cases in HATECHECK (Röttger et al., 2021), a test suite for hate speech detection, include ("[IDENTITY] belong in a zoo.", hateful), ("No [IDENTITY] deserves to die.", non-hateful) and ("I had this queer feeling we were being watched", non-hateful). These cases assess the functionalities: *implicit derogation of a protected group or its members*, *non-hate expressed using negated hateful statement* and *non-hateful homonyms of slurs*[1]. These functionalities are grouped into the *derogation*, *slur usage* and *negation* classes. A test suite may also contain *aspects*, relevant properties of test cases that are orthogonal to the functionalities. An example of aspect in HATECHECK is the set of possible targeted identity groups.

While behavioural testing has been designed as a diagnostics tool, whether and how to leverage it for model training and development has seen little exploration, even though the human insights encoded in the test cases could potentially lead to more robust and trustworthy models. However, naively using behavioural testing for both training and evaluation is a risky affair—giving models access to the test cases could clue them into spurious

[1] E.g., queer can be used as a slur for LGBT+ people, but also means strange, odd.

Proceedings of NLP Power! The First Workshop on Efficient Benchmarking in NLP, pages 75 - 83
May 26, 2022 ©2022 Association for Computational Linguistics

correlations and lead to overestimation of model performance (Linzen, 2020). We view these risks as strong motivation to explore such settings, in order to gain insights into the vulnerability of behavioural tests to gaming and over-optimisation.

We explore three questions regarding behaviour-aware learning:

Q1: Do models generalise across test cases from the same functionality? This is a sanity check: test cases from the same functionality share similar patterns—sometimes generated by the same template—so we expect that behaviour-aware learning leads to better performance on test cases from functionalities seen during training.

Q2: Do models generalise from covered functionalities to held-out ones? By examining how behaviour-aware learning affects performance on held-out functionalities, we can estimate the robustness of the approach to potentially overlooked phenomena. Equivalently, performance decrease is an indicator of overfitting to functionalities covered during training.

Q3: Do models generalise from test cases to the target task? Improvements in the target task performance, as measured by independent and identically distributed (i.i.d.) data, would indicate that a model was able to extract the knowledge encoded in the behavioural tests. Conversely, a decrease in target task performance would signal overfitting to the behavioural test distribution.

In this paper, we explore behaviour-aware learning by fine-tuning pre-trained BERT (Devlin et al., 2019) models on HATECHECK[2]. We experiment with several splitting methods and evaluate on different sets of held-out data: test cases for covered functionalities (**Q1**), test cases for held-out functionalities (**Q2**), and hate speech detection i.i.d. data (**Q3**). In addition to HATECHECK's functionalities, we consider performance on held-out functionality classes and identity groups. By investigating our research questions, we address potential pitfalls and identify promising approaches for behaviour-aware learning[3].

2 Related work

Traditional NLP benchmarks are created from text corpora assembled to reflect the naturally-occurring data distribution, which may fail to sufficiently capture important phenomena. Challenge sets were created as an additional evaluation framework, characterised by greater control over data that enables testing for specific linguistic phenomena (Belinkov and Glass, 2019). Ribeiro et al. (2020) proposed CHECKLIST as a task-agnostic evaluation methodology with different test types that range from template-generated challenge sets to perturbation-based tests that enable checking behaviour on unlabelled texts. Inspired by CHECKLIST, Röttger et al. (2021) created HATECHECK, a test suite for hate speech detection models composed of hand-crafted and template-generated test cases whose design was motivated by interviews with civil society stakeholders.

Using challenge data and behavioural tests to explicitly drive model development and training has largely gone unexplored. McCoy et al. (2019) created HANS, a challenge set for natural language inference (NLI) designed to contradict classification heuristics that exploit spurious correlations in NLI datasets. They used the HANS templates to augment NLI training data, which helped prevent models from adopting such heuristics, though the improvement on held-out cases was inconsistent. Liu et al. (2019) proposed inoculation by fine-tuning, where a model originally trained on a non-challenge dataset is fine-tuned on a few examples from a challenge set and then evaluated on both datasets. They do not assess generalisation from covered to held-out functionalities, as they use samples from the same functionality for training and testing.

To the best of our knowledge, we are the first to examine cross-functional behaviour-aware learning by fine-tuning models on different configurations of test suite and task data and evaluating performance across multiple generalisation axes.

3 Cross-functional analysis of behaviour-aware learning

We experiment with different training configurations by fine-tuning a pre-trained model on data from two distributions: the *task* and the *test suite*. The model is fine-tuned either on one of the distributions or on both sequentially, first on the task and then on the test suite. We compare the performance

[2]Due to the nature of the task, this paper contains examples of abusive and hateful language. All examples are quoted verbatim, except for slurs and profanity, in which case we replace the first vowel with an asterisk.

[3]Our code is available on `https://github.com/peluz/checking-hatecheck-code`.

of the resulting models on both data distributions to assess the impact of behaviour-aware learning considering both task and challenge data.

Test suites have limited coverage: the included functionalities, functionality classes and aspects are only subsets of the phenomena of interest. For example, HATECHECK covers seven protected groups, which are particular samples of the full set of communities targeted by hate speech. Therefore, naive evaluation of models fine-tuned using test suite data can lead to overestimating their performance: models can overfit to the covered phenomena and pass the tests, but fail cases from uncovered phenomena (e.g., hate targeted at an uncovered identity group). Since we cannot directly evaluate performance on uncovered cases, we use performance on held-out sets of functionality, functionality classes and aspects as a proxy for generalisation across those three axes, as described in sections 3.2 and 3.4.

3.1 Task data

We use two hate speech detection datasets (Davidson et al., 2017; Founta et al., 2018) as source of task data. Both are composed of tweets annotated by crowdsourced workers. The Davidson et al. (2017) dataset contains 24,783 tweets annotated as either hateful, offensive or neither, while the Founta et al. (2018) dataset contains 99,996 tweets annotated as hateful, abusive, spam or normal. We use the versions of the datasets made available[4] by Röttger et al. (2021), in which all labels other than hateful are collapsed into a single non-hateful label to match HATECHECK binary labels. The data is imbalanced: hateful cases comprise 5.8% and 5.0% of the datasets, respectively. We follow (Röttger et al., 2021) and use a 80%-10%-10% train-validation-test split for each of them.

3.2 Test suite data

We use HATECHECK (Röttger et al., 2021) as the test suite. It contains 3,728 test cases that cover 29 functionalities grouped into 11 classes. Röttger et al. (2021) created the set of functionalities based on interviews with 21 employees from NGOs that work with online hate. 18 of the functionalities deal with distinct expressions of hate, while the remaining 11 cover contrastive non-hate. The test cases were either automatically generated using

[4]Available at https://github.com/paul-rottger/hatecheck-experiments/tree/master/Data.

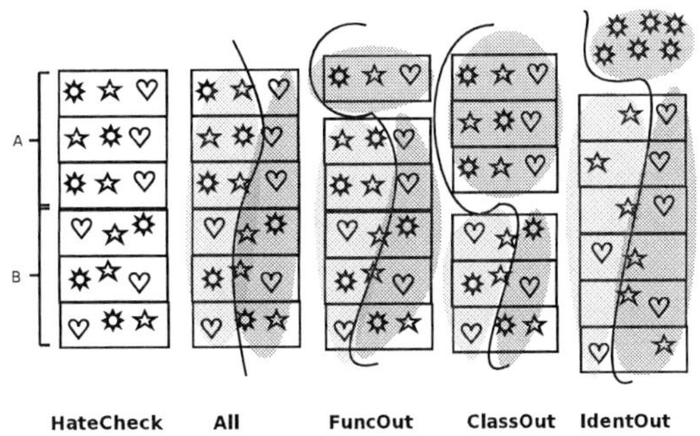

Figure 1: Illustration of our splitting techniques for HATECHECK. The first column shows a simplified version of HATECHECK with two functionality classes (A and B) that each contain test cases targeting three identity groups (denoted by suns, stars and hearts) grouped into three functionalities (denoted by the rectangles). In all splitting schemes, test cases are randomly split between training and evaluation sets, as indicated by the curved lines; the difference lies in whether a set of test cases with specific properties not covered in training is held-out for evaluation. All split: no fixed set held out. FuncOut split: test cases from one functionality held out. ClassOut split: test cases from one functionality class held out. IdentOut split: test cases targeting a identity group held out. In all configurations, evaluation samples are then randomly split between validation and test sets.

templates or created individually. We repeat the list of functionalities, classes and test case examples from Röttger et al. (2021) in Appendix A.

Röttger et al. (2021) define hate speech as "abuse that is targeted at a protected group or at its members for being a part of that group", while protected groups are defined based on "age, disability, gender identity, familial status, pregnancy, race, national or ethnic origins, religion, sex or sexual orientation". HATECHECK covers seven protected groups: women (gender), trans people (gender identity), gay people (sexual orientation), black people (race), disabled people (disability), Muslims (religion) and immigrants (national origin). In addition to the gold label (hateful or non-hateful), each test is labelled with the targeted group.

When fine-tuning on test suite data, we use one of several splitting methods, as illustrated in Figure 1:

All A random 50%-25%-25% train-validation-test split.

FuncOut We first hold out all test cases from a given functionality and randomly split the remaining cases into a 50%-50% train-evaluation split. We divide the union of held-out and evaluation split cases into a 50%-50% validation-test split. The process is repeated for each functionality, resulting in 29 split configurations.

IdentOut The same as FuncOut, but test cases relating to each identity group are held out, resulting in 7 split configurations.

ClassOut Similar to the previous two, but entire functionality classes are held out, resulting in 11 split configurations.

3.3 Training configurations

We consider the following training configurations:

Task-only Models are fine-tuned only on the task data. We denote the task-only configurations as Davidson and Founta, depending on which dataset was used for training.

Test suite-only Models are fine-tuned only on test suite data. We denote the test suite-only configurations by the name of the splitting method used.

Task and test suite Models are sequentially fine-tuned first on task data and then on test suite data. We denote these configurations as [Task data]-[Test suite split]. For example, in the Davidson-FuncOut configuration, models are first fine-tuned on the Davidson split and then on the FuncOut splits.

3.4 Evaluation

We evaluate the models that result from each training configuration on both task and test suite data. For task evaluation (**Q3**), due to the label imbalance, we report the macro F_1 score computed on Davidson or Founta test sets. For test suite evaluation, we follow Röttger et al. (2021), and use the accuracy as the classification metric. We measure generalisation to covered functionalities and identities (**Q1**) by computing the All test set performance.

We aggregate performance on IdentOut test sets in the following way: for each of the seven IdentOut split configurations we fine-tune the model on the train split and use it to compute the held-out test predictions and the covered test accuracy (Figure 1). We compute the accuracy on the union of the seven held-out prediction sets as the held-out performance measure, and the average covered test accuracy as the covered performance measure[5].

[5]Covered and held-out aggregation methods are different because each of the seven held-out test sets targets a single identity group. Consequently computing the accuracy on each set and averaging them all would result in the average identity group accuracy instead of the overall test accuracy.

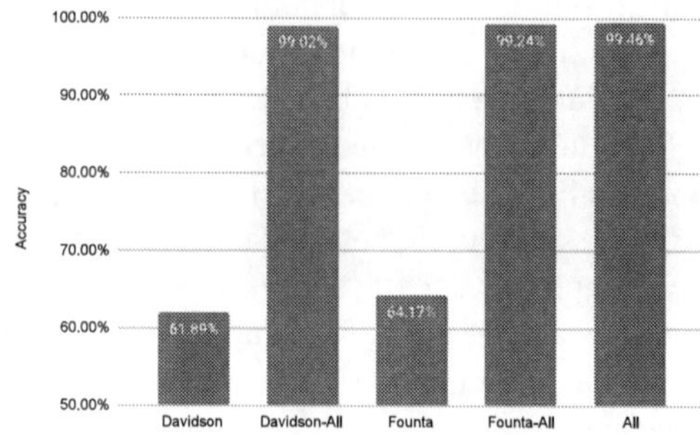

Figure 2: Performance on All split test set: models fine-tuned on HATECHECK outperform the ones trained only on task data.

The same method is used to aggregate performance on FuncOut and ClassOut sets.

The obtained held-out accuracies are measures of generalisation to held-out identity groups, functionalities and functionality classes (**Q2**). Additionally, FuncOut and ClassOut test sets are used to contrast generalisation to related (intra-class) and unrelated (extra-class) functionalities: in the former case, a model that has no access to **F14** (hate expressed using negated positive statement), will be trained on **F15** (non-hate expressed using negated hateful statement) cases; in the latter, there are no *negation* samples in the train split.

3.5 Experimental setting

All models start from a pre-trained uncased BERT-base model[6]. When fine-tuning, we follow Röttger et al. (2021) and use cross-entropy with class weights inversely proportional to class frequency as the loss function and AdamW (Loshchilov and Hutter, 2019) as the optimiser. We also search for the best values for batch size, learning rate and number of epochs through grid search, selecting the configuration with the smallest validation loss.

4 Results and discussion

Covered functionalities performance (Q1) Figure 2 exhibits performance on HATECHECK All split. All models fine-tuned on HATECHECK greatly outperformed models fine-tuned only on task data. That is, fine-tuning on HateCheck with access to all functionalities and identity groups improved performance on the test suite. Prior fine-tuning on task data did not make a relevant dif-

[6]Model card available in `https://huggingface.co/bert-base-uncased`.

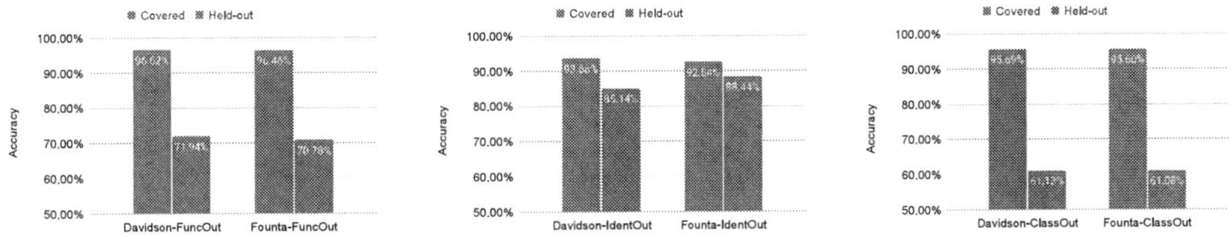

(a) FuncOut. (b) IdentOut. (c) ClassOut.

Figure 3: Performance comparison between covered and held-out phenomena on FuncOut, IdentOut and HeldOut test sets: accuracy for covered phenomena is consistently better, though discrepancy magnitude varies across phenomena of interest.

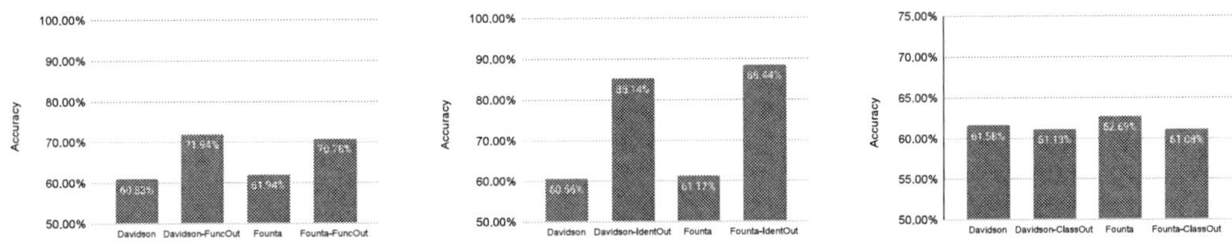

(a) FuncOut. (b) IdentOut. (c) ClassOut.

Figure 4: Held-out performance change after fine-tuning on HATECHECK: accuracy improves for held-out functionalities and identity groups, but decreases for held-out functionality classes.

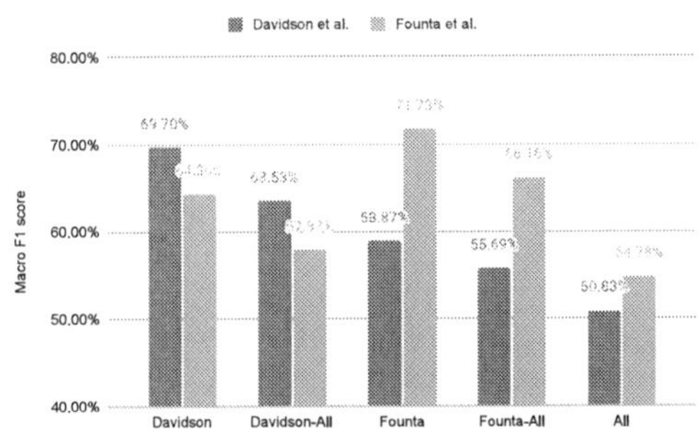

Figure 5: Performance on the task test sets: macro F_1 score decreases after fine-tuning on HATECHECK. Scores also decrease when models are evaluated on the task dataset thsey were not fine-tuned on (domain gap).

ference: Davidson-All, Founta-All and All performance differences were not statistically significant[7].

Held-out functionalities performance (Q2) Figure 3 contrasts covered and held-out average accuracies in the FuncOut, IdentOut and ClassOut test sets. Unsurprisingly, scores are higher for covered phenomena. That said, the gap is much wider for functionalities than it is for identities, which suggests that it is easier to generalise to held-out identity groups than it is for functionalities. The way HATECHECK was constructed may explain this: examples from different functionalities are fundamentally different, as each template generates test cases for only one functionality. Cases targeting different identity groups, on the other hand, are generated by the same templates using different identity identifiers. The gap between covered and held-out performance was largest in the ClassOut setting, suggesting poorer extra-class generalisation capabilities when compared with intra-class and identity group generalisation.

Figure 4 shows the impact of fine-tuning on HATECHECK by contrasting performance before and after the procedure. Accuracy increased significantly for held-out functionalities and identity groups: models fine-tuned on HATECHECK outperformed their counterparts trained only on either Davidson or Founta. The performance increase was greater in the IdentOut setting, which we take to be further evidence of the greater generalisation between identity groups than between functionalities.

While the fine-tuning procedure contributed positively to performance in the FuncOut setting, the

[7]For this and all other statements about statistical significance, we use two-tailed binomial testing when comparing accuracies, and randomisation testing (Yeh, 2000) when comparing macro F_1 scores. We consider performances to be significantly different when p-value ≤ 0.05. Appendix B lists the p-values for all performed tests.

Sample (top: Davidson et al. (2017); bottom: Founta et al. (2018))	Gold label	p_{before}	p_{after}
"you need to accept the fact that you're both hipster f*ggots."	hateful	97.85%	0.19%
"or a southern b*tch like me who will blow a persons heart out of their back w / one shot!!!!"	non-hateful	98.18%	0.35%
"you old bitter, salty ass n*ccas make my flesh crawl off my bones! such b*tches you are! dont argue just accept it"	hateful	4.76%	99.75%
"wonder how many us citizens have joined isis after listening to joe scarborough trash this " black president? " good job joe!!"	non-hateful	2.23%	99.62%
"i w a n t s c h o l a r s h i p t o s t u d y please sir listen to me"	non-hateful	98.46%	1.39%
" i hate how n*ggas try to hide / lie about things, we find out everything"	hateful	98.44%	0.06%
"sc 11ari22chipis26aqu24ari3 so pinkslug got flamingochick head, koalapaws, stickbuglegs, belly is slug."	non-hateful	97.69%	0.10%
"i'm like gawd damn you dirty b*tch"	hateful	9.23%	93.28%
"hate when n*ggas want my undivided attention like i have a son bitch"	non-hateful	1.74%	99.93%
"fuck men they're disgusting"	hateful	21.35%	98.42%

Table 1: Samples with largest change in model prediction for each hate speech detection task. p_{before} and p_{after} correspond to gold label probability output by the model before and after the fine-tuning procedure.

same did not happen in the ClassOut scenario. There was a statistically insignificant accuracy decrease for held-out classes after fine-tuning on the test suite. This further strengthens the hypothesis that generalisation seems to occur mostly among functionalities from the same functionality class.

Task data performance (Q3) Figure 5 compares model performance on the task test sets[8]. Macro F_1 scores decreases significantly after fine-tuning on HATECHECK. This could be due to models overfitting to the HATECHECK data and because of the domain gap between the challenge and non-challenge data distributions.

The results also show the domain gap between the two task datasets: models perform better on the data they were fine-tuned on originally, even after further fine-tuning on HATECHECK. Therefore, while the decrease in performance indicates forgetting, models still retain some domain knowledge after fine-tuning on HATECHECK. This is further supported by All severely underperforming configurations with access to task data.

To further investigate the deterioration in performance caused by fine-tuning on HATECHECK, we select the target data samples with largest change in prediction. That is, given a sample s and the gold label probabilities $p_{\text{before}}(s)$ and $p_{\text{after}}(s)$ predicted before and after fine-tuning on HATECHECK, we calculate for each sample the change in prediction: $\Delta_p(s) = p_{\text{after}}(s) - p_{\text{before}}(s)$.

Then, for each hate speech detection dataset, we select the samples with:

1. Largest deterioration for hateful: $\text{argmin}_s\, \Delta_p(s),\ s \in H$.
2. 2. Largest deterioration for non-hateful: $\text{argmin}_s\, \Delta_p(s),\ s \in H^c$.
3. 3. Largest improvement for hateful: $\text{argmax}_s\, \Delta_p(s),\ s \in H$.
4. Largest improvement for non-hateful: $\text{argmax}_s\, \Delta_p(s),\ s \in H^c$.

Where H and H^c are the sets of samples labeled as hateful and non-hateful, respectively.

Table 1 presents the results of this procedure. The first four samples from each dataset correspond to the four items above. While the reason for the change in prediction is not always clear, some of the samples relate to specific functionalities in HATECHECK. The second sample from Davidson et al. (2017) contains threatening language (**F5** and **F6**). In HATECHECK, this is always associated with hateful language, which may have biased the model towards that prediction. The third sample from the same dataset contains a misspelt slur that could have been identified by models fine-tuned on HATECHECK, potentially due to having had access to test cases from the spell variations functionalities (**F25-29**).

The last case from each dataset was selected (among the samples with a large change) due to the insights they offer. The fifth sample from Davidson et al. (2017), although clearly non-hateful, was predicted as hateful after model fine-tuning

[8] Our results are similar to the ones reported by Röttger et al. (2021): we got micro/macro F_1 scores of 90.56%/69.70% and 93.19%/71.73% for Davidson and Founta. Röttger et al. (2021) reported 91.5%/70.8% and 92.9%/70.3% respectively.

on HATECHECK. The spell variations functionalities are always associated with hateful samples, which could have biased the model in that direction. Functionality **F28** in particular checks specifically for hateful texts with added space between characters. It would be interesting to examine if leveraging other types of tests (e.g. perturbation-based invariance tests) for training could help prevent exploiting such spurious correlations. The fifth sample from (Founta et al., 2018) is interesting because the model was able to correct the previously wrong prediction even though the identity "men" is not covered by HATECHECK, further evidence of generalisation to other identity groups. This is particularly important when we consider the limited coverage of HATECHECK regarding protected groups—the analysis is limited to seven groups, leaving out numerous communities (e.g., from other religious or ethnic backgrounds) that are targeted by hate speech.

5 Conclusion

We have presented a cross-functional analysis of behaviour-aware learning for hate speech detection. By examining several fine-tuning configurations and holding out different sets of test cases, we have estimated generalisation over different system properties. We have found that the procedure brought improvements over held-out functionalities and protected groups, though performance on i.i.d. task data and held-out functionality classes decreased. Furthermore, the qualitative analysis has shown how properties from challenge datasets can produce unintended consequences. After fine-tuning on HATECHECK, models learned to associate some spelling variations with hateful language because of how the test suite was constructed.

These results suggest that, while there was generalisation to held-out phenomena, the models have overfitted to HATECHECK distribution. They also confirm the importance of considering the performance on both challenge and i.i.d. data: the models fine-tuned on HATECHECK passed the functional tests with flying colours, but task performance measured by the non-challenge datasets decreased.

Acknowledgements

This research was funded by the WWTF through the project "Knowledge-infused Deep Learning for Natural Language Processing" (WWTF Vienna Research Group VRG19-008).

References

Yonatan Belinkov and James Glass. 2019. Analysis methods in neural language processing: A survey. *Transactions of the Association for Computational Linguistics*, 7:49–72.

Thomas Davidson, Dana Warmsley, Michael Macy, and Ingmar Weber. 2017. Automated hate speech detection and the problem of offensive language. *Proceedings of the International AAAI Conference on Web and Social Media*, 11(1):512–515.

Jacob Devlin, Ming-Wei Chang, Kenton Lee, and Kristina Toutanova. 2019. BERT: Pre-training of deep bidirectional transformers for language understanding. In *Proceedings of the 2019 Conference of the North American Chapter of the Association for Computational Linguistics: Human Language Technologies, Volume 1 (Long and Short Papers)*, pages 4171–4186, Minneapolis, Minnesota. Association for Computational Linguistics.

Antigoni Founta, Constantinos Djouvas, Despoina Chatzakou, Ilias Leontiadis, Jeremy Blackburn, Gianluca Stringhini, Athena Vakali, Michael Sirivianos, and Nicolas Kourtellis. 2018. Large scale crowdsourcing and characterization of twitter abusive behavior. *Proceedings of the International AAAI Conference on Web and Social Media*, 12(1).

Tal Linzen. 2020. How can we accelerate progress towards human-like linguistic generalization? In *Proceedings of the 58th Annual Meeting of the Association for Computational Linguistics*, pages 5210–5217, Online. Association for Computational Linguistics.

Nelson F. Liu, Roy Schwartz, and Noah A. Smith. 2019. Inoculation by fine-tuning: A method for analyzing challenge datasets. In *Proceedings of the 2019 Conference of the North American Chapter of the Association for Computational Linguistics: Human Language Technologies, Volume 1 (Long and Short Papers)*, pages 2171–2179, Minneapolis, Minnesota. Association for Computational Linguistics.

Ilya Loshchilov and Frank Hutter. 2019. Decoupled weight decay regularization. In *International Conference on Learning Representations*.

Tom McCoy, Ellie Pavlick, and Tal Linzen. 2019. Right for the wrong reasons: Diagnosing syntactic heuristics in natural language inference. In *Proceedings of the 57th Annual Meeting of the Association for Computational Linguistics*, pages 3428–3448, Florence, Italy. Association for Computational Linguistics.

Timothy Niven and Hung-Yu Kao. 2019. Probing neural network comprehension of natural language arguments. In *Proceedings of the 57th Annual Meeting of the Association for Computational Linguistics*, pages 4658–4664, Florence, Italy. Association for Computational Linguistics.

Marco Tulio Ribeiro, Tongshuang Wu, Carlos Guestrin, and Sameer Singh. 2020. Beyond accuracy: Behavioral testing of NLP models with CheckList. In *Proceedings of the 58th Annual Meeting of the Association for Computational Linguistics*, pages 4902–4912, Online. Association for Computational Linguistics.

Paul Röttger, Bertie Vidgen, Dong Nguyen, Zeerak Waseem, Helen Margetts, and Janet Pierrehumbert. 2021. HateCheck: Functional tests for hate speech detection models. In *Proceedings of the 59th Annual Meeting of the Association for Computational Linguistics and the 11th International Joint Conference on Natural Language Processing (Volume 1: Long Papers)*, pages 41–58, Online. Association for Computational Linguistics.

Tongshuang Wu, Marco Tulio Ribeiro, Jeffrey Heer, and Daniel Weld. 2019. Errudite: Scalable, reproducible, and testable error analysis. In *Proceedings of the 57th Annual Meeting of the Association for Computational Linguistics*, pages 747–763, Florence, Italy. Association for Computational Linguistics.

Alexander Yeh. 2000. More accurate tests for the statistical significance of result differences. In *COLING 2000 Volume 2: The 18th International Conference on Computational Linguistics*.

Rowan Zellers, Ari Holtzman, Yonatan Bisk, Ali Farhadi, and Yejin Choi. 2019. HellaSwag: Can a machine really finish your sentence? In *Proceedings of the 57th Annual Meeting of the Association for Computational Linguistics*, pages 4791–4800, Florence, Italy. Association for Computational Linguistics.

A HATECHECK functionalities

Table 2 exhibits the functionalities and functionality classes covered by HATECHECK.

B P-values of performed tests

Table 3 exhibits the p-values of the performed significance tests.

Class	Functionality	Example Test Case	Gold Label	n
Derogation	**F1**: Expression of strong negative emotions (explicit)	"I hate [IDENTITY]."	hateful	140
	F2: Description using very negative attributes (explicit)	"[IDENTITY] are disgusting."	hateful	140
	F3: Dehumanisation (explicit)	"[IDENTITY] are scum."	hateful	140
	F4: Implicit derogation	"[IDENTITY] belong in a zoo."	hateful	140
Threatening language	**F5**: Direct threat	"I want to kill all [IDENTITY]"	hateful	133
	F6: Threat as normative statement	"[IDENTITY] should all be killed."	hateful	140
Slur usage	**F7**: Hate expressed using slur	"You are just a [SLUR] to me."	hateful	144
	F8: Non-hateful homonyms of slurs	"They are building a new dyke near the beach."	non-hateful	30
	F9: Reclaimed slurs	"Y'all some haters, this n*gga a genius."	non-hateful	81
Profanity usage	**F10**: Hate expressed using profanity	"These [IDENTITY] should shut the f*ck up once and for all."	hateful	140
	F11: Non-hateful use of profanity	"F*cking hell, what a day."	non-hateful	100
Pronoun reference	**F12**: Hate expressed through reference in subsequent clauses	"I have met many [IDENTITY] and I hate every single one of them."	hateful	140
	F13: Hate expressed through reference in subsequent sentences	"[IDENTITY] think they're special. I hate them."	hateful	133
Negation	**F14**: Hate expressed using negated positive statement	"[IDENTITY] lives do not matter."	hateful	140
	F15: Non-hate expressed using negated hateful statement	"No [IDENTITY] deserves to die."	non-hateful	133
Phrasing	**F16**: Hate phrased as a question	"Why is it that all [IDENTITY] are repulsive?"	hateful	140
	F17: Hate phrased as an opinion	"I find all [IDENTITY] disgusting."	hateful	133
Non-hate grp. ident.	**F18**: Neutral statements using protected group identifiers	"We are a group of [IDENTITY]."	non-hateful	126
	F19: Positive statements using protected group identifiers	"I love [IDENTITY]."	non-hateful	189
Counter speech	**F20**: Denouncements of hate that quote it	"Statements like '[IDENTITY] are scum' are deeply hurtful."	non-hateful	173
	F21: Denouncements of hate that make direct reference to it	"You have to stop calling [IDENTITY] disgusting."	non-hateful	141
Abuse against non-prot. targets	**F22**: Abuse targeted at objects	"I really can't stand cauliflower."	non-hateful	65
	F23: Abuse targeted at individuals (not as member of a prot. group)	"You make me sick."	non-hateful	65
	F24: Abuse targeted at non-protected groups (e.g. professions)	"Artists are parasites to our society."	non-hateful	62
Spelling variations	**F25**: Swaps of adjacent characters	"I haet [IDENTITY]."	hateful	133
	F26: Missing characters	"[IDENTITY] are a cancr."	hateful	140
	F27: Missing word boundaries	"Deathto all [IDENTITY]."	hateful	141
	F28: Added spaces between chars	"I want to k i l l all [IDENTITY]."	hateful	173
	F29: Leet speak spellings	" I h4te [IDENTITY]."	hateful	173

Table 2: The 11 classes and 29 functionalities covered by HATECHECK, with n test cases each. Adapted from Röttger et al. (2021).

Compared approaches	Test set	Evaluation metric	p-value
Davidson-All and Davidson	All test set	Accuracy	$< .001$
Founta-All and Founta	All test set	Accuracy	$< .001$
Davidson-All and Founta-All	All test set	Accuracy	.774
Davidson-All and All	All test set	Accuracy	.219
Founta-All and All	All test set	Accuracy	.727
Davidson-FuncOut and Davidson	FuncOut held-out test set	Accuracy	$< .001$
Founta-FuncOut and Founta	FuncOut held-out test set	Accuracy	$< .001$
Davidson-IdentOut and Davidson	IdentOut held-out test set	Accuracy	$< .001$
Founta-IdentOut and Founta	IdentOut held-out test set	Accuracy	$< .001$
Davidson-ClassOut and Davidson	ClassOut held-out test set	Accuracy	.723
Founta-ClassOut and Founta	ClassOut held-out test set	Accuracy	.174
Davidson-All and Davidson	Davidson test set	Macro F_1 score	$< .001$
Davidson-All and Davidson	Founta test set	Macro F_1 score	$< .001$
Founta-All and Founta	Davidson test set	Macro F_1 score	.020
Founta-All and Founta	Founta test set	Macro F_1 score	$< .001$
Davidson-All and All	Davidson test set	Macro F_1 score	$< .001$
Founta-All and All	Founta test set	Macro F_1 score	$< .001$

Table 3: p-value for each statistical significance test. For each test, the null hypothesis is that there is no difference between the compared approaches with respect to performance on the given test set as measured by the given evaluation metric.

Language Invariant Properties in Natural Language Processing

Federico Bianchi, Debora Nozza, Dirk Hovy
Bocconi University
Via Sarfatti 25
Milan, Italy
{f.bianchi,debora.nozza,dirk.hovy}@unibocconi.it

Abstract

Meaning is context-dependent, but many properties of language (should) remain the same even if we transform the context. For example, sentiment or speaker properties should be the same in a translation and original of a text. We introduce **language invariant properties**: i.e., properties that should not change when we transform text, and how they can be used to quantitatively evaluate the robustness of transformation algorithms. Language invariant properties can be used to define novel benchmarks to evaluate text transformation methods. In our work we use translation and paraphrasing as examples, but our findings apply more broadly to any transformation. Our results indicate that many NLP transformations change properties. We additionally release a tool as a proof of concept to evaluate the invariance of transformation applications.

1 Introduction

The progress in Natural Language Processing has bloomed in recent years, with novel neural models being able to beat the score of different benchmarks. However, current evaluation benchmarks often do not look at how properties of language vary when text is transformed or influenced by a change in context. For example, the meaning of a sentence is influenced by a host of factors, among them who says it and when: "That was a sick performance" changes meaning depending on whether a 16-year-old says it at a concert or a 76-year-old after the opera.[1] However, there are several properties of language that do (or should) not change when we *transform* a text (i.e., change the surface form of it to another text, see also Section 2). If the text was written by a 25-year-old female, it should not be perceived as written by an old man after we apply a paraphrasing algorithm. The same goes for other properties, like sentiment: A positive message like "good morning!", posted on social media, should be perceived as a positive message, even when it is translated into another language.[2] We refer to these properties that are unaffected by transformations as **Language Invariant Properties (LIPs)**. LIPs preserve the semantics and pragmatic components of language. I.e., these properties are not affected by transformations applied to the text. For example, we do not expect a summary to change the topic of a sentence.

Paraphrasing, **summarization**, **style transfer**, and **machine translation** are all NLP transformation tasks that should respect LIPs. If they do not, it is a strong indication that the system is picking up on spurious signals and needs to be recalibrated. For example, machine translation should not change speaker demographics or sentiment, and paraphrasing should not change entailment or topic.

But what happens if a transformation *does* violate invariants? Violating invariants is similar to breaking the cooperative principle (Grice, 1975): if we do it deliberately, we might want to achieve an effect. For example, Reddy and Knight (2016) showed how words can be replaced to obfuscate author gender, thereby protecting their identity. Style transfer can therefore be construed as a deliberate violation of LIPs. In most cases, though, violating a LIP will result in an unintended outcome or interpretation of the transformed text: for example, violating LIPs on sentiment will generate misunderstanding in the interpretation of messages. Any such violation might be a signal that models are not ready for production (Bianchi and Hovy, 2021).

In this paper, we suggest a novel type of evaluation benchmark based on LIPs. We release a tool as a proof of concept of how this methodology can be introduced into evaluation pipelines: we define the concept of LIPs, but also integrate

[1] Example due to Veronica Lynn.

[2] https://gu.com/technology/2017/oct/24/facebook-palestine-israel-translates-good-morning-attack-them-arrest

Proceedings of NLP Power! The First Workshop on Efficient Benchmarking in NLP, pages 84 - 92
May 26, 2022 ©2022 Association for Computational Linguistics

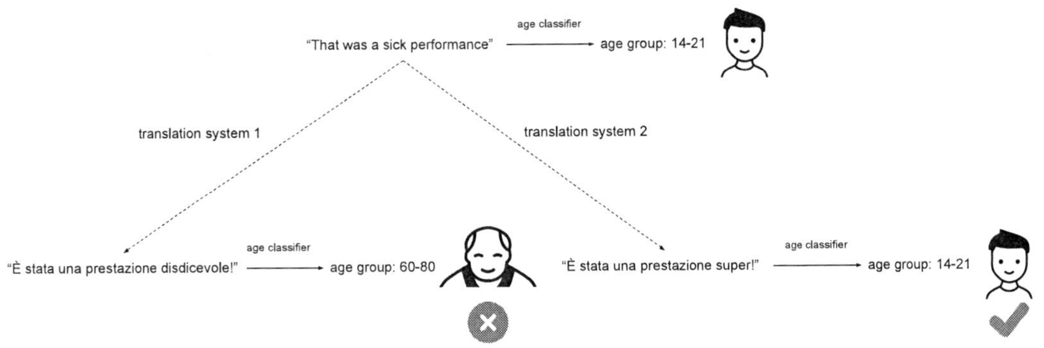

Figure 1: Author age is a Language Invariant Property (LIP). Translation system 1 fails to account for this and provides a translation that can give the wrong interpretation to the sentence. Translation system 2 is instead providing a more correct interpretation.

insights from Hovy et al. (2020), defining an initial benchmark to study LIPs in two of the most well-known transformation tasks: machine translation and paraphrasing. We apply those principles more broadly to transformations in NLP as a whole.

Contributions. We introduce LIPs: properties of language that should not change during a transformation. Our contribution also focuses on the proposal of an evaluation methodology for LIPs and the release of a Python application that can be used to test how well systems can preserve LIPs.[3] We believe that this contribution can help the community to work on benchmarking and understanding how properties change when text is transformed.

2 Language Invariant Properties

To use the concept of LIPs, we first need to make clear what we mean by it. We formally define LIPs and transformations below.

Assume the existence of a set S of all the possible utterable sentences. Let us define A and B as subsets of S. These can be in the same or different languages. Now, let's define a mapping function

$$t : A \rightarrow B$$

i.e., $t(\cdot)$ is a **transformation** that changes the surface form of the text A into B.

A *language property* p is a function that maps elements of S to a set P of property values. p is **invariant** if and only if

$$\forall a \in A \;\; p(a) = p(t(a)) = p(b)$$

[3]https://github.com/MilaNLProc/language-invariant-properties

where $b \in B$, and $t(a) = b$. I.e., if applying $p(\cdot)$ to both an utterance and its transformation still maps to the same property. We do not provide an exhaustive list of these properties, but suggest to include at least **meaning**, **topic**, **sentiment**, **speaker demographics**, and **logical entailment**.

LIPs are thus based on the concept of text transformations. Machine translation (MT) is a salient example of a transformation and a prime example of a task for which LIPs are important. MT can be viewed as a transformation between two languages where the main fundamental LIP that should not be broken is meaning.

However, LIPs are not restricted to MT but have broader applicability, e.g., in style transfer. In that case, though, some context has to be defined. When applying a *formal* to *polite* transfer, this function is by definition *not* invariant anymore. Nonetheless, many other properties should not be influenced by this transformation. Finally, for paraphrasing, we have only one language, but we have the additional constraint that $t(a) \neq a$. For summarization, the constraint instead is that $len(t(a)) < len(a)$.

LIPs are also what make some tasks in language more difficult than others: for example, data augmentation (Feng et al., 2021) cannot be as easily implemented in text data as in image processing, since even subtle changes to a sentence can affect meaning and style. Changing the slant or skew of a photo will still show the same object, but for example word replacement easily breaks LIPs, since the final meaning of the final sentence and the perceived characteristics can differ. Even replacing a word with one that is similar can affect LIPs. For example, consider machine translation with a parallel corpus: "the dogs are running" can be paired with the translation "I cani stanno correndo" in Italian. If we were to do augmentation, replacing *dogs* with its hyperonym *animals* does not corrupt the overall meaning, as the new English sentence still entails all that is entailed by the old one. However, the Italian example is no longer a correct translation of the new sentence, since *cani* is not the word for animals.

LIPs are also part of the communication between speakers. The information encoded in a sentence uttered by one speaker contains LIPs that are important for efficient communication, as misunderstanding a positive comment as a negative one can create issues between communication partners.

Note that we are not interested in evaluating the *quality* of the transformation (e.g., the translation or paraphrase). There are many different metrics and evaluation benchmarks for that (BLEU, ROUGE, BERTscore etc.: Papineni et al., 2002; Lin, 2004; Zhang et al., 2020b). Our analysis concerns another aspect of communication for which we wish to propose an initial benchmark.

3 Related Work

There have been different works in NLP that have investigated issues arising from language technology (Hovy and Spruit, 2016; Blodgett et al., 2020; Bianchi and Hovy, 2021; Bolukbasi et al., 2016; Gonen and Goldberg, 2019; Lauscher et al., 2020; Bianchi et al., 2021a; Dev et al., 2020; Sheng et al., 2019; Nozza et al., 2021, 2022). In our paper, we focus on issues that can arise from the usage of text transformation algorithms (for example, we will see examples of gender bias in transformation, inspired by (Hovy et al., 2020), in Section 5) and we describe a method that can allow us to analyze them.

The idea that drives LIPs have spawned across different work in the NLP literature; For example, Poncelas et al. (2020) discuss the effect that machine translation can have on sentiment classifiers. At the same time, ideas of conserving meaning during style transfer are also presented in the work by Hu et al. (2020). We propose LIPs as a term to give a unified view on the problem of preserving these properties during transformation.

LIPs share some notions with the checklist by Ribeiro et al. (2020) and the adversarial reliability checks by Tan et al. (2021). However, LIPs evaluate how well fundamental properties of discourse are preserved in a transformation, the checklist is made to guide users in a fine-grained analysis of the model performance to better understand bugs in the applications with the use of templates. As we will show later, LIPs can be quickly tested to any new annotated dataset. Some of the checklist's tests, like *Replace neutral words with other neutral words*, can be seen as LIPs. The general idea of adversarial attacks, meanwhile, also requires LIPs to hold in order to work. Nonetheless, we think the frameworks are complementary.

4 Benchmarking Transformation Invariance

For ease of reading, we will use translation as an example of a transformation in the following. However, the concept can be applied to any of the transformations we mentioned above.

We start with a set of original texts A to translate into a set of texts B.[4] We thus need a translation model t from the source language of A to a target language of B. To test the transformation wrt a LIP, A should be annotated with that language property of interest, this is our ground truth and we are going to refer to this as $\hat{p}(A)$. We also need a classifier for the LIP of interest, which serves as language property function p. For example, a LIP classifier could be a gender classifier that, given an input text, returns the inferred gender of the speaker. Here, we need one cross-lingual classifier, or two classifiers, one in the source and one in the target language.[5]

Once we apply the translation, we can use the LIP classifier on the original data A and the new set of translated data B obtaining respectively, $p(A)$ and $p(B)$.

We can then compare the difference between the distribution of the LIP in the original data and either prediction. I.e., we compare the differences in distribution of $\hat{p}(A) - p(A)$ to $\hat{p}(A) - p(B)$ to understand the effect of the transformations. We show a visual explanation on how to benchmark LIPs in Figure 2.

Note that we are *not* interested in the actual performance of the classifiers, but in the difference in performance on the two datasets. We observe two possible phenomena (as in Hovy et al. (2020)):

[4]We slightly abuse of notation here and interpret A has the set of original texts instead of the set of the possible utterances.

[5]For all other transformations, which stay in the same language, we only need one classifier. (Paraphrasing or summarization can be viewed as a transformation from English to English).

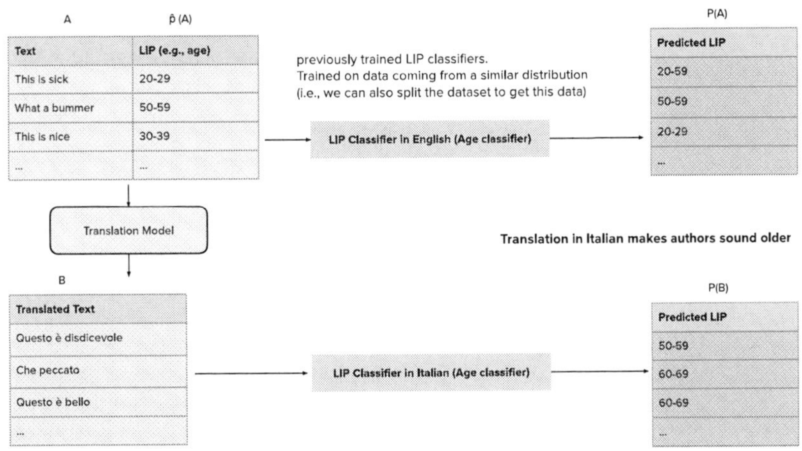

Figure 2: A visual explanation on how to benchmark LIPs.

1) If there is a *classifier bias*, both the predictions based on the original language and the predictions based on the translations should be skewed in the **same** direction with respect to the distribution in A. E.g., for gender classification, both classifiers predict a higher rate of male authors in the original and the translated text. 2) Instead, if there is a *transformation bias*, then the distribution of the translated predictions should be skewed in a different direction than the one based on the original language. E.g., the gender distribution in the original language should be less skewed than the gender ratio in the translation.

Note that we assume that the LIP classifiers used for the source and one in the target language have similar biases; if this were not true and the classifiers had different biases phenomena 1) could be caused both by the bias in translations or bias in the models. This mostly depends on the quality of the classifiers, that has to be assessed before the evaluation of the LIPs.

4.1 Datasets

Here, we evaluate machine translation and paraphrasing as transformation tasks. Our first release of this benchmark tool contains the datasets from Hovy et al. (2020), annotated with gender[6] and age categories, and the SemEval dataset from Mohammad et al. (2018) annotated with emotion recognition. Moreover, we include the English dataset from HatEval (Basile et al., 2019) containing tweets for hate speech detection. These datasets come with training and test splits and we use the training data to train the LIP classifiers.

Nonetheless, our benchmark can be easily extended with new datasets encoding other LIPs.

4.2 TrustPilot

We use a subset of the dataset by Hovy et al. (2015). It contains TrustPilot reviews in English, Italian, German, French, and Dutch with demographic information about the user's age and gender. Training data for the different languages consists of 5k samples (balanced for gender) and can be used to build the LIP classifiers. The dataset can be used to evaluate the LIPs AUTHOR-GENDER and AUTHOR-AGE.

4.3 HatEval

We use the English tweet data from HatEval (Basile et al., 2019). We take the training and test set (3k examples). Each tweet comes with a value that indicates if the tweet contains hate speech. The dataset can be used to evaluate the LIP HATEFULNESS.

4.4 Affects in Tweets (AiT)

We use the Affect in Tweets dataset (AiT) (Mohammad et al., 2018), which contains tweets annotated with emotions. We reduce the number of possible classes by only keeping emotions in the set $\{$*fear, joy, anger, sadness*$\}$ to allow for future comparisons with other datasets. We then map *joy* to *positive* and the other emotions to *negative* for deriving the sentiment following Bianchi et al. (2021b, 2022). The data we collected comes in English (train: 4,257, test: 2,149) and Spanish (train:

[6]The dataset comes with binary gender, but this is not an indication of our views or the capabilities of the tool.

Method	L1	L2	$KL_{A,p(A)}$	$KL_{B,p(B)}$	Dist $\hat{p}(A)$	Dist $p(A)$	Dist $p(B)$
SE	IT	EN	0.004	0.034	M: 0.52, F: 0.48	M: 0.56, F: 0.44	M: **0.64**, F: 0.36
TF	IT	EN	0.000	0.034	M: 0.52, F: 0.48	M: 0.53, F: 0.47	M: **0.64**, F: 0.36
SE	DE	EN	0.000	0.030	M: 0.50, F: 0.50	M: 0.49, F: 0.51	M: **0.61**, F: 0.39
TF	DE	EN	0.001	0.022	M: 0.50, F: 0.50	M: 0.52, F: 0.48	M: **0.60**, F: 0.40

Table 1: Results on TrustPilot dataset translating IT/DE–EN. TF = logistic regression classifier with TF-IDF (TF), SE = (cross-lingual) embedding model. Translation breaks the LIP AUTHOR-GENDER

2,366, test: 1,908). The dataset can be used to evaluate the LIP SENTIMENT.

4.5 Methods

Classifiers As default classifier we use L2-regularized Logistic Regression models over 2-6 TF-IDF character-grams (Hovy et al., 2020). Due to the great recent results of pre-trained language models (Nozza et al., 2020), we also use SBERT (Reimers and Gurevych, 2019) to generate sentence embeddings and use these representations as input to a logistic regression (L2 regularization and balance weights). The two classification methods are referred to as TF (TF-IDF) and SE (Sentence Embeddings). Our framework supports the use of any classifiers. The advantage of this setup is that it is generally fast to set up, but interested user can also use more complex transformer models. The replicability details appear in the Appendix.

Scoring Standard metrics for classification evaluation can be used to assess how much LIPs are preserved during a transformation. Following Hovy et al. (2020) we use the KL divergence to compute the distance - in terms of the distribution divergence - between the two predicted distributions. The benchmark also outputs the X^2 test to assess if there is a significant difference in the predicted distributions. It is also possible to look at the plots of the distribution to understand the effects of the transformations (see following examples in Figures 3, 4 and 5).

5 Evaluation

We evaluate four tasks, i.e., combinations of transformations and LIPs; the combination is determined by the availability of the particular property in the respective dataset.

5.1 TrustPilot Translation - LIP: AUTHOR-GENDER

We use the TrustPilot dataset to study the author-gender LIP during translation. We use the Google translated documents provided by the authors. We are essentially recomputing the results that appear in the work by Hovy et al. (2020). As shown in Table 1, our experiments with both TF and SE confirm the one in the paper: it is easy to see that the translations from both Italian and German into English are more likely to be predicted as male (this can be seen by the change in the distribution), breaking the LIP AUTHOR-GENDER.

5.2 AiT Translation - LIP: SENTIMENT

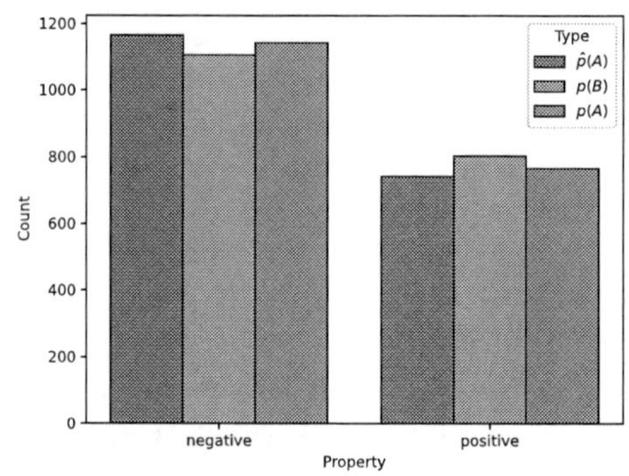

Figure 3: Translation ES–EN on AiT sentiment analysis. Translation respects the LIP SENTIMENT

We use the AiT dataset to test the sentiment LIP during translation. We translate the tweets from Spanish to English using DeepL. We use SE as our embedding method. As shown in Figure 3, SENTIMENT is a LIP that seems to be easily kept during translations. This is expected, as sentiment is a fundamental part of the meaning of a sentence and has to be translated accordingly.

5.3 TrustPilot Paraphrasing - LIP: AUTHOR-GENDER

When we apply paraphrasing on the TrustPilot data, the SE classifier on the transformed data predicts more samples as male (see Figure 4 that plots the distribution). $KL_{A,p(B)} = 0.018$, difference sig-

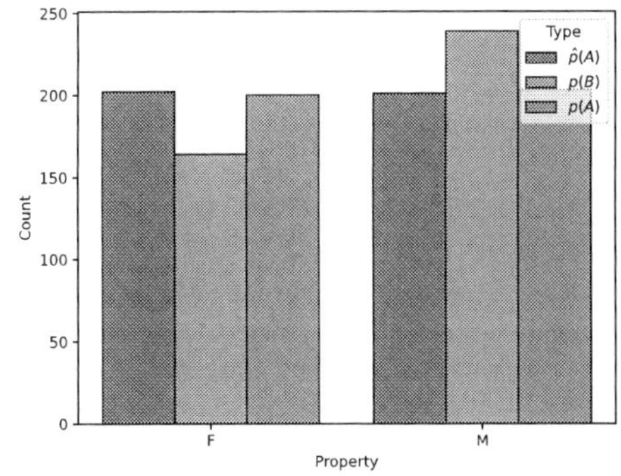

Figure 4: Paraphrasing on TrustPilot English data. Paraphrasing breaks the LIP AUTHOR-GENDER

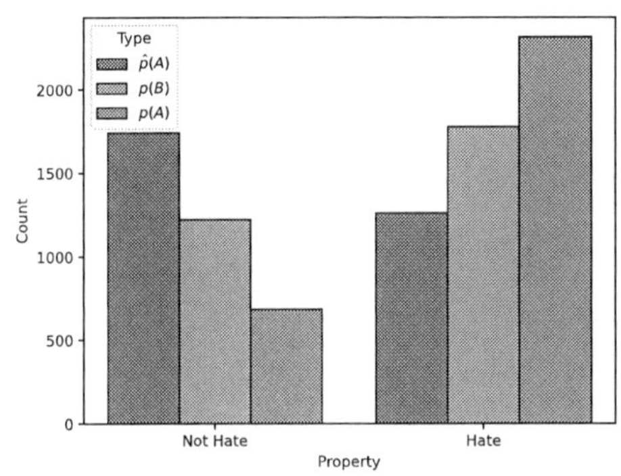

Figure 5: Paraphrasing on HatEval English data. Paraphrasing breaks the LIP HATEFULNESS

nificant for X^2 with $p < 0.01$, resulting in a break of the LIP HATEFULNESS.

5.4 HatEval Paraphrasing - LIP: HATEFULNESS

We use the HatEval data to study the hatefulness LIP after paraphrasing. We use SE as our embedding method. Figure 5 shows that the SE classifier predicted a high amount of hateful tweets in $p(A)$ (a problem due to the differences between the training and the test in HatEval (Basile et al., 2019; Nozza, 2021)), this number is drastically reduced in $p(B)$, suggesting that paraphrasing reduces hatefulness, breaking the LIP. As an example of paraphrased text, *Savage Indians living up to their reputation* was transformed to *Indians are living up to their reputation.* While the message still internalizes bias, removing the term *Savage* has reduced its strength. It is important to remark that we are not currently evaluating the *quality* of the transformation—that is another task. The results we obtain are in part due to the paraphrasing tool we used,[7] but they still indicate a limit in the model capabilities.

6 Benchmark Tool

We release an extensible benchmark tool[8] that can be used to quickly assess a model's capability to handle LIPs. The benchmark has been designed to provide a high-level API that can be integrated into any transformation pipeline. Users can access the dataset text, transform, and score it (see Figure 6). Thus, this pipeline should be very easy to use. The tool allows the users to run the experiments multiple time to also understand the variations that depends on the model themselves.

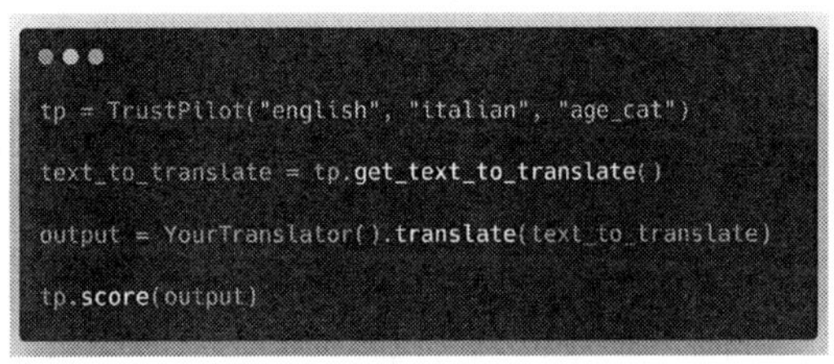

Figure 6: The benchmark has been designed to provide a high-level API that can be integrated in any transformation pipeline. Users can access the dataset text, transform, and score it.

We hope this benchmark tool can be of help, even as an initial prototype, in designing evaluation pipelines meant at studying how LIPs are preserved in text.

7 Conclusion

This paper introduces the concept of Language Invariant Properties, properties in language that should not change during transformations. We also describe a possible evaluation pipeline for LIPs showcasing that some of the language transformation technologies we use suffer from limitations and that they cannot often preserve important LIPs.

We believe that the study of LIPs can improve the performance of different NLP tasks and to provide better support in this direction we release a benchmark that can help researchers and practitioners understand how well their models handle LIPs.

[7] https://huggingface.co/tuner007/pegasus_paraphrase

[8] This will be a link to a GitHub Repo

8 Limitations

The tool we implemented comes with some limitations. We cannot completely remove the learned bias in the classifiers and we always assume that when there are two classifiers, these two perform reliably well on both languages so that we can compare the output.

To reduce one of the possible sources of bias, the classifiers are currently trained with data coming from a similar distribution to the one used at test time, ideally from the same collection.

Ethical Considerations

We are aware that our work assumes that it is easy to classify text in different languages even when considering cultural differences and we do not aim to ignore this. We know that cultural differences can make it more difficult to preserve LIPs (Hovy and Yang, 2021): it might not be possible to effectively translate a positive message into a language that does not share the same appreciation/valence for the same things. However, we also believe this is a more general limitation of machine translation. The speaker's intentions are to keep the message consistent - in terms of LIPs - even when translated.

Acknowledgments

We thank Giovanni Cassani and Amanda Curry for the comments on an early draft of this work. This project has partially received funding from the European Research Council (ERC) under the European Union's Horizon 2020 research and innovation program (grant agreement No. 949944, INTEGRATOR), and by Fondazione Cariplo (grant No. 2020-4288, MONICA). The authors are members of the Data and Marketing Insights Unit of the Bocconi Institute for Data Science and Analysis.

References

Valerio Basile, Cristina Bosco, Elisabetta Fersini, Debora Nozza, Viviana Patti, Francisco Manuel Rangel Pardo, Paolo Rosso, and Manuela Sanguinetti. 2019. SemEval-2019 task 5: Multilingual detection of hate speech against immigrants and women in Twitter. In *Proceedings of the 13th International Workshop on Semantic Evaluation*, pages 54–63, Minneapolis, Minnesota, USA. Association for Computational Linguistics.

Federico Bianchi and Dirk Hovy. 2021. On the gap between adoption and understanding in NLP. In *Findings of the Association for Computational Linguistics: ACL-IJCNLP 2021*, pages 3895–3901, Online. Association for Computational Linguistics.

Federico Bianchi, Marco Marelli, Paolo Nicoli, and Matteo Palmonari. 2021a. SWEAT: Scoring polarization of topics across different corpora. In *Proceedings of the 2021 Conference on Empirical Methods in Natural Language Processing*, pages 10065–10072, Online and Punta Cana, Dominican Republic. Association for Computational Linguistics.

Federico Bianchi, Debora Nozza, and Dirk Hovy. 2021b. FEEL-IT: Emotion and sentiment classification for the Italian language. In *Proceedings of the Eleventh Workshop on Computational Approaches to Subjectivity, Sentiment and Social Media Analysis*, pages 76–83, Online. Association for Computational Linguistics.

Federico Bianchi, Debora Nozza, and Dirk Hovy. 2022. XLM-EMO: Multilingual Emotion Prediction in Social Media Text. In *Proceedings of the 12th Workshop on Computational Approaches to Subjectivity, Sentiment and Social Media Analysis*. Association for Computational Linguistics.

Su Lin Blodgett, Solon Barocas, Hal Daumé III, and Hanna Wallach. 2020. Language (technology) is power: A critical survey of "bias" in NLP. In *Proceedings of the 58th Annual Meeting of the Association for Computational Linguistics*, pages 5454–5476, Online. Association for Computational Linguistics.

Tolga Bolukbasi, Kai-Wei Chang, James Y. Zou, Venkatesh Saligrama, and Adam Tauman Kalai. 2016. Man is to computer programmer as woman is to homemaker? debiasing word embeddings. In *Advances in Neural Information Processing Systems 29: Annual Conference on Neural Information Processing Systems 2016, December 5-10, 2016, Barcelona, Spain*, pages 4349–4357.

Sunipa Dev, Tao Li, Jeff M. Phillips, and Vivek Srikumar. 2020. On measuring and mitigating biased inferences of word embeddings. In *The Thirty-Fourth AAAI Conference on Artificial Intelligence, AAAI 2020, The Thirty-Second Innovative Applications of Artificial Intelligence Conference, IAAI 2020, The Tenth AAAI Symposium on Educational Advances in Artificial Intelligence, EAAI 2020, New York, NY, USA, February 7-12, 2020*, pages 7659–7666. AAAI Press.

Steven Y. Feng, Varun Gangal, Jason Wei, Sarath Chandar, Soroush Vosoughi, Teruko Mitamura, and Eduard Hovy. 2021. A survey of data augmentation approaches for NLP. In *Findings of the Association for Computational Linguistics: ACL-IJCNLP 2021*, pages 968–988, Online. Association for Computational Linguistics.

Hila Gonen and Yoav Goldberg. 2019. Lipstick on a pig: Debiasing methods cover up systematic gender biases in word embeddings but do not remove them. In *Proceedings of the 2019 Workshop on Widening NLP*, pages 60–63, Florence, Italy. Association for Computational Linguistics.

Paul Grice. 1975. Logic and conversation. In *Syntax and semantics. 3: Speech acts*, pages 41–58. New York: Academic Press.

Dirk Hovy, Federico Bianchi, and Tommaso Fornaciari. 2020. "you sound just like your father" commercial machine translation systems include stylistic biases. In *Proceedings of the 58th Annual Meeting of the Association for Computational Linguistics*, pages 1686–1690, Online. Association for Computational Linguistics.

Dirk Hovy, Anders Johannsen, and Anders Søgaard. 2015. User review sites as a resource for large-scale sociolinguistic studies. In *Proceedings of the 24th International Conference on World Wide Web*, WWW '15, page 452–461. International World Wide Web Conferences Steering Committee.

Dirk Hovy and Shannon L. Spruit. 2016. The social impact of natural language processing. In *Proceedings of the 54th Annual Meeting of the Association for Computational Linguistics (Volume 2: Short Papers)*, pages 591–598, Berlin, Germany. Association for Computational Linguistics.

Dirk Hovy and Diyi Yang. 2021. The importance of modeling social factors of language: Theory and practice. In *Proceedings of the 2021 Conference of the North American Chapter of the Association for Computational Linguistics: Human Language Technologies*, pages 588–602, Online. Association for Computational Linguistics.

Zhiqiang Hu, Roy Ka-Wei Lee, Charu C Aggarwal, and Aston Zhang. 2020. Text style transfer: A review and experimental evaluation. *arXiv preprint arXiv:2010.12742*.

Anne Lauscher, Goran Glavaš, Simone Paolo Ponzetto, and Ivan Vulić. 2020. A general framework for implicit and explicit debiasing of distributional word vector spaces. In *Proceedings of the AAAI Conference on Artificial Intelligence*, pages 8131–8138.

Chin-Yew Lin. 2004. ROUGE: A package for automatic evaluation of summaries. In *Text Summarization Branches Out*, pages 74–81, Barcelona, Spain. Association for Computational Linguistics.

Saif Mohammad, Felipe Bravo-Marquez, Mohammad Salameh, and Svetlana Kiritchenko. 2018. SemEval-2018 task 1: Affect in tweets. In *Proceedings of The 12th International Workshop on Semantic Evaluation*, pages 1–17, New Orleans, Louisiana. Association for Computational Linguistics.

Debora Nozza. 2021. Exposing the limits of zero-shot cross-lingual hate speech detection. In *Proceedings of the 59th Annual Meeting of the Association for Computational Linguistics and the 11th International Joint Conference on Natural Language Processing (Volume 2: Short Papers)*, pages 907–914, Online. Association for Computational Linguistics.

Debora Nozza, Federico Bianchi, and Dirk Hovy. 2020. What the [MASK]? Making Sense of Language-Specific BERT Models. *arXiv preprint arXiv:2003.02912*.

Debora Nozza, Federico Bianchi, and Dirk Hovy. 2021. "HONEST: Measuring hurtful sentence completion in language models". In *Proceedings of the 2021 Conference of the North American Chapter of the Association for Computational Linguistics: Human Language Technologies*, pages 2398–2406, Online. Association for Computational Linguistics.

Debora Nozza, Federico Bianchi, Anne Lauscher, and Dirk Hovy. 2022. Measuring Harmful Sentence Completion in Language Models for LGBTQIA+ Individuals. In *Proceedings of the Second Workshop on Language Technology for Equality, Diversity and Inclusion*. Association for Computational Linguistics.

Kishore Papineni, Salim Roukos, Todd Ward, and Wei-Jing Zhu. 2002. Bleu: a method for automatic evaluation of machine translation. In *Proceedings of the 40th Annual Meeting of the Association for Computational Linguistics*, pages 311–318, Philadelphia, Pennsylvania, USA. Association for Computational Linguistics.

Alberto Poncelas, Pintu Lohar, James Hadley, and Andy Way. 2020. The impact of indirect machine translation on sentiment classification. In *Proceedings of the 14th Conference of the Association for Machine Translation in the Americas (Volume 1: Research Track)*, pages 78–88, Virtual. Association for Machine Translation in the Americas.

Sravana Reddy and Kevin Knight. 2016. Obfuscating gender in social media writing. In *Proceedings of the First Workshop on NLP and Computational Social Science*, pages 17–26, Austin, Texas. Association for Computational Linguistics.

Nils Reimers and Iryna Gurevych. 2019. Sentence-BERT: Sentence embeddings using Siamese BERT-networks. In *Proceedings of the 2019 Conference on Empirical Methods in Natural Language Processing and the 9th International Joint Conference on Natural Language Processing (EMNLP-IJCNLP)*, pages 3982–3992, Hong Kong, China. Association for Computational Linguistics.

Marco Tulio Ribeiro, Tongshuang Wu, Carlos Guestrin, and Sameer Singh. 2020. Beyond accuracy: Behavioral testing of NLP models with CheckList. In *Proceedings of the 58th Annual Meeting of the Association for Computational Linguistics*, pages 4902–4912, Online. Association for Computational Linguistics.

Emily Sheng, Kai-Wei Chang, Premkumar Natarajan, and Nanyun Peng. 2019. The woman worked as a babysitter: On biases in language generation. In *Proceedings of the 2019 Conference on Empirical Methods in Natural Language Processing and the*

9th International Joint Conference on Natural Language Processing (EMNLP-IJCNLP), pages 3407–3412, Hong Kong, China. Association for Computational Linguistics.

Samson Tan, Shafiq Joty, Kathy Baxter, Araz Taeihagh, Gregory A. Bennett, and Min-Yen Kan. 2021. Reliability testing for natural language processing systems. In *Proceedings of the 59th Annual Meeting of the Association for Computational Linguistics and the 11th International Joint Conference on Natural Language Processing (Volume 1: Long Papers)*, pages 4153–4169, Online. Association for Computational Linguistics.

Jingqing Zhang, Yao Zhao, Mohammad Saleh, and Peter J. Liu. 2020a. PEGASUS: pre-training with extracted gap-sentences for abstractive summarization. In *Proceedings of the 37th International Conference on Machine Learning, ICML 2020, 13-18 July 2020, Virtual Event*, volume 119, pages 11328–11339. PMLR.

Tianyi Zhang, Varsha Kishore, Felix Wu, Kilian Q. Weinberger, and Yoav Artzi. 2020b. Bertscore: Evaluating text generation with BERT. In *8th International Conference on Learning Representations, ICLR 2020, Addis Ababa, Ethiopia, April 26-30, 2020*. OpenReview.net.

A Logistic Regression Setup

We use a 5 fold cross-validation on the training data to select the best parameters of the logisitic regression. Class weights are balanced and we use L2 Regularization. We search the best C value in [5.0, 2.0, 1.0, 0.5, 0.1]. The solver used is *saga*.

When using TF-IDF we use the following parameters: ngram range=(2, 6), sublinear tf=True, min df=0.001, max df=0.8.

Nevertheless, the tool we will share will contain all the parameters (the tool is versioned, so it is easy to track the changes and check which parameters have been used to run the experiments).

B Models Used

B.1 TrustPilot Paraphrase

We use the same classifier for the original and the transformed text. We generate the representations with SBERT. The model used is *paraphrase-distilroberta-base-v2*.[9]

As paraphrase model, we use a fine-tuned Pegasus (Zhang et al., 2020a) model, pegasus paraphrase,[10] that at the time of writing is one of the most downloaded on the HuggingFace Hub.

[9] `https://sbert.net`

[10] `https://huggingface.co/tuner007/pegasus_paraphrase`

B.2 AiT Translation

We translated the tweets using the DeepL APIs.[11] As classifiers we use the cross-lingual model for both languages, each language has its language-specific classifier. The cross-lingual sentence embedding method used is *paraphrase-multilingual-mpnet-base-v2*, from the SBERT package.

B.3 TrustPilot Translation

As translation we use the already translated sentences from the TrustPilot dataset provided by Hovy et al. (2020). We use both the TF-IDF based and the cross-lingual classifier, as shown in Table 1, each language has its own language-specific classifier. The cross-lingual sentence embedding method used is *paraphrase-multilingual-mpnet-base-v2*, from the SBERT package.

B.4 HatEval Paraphrasing

We use the same classifier for the original and the transformed text. We generate the representations with SBERT. The model used is *paraphrase-distilroberta-base-v2*. Users are replaced with @*user*, hashtags are removed.

As paraphrase model, we use a fine-tuned Pegasus (Zhang et al., 2020a) model, pegasus paraphrase, that at the time of writing is one of the most downloaded on the HuggingFace Hub.

[11] `https://deepl.com/`

DACT-BERT: Differentiable Adaptive Computation Time for an Efficient BERT Inference

Cristóbal Eyzaguirre[1,*], **Felipe del Río**[1], **Vladimir Araujo**[1,2], **Alvaro Soto**[1]
[1]Pontificia Universidad Católica de Chile, [2]KU Leuven
ceyzagui@stanford.edu, {fidelrio,vgaraujo}@uc.cl,
asoto@ing.puc.cl

Abstract

Large-scale pre-trained language models have shown remarkable results in diverse NLP applications. However, these performance gains have been accompanied by a significant increase in computation time and model size, stressing the need to develop new or complementary strategies to increase the efficiency of these models. This paper proposes DACT-BERT, a differentiable adaptive computation time strategy for BERT-like models. DACT-BERT adds an adaptive computational mechanism to BERT's regular processing pipeline, which controls the number of Transformer blocks that need to be executed at inference time. By doing this, the model learns to combine the most appropriate intermediate representations for the task at hand. Our experiments demonstrate that our approach, when compared to the baselines, excels on a reduced computational regime and is competitive in other less restrictive ones. Code available at https://github.com/ceyzaguirre4/dact_bert.

1 Introduction

The use of pre-trained language models based on large-scale Transformers (Vaswani et al., 2017) has gained popularity after the release of BERT (Devlin et al., 2019). The usual pipeline consists of fine-tuning BERT by adapting and retraining its classification head to meet the requirements of a specific NLP task. Unfortunately, the benefits of using a powerful model are also accompanied by a highly demanding computational load. In effect, current pre-trained language models such as BERT have millions of parameters, making them computationally intensive both during training and inference.

While high accuracy is usually the ultimate goal, computational efficiency is also desirable. The use of a demanding model not only causes longer processing times and limits applicability to low-end devices, but it also has major implications in terms of the environmental impact of AI technologies (Schwartz et al., 2020). As an example, Strubell et al. (2019) provides an estimation of the carbon footprint of several large NLP models, including BERT, concluding that they are becoming unfriendly to the environment.

Recent works have shown that behind BERT's immense capacity, there is considerable redundancy and over-parametrization (Kovaleva et al., 2019; Rogers et al., 2020). Consequently, others works have explored strategies to develop efficient and compact versions of BERT. One such strategy known as dynamic Transformers consists of providing BERT with an adaptive mechanism to control how many Transformers blocks are used (Xin et al., 2020; Liu et al., 2020; Zhou et al., 2020).

In this paper, we present DACT-BERT, an alternative to current dynamic Transformers that uses an Adaptive Computation Time (ACT) mechanism (Graves, 2016) to control the complexity of the processing pipeline of BERT. This mechanism controls the number of Transformer blocks executed at inference time by using additional classifiers. This allows resulting models to take advantage of the information already encoded in intermediate layers without the need to run all layers. Specifically, our model integrates DACT, a fully differentiable variant of the adaptive computation module (Eyzaguirre and Soto, 2020) that allows us to train a halting neuron after each Transformer block. This neuron indicates the confidence the model has on returning the correct answer after executing said block. We use the DACT algorithm to determine when the answer stabilizes in a given output using the halting neuron and halt once it is sure running more blocks cannot change the output.

2 Related Work

Several architectures have been designed to avoid overcomputing in Transformer-based models. According to Zhou et al. (2020), there are two groups.

[*]Work done at Pontificia Universidad Católica de Chile.

Proceedings of NLP Power! The First Workshop on Efficient Benchmarking in NLP, pages 93 - 99
May 26, 2022 ©2022 Association for Computational Linguistics

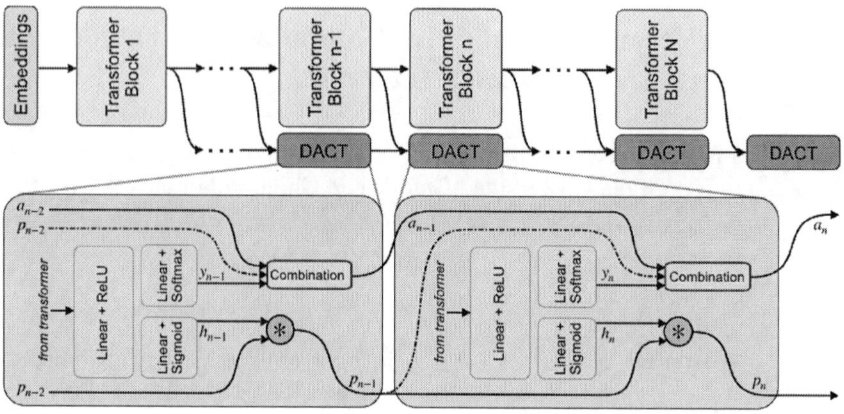

Figure 1: DACT-BERT adds an additional classification layer after each Transformer block, along with a sigmoidal *confidence function*. DACT-BERT combines the Transformer hidden state and the outputs and confidences of all earlier layers into an accumulated answer a_n. Later, during inference, the model is halted once $a_n \approx a_N$.

2.1 Static Efficient Transformers

One such strategy is to use lightweight architectures that are trained from scratch. As an example, ALBERT (Lan et al., 2020) and Universal Transformer (Dehghani et al., 2019) propose cross-layer parameter sharing as a way to improve model efficiency. The latter also includes an ACT-based (Graves, 2016) halting mechanism that is not fully differentiable as DACT-BERT is.

A second strategy is to distill the knowledge of pretrained models into a more compact "student". Models such as PKD-BERT (Sun et al., 2019), TinyBERT (Jiao et al., 2020), and DistilBERT (Sanh et al., 2020) compress the knowledge of large models, the "teachers", into more compact or efficient ones to obtain similar performance at a reduced computation or memory cost. While these approaches effectively reduce the total calculation needed to execute the model, they are limited in the same way as BERT, they do not take into account that some examples could be less complicated than others and use the same amount of computation.

2.2 Dynamic Transformers

Recently, a series of algorithms have been proposed to reduce computation in Transformer language models based on early exiting (Kaya et al., 2019; Han et al., 2021). Models such as DeeBERT (Xin et al., 2020), FastBert (Liu et al., 2020), PABEE (Zhou et al., 2020), and Depths Transformers (Elbayad et al., 2020) introduce intermediate classifiers after each Transformer block. At inference, a "halting criterion" is used to dynamically determine the number of blocks needed to perform a specific prediction. Instead of using a confidence approach (Guo et al., 2017) to determine when to stop, recent approaches rely on computing a particular heuristic (such as Shannon's entropy or Mutual Information) (Liu et al., 2020; Xin et al., 2020; Liu et al., 2021), an agreement between intermediate classifiers (Zhou et al., 2020), a trained confidence predictor (Xin et al., 2021), or directly the amount of steps based on an heuristic based training (Elbayad et al., 2020).

Unlike previous works that use heuristic proxies of models confidence to decide when to halt, DACT-BERT is based on a learning scheme that induces the model to halt when it predicts that its current answer will not change with further processing. As an illustrative example consider a difficult input. Here, our model could "understand" that further processing steps are superfluous and decide to stop early, even if its current answer has a low confidence. On the other hand, existing early stopping models would keep wasting computation because their confidence is low.

3 DACT-BERT: Differentiable Adaptive Computation Time for BERT

Dynamic early stopping methods use a proxy of model confidence to decide when it is safe to cut computation. In this work our signaling module, DACT, approximates this gating mechanism with a soft variant that allows our model to independently learn the confidence function. This mechanism can then be used to detect when stable results are obtained, allowing for the reduction of the total number of steps necessary for a given prediction.

The original formulation of DACT (Eyzaguirre and Soto, 2020) applies this module to recurrent models. In our case, we adapt the formulation to the case of Transformer based architectures, mainly BERT.

3.1 Method Description

As shown in Figure 1 and detailed in Algorithm 1, DACT-BERT introduces additional linear layers after each computational unit, similar to the *off-ramps* in DeeBERT (Xin et al., 2020) or the student classifiers in the work of Liu et al. (2020). However, differently from previous approaches, each n-th DACT module also computes an scalar confidence score, or halting value h_n, in addition to the output vector y_n. Following Devlin et al. (2019), both, y_n and h_n, are estimated by using the classification token ($[CLS]$) that is included in BERT as part of the output representation of each layer.

During training, all the output vectors and halting values are accumulated to obtain a_n *i.e.*, encoding the model's best guess after unrolling n Transformer layers. It is combined using the final predicted probabilities p_n, allowing it to be rewritten as the weighted average of all intermediate outputs y_n multiplied by a function of the confidences of earlier blocks. Line 8 shows how the output vectors are combined using a function of the halting values, to obtain the final predicted probabilities.

The model output is built inductively by using a monotonically decreasing function of the model confidence, p_n, to interpolate between the current step's answer and the result of the same operation from the previous step. We then train the model to reduce the classification loss of the final output with a regularizer that induces a bias towards reduced computation. Unlike the regularizer used by Eyzaguirre and Soto (2020), we use:

$$\hat{L}(x, y) = L(x, y) + \tau \sum_{i=1}^{n} h_i \quad (1)$$

where τ is a hyper-parameter used to moderate the trade-off between complexity and error. We find empirically that our changes help convergence and further binarize the halting probabilities.

Notably, the formulation is end-to-end differentiable. This allows to fine-tune the weights of the underlying backbone, *i.e.* the Transformer and embedding layers, using a joint optimization with the process that trains the intermediate classifiers.

Algorithm 1 *DACT*

Input: M model with N blocks
Input: $is\_training \in \{\texttt{True}, \texttt{False}\}$
1: $p_n \leftarrow 1$
2: $a_n \leftarrow \vec{0}$
3: **for** step $n = 1, 2, \ldots N$ **do**
4:     *# Get output and confidence*
5:     $y_n \leftarrow GetOutputModule(M, n)$
6:     $h_n \leftarrow GetHaltModule(M, n)$
7:     *# Combine with previous outputs*
8:     $a_n \leftarrow (y_n * p_{n-1}) + (a_n * (1 - p_{n-1}))$
9:     *# Update halting probability*
10:     $p_n \leftarrow p_{n-1} * h_n$
11:     *# Stop computation during inference*
12:     **if** not $is\_training$ **then**
13:         **if** $AnsCantChange()$ **then**
14:             **break loop**
15:         **end if**
16:     **end if**
17: **end for**
Output: Approximate final answer a_n

3.2 Dynamic Computation at Inference

The inductive formulation of a_n lends itself to calculating upper and lower bounds on the probabilities of the output classes. At inference, execution halts once the predicted probabilities for the top-class c^* in a_n after running all $N - n$ remaining steps is still higher than the highest value for the runner-up class c^{ru}, and by extension of any other class, then halting doesn't change the output:

$$\Pr(c^*, n)(1 - p_n)^{N-n} \geq \Pr(c^{ru}, n) + p_n(N - n) \quad (2)$$

That is, the model stops executing additional blocks once it finds that doing so will not change the class with maximum probability in the output because the difference between the top class and the rest is insurmountable. Therefore, the *halting condition* remains the same as the original DACT formulation (Eyzaguirre and Soto, 2020).

3.3 Training

The training of the module follows a two step process. First, the underlying Transformer model must be tuned to the objective task. This ensures a good starting point onto which the DACT module can then be adapted to and speeding up convergence. This is followed by a second fine-tuning phase where the complete model is jointly trained for the task. This differs slightly from existing dynamic Transformer methods, which first pre-train the backbone and then freeze it to modify only the classifier weights.

4 Results

4.1 Experimental Setup

We tested our method using both BERT and RoBERTa backbones, evaluating both models on six different tasks from the GLUE benchmark (Wang et al., 2018). We use DeeBERT (Xin et al., 2020) and PABEE (Zhou et al., 2020) as our dynamic baselines, using the same backbones for a fair comparison, and the respective non-adaptive backbones along with DistilBERT (Sanh et al., 2020) as static baselines.

4.2 Implementation Details

Our model was developed using PyTorch (Paszke et al., 2017) on top of the implementations released by Xin et al. (2020) and Zhou et al. (2020), as well as the HuggingFace Transformers library (Wolf et al., 2020). Because the focus of this paper was to introduce an alternative architecture of dynamic Transformers and not achieve state of the art results we use the default parameters and architectures from the Transformers library.

Both DeeBERT and DACT-BERT experiments were repeated three times to obtain the confidence intervals (95% confidence) shown in Figure 2, each time using a different random initialization for the weights in the auxiliary classifiers [1]. Results for FastBERT (Liu et al., 2020) are not reported since both DeeBERT and FastBERT use the same entropy-threshold halting criterion.

Each experiment was run using a single 11GB NVIDIA graphics accelerator, which allows for training on the complete batch using 32-bit precision and without needing gradient accumulation.

4.3 Computational Efficiency

To compare the trade-off that exists between computation efficiency and the performances obtained with it, we computed efficiency-performance diagrams for the validation set. Efficiency was measured as the proportion of Transformer layers used compared to the total number of layers in their static counterparts. The specific metrics for performance are those suggested in the GLUE paper (Wang et al., 2018) for each task.

In our experiments we fine-tune the backbone model for the GLUE tasks using the default values of the hyper-parameters. For the second stage we vary the value of τ in Equation (1) to compute our computation-performance diagram curves, selecting from a set of fixed values for all the experiments: $\tau \in \{5 \cdot 10^{-5}, 5 \cdot 10^{-4}, 5 \cdot 10^{-3}, 5 \cdot 10^{-2}, 5 \cdot 10^{-1}\}$. By modifying this hyperparameter in DACT we can manage the amount of computation the model will perform and record the performance it managed to achieve at this level.

Similarly, using DeeBERT to create the computation-performance diagrams the entropy threshold was varied continuously in increments of 0.05. For PaBEE we fluctuate the patience value between 1 and 12, effectively trying out the full range. The results for the unmodified static backbones are also included as a reference, as are the results obtained by the half-depth DistilBERT pretrained model.

The area under the curve (AUC) in the Performance vs. Efficiency plot shown in Figure 2 shows our approach improves the trade-off between precision and computation. As was to be expected, all models perform similarly when saving little computation as they replicate the results achieved by the non-adaptive BERT backbone that performs a similar number of steps. On the other hand, when using limited amounts of computation our model outperforms the alternatives in almost every task, especially in tasks for with more training data available. We attribute this advantage in trading off computation and performance to fine-tuning of the backbone weights for reduced computation. Intuitively, as we move away from the 12 step regime for which the underlying static model was trained, more modification of the weights is required. Recall that of all the Dynamic Transformer algorithms only DACT-BERT can modify the Transformer weights because of its full-differentiability.

Importantly, because our model learns to regulate itself, it shows remarkable stability in the amount of calculation saved. As the same values of ponder penalties give rise to similar efficiency outputs. By contrast, DeeBERT proves to be highly sensitive to the chosen value for the entropy hyperparameter. The robustness of our model appears to come from learning the efficiency mechanism rather than relying on a somewhat arbitrary heuristic for its control.

In addition, we find our model uses less lay-

[1]The random seeds were saved and will be published along with the code to facilitate replicating the results.

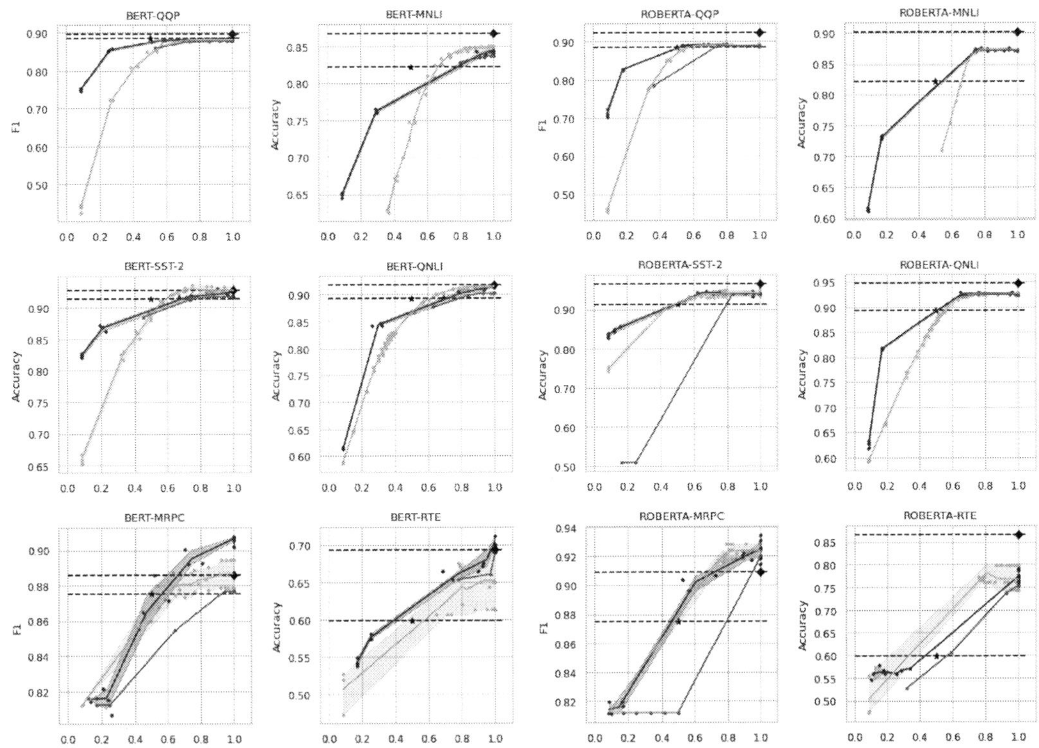

Figure 2: Performance vs efficiency trade-offs for BERT-base and RoBERTa-base models using DACT-BERT (blue), DeeBERT (orange) and PaBEE (green). DACT-BERT and DeeBERT experiments were repeated three times for each hyper-parameter. Individual runs are shown with colored dots, and the average along with its confidence interval is shown using a band. In all figures the **x-axis** shows computation measured as the fraction of the layers used by the respective static backbone (shown as a black diamond). **DistilBERT's** relative perfomance is shown at the 50% computation mark using a black star.

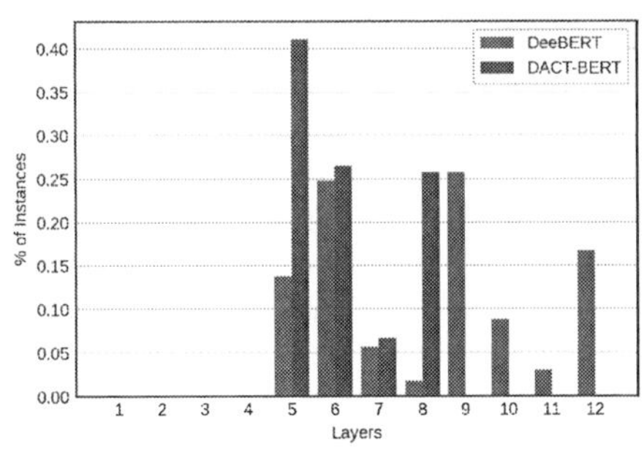

Figure 3: Frequency each Transformer block is used.

ers compared to DeeBERT (see example at Fig. 3), allowing us to prune the final layers. We explain this difference by noting that the entropy will remain high throughout the whole model for the case of difficult questions as it will be uncertain about the answer. On the other hand, any layer in DACT-BERT is capable of quitting computation if it believes future layers cannot answer with more certainty than its own, regardless of how certain the model actually is.

5 Conclusions

This work explored the value of using the DACT algorithm with pre-trained Transformer architectures. This results in a fully differentiable model that explicitly learns how many Transformers blocks it needs to perform a specific task. Our results show that our approach, DACT-BERT, outperforms the current dynamic Transformer architectures in several tasks when significantly reducing computation.

Acknowledgements

This work was partially funded by the Centro Nacional de Inteligencia Artificial CENIA, FB210017, BASAL, ANID.

References

Mostafa Dehghani, Stephan Gouws, Oriol Vinyals, Jakob Uszkoreit, and Lukasz Kaiser. 2019. Universal transformers. In *International Conference on Learning Representations*.

Jacob Devlin, Ming-Wei Chang, Kenton Lee, and Kristina Toutanova. 2019. BERT: Pre-training of deep bidirectional transformers for language understanding. In *Proceedings of the 2019 Conference of the North American Chapter of the Association for Computational Linguistics: Human Language Technologies, Volume 1 (Long and Short Papers)*, pages 4171–4186, Minneapolis, Minnesota. Association for Computational Linguistics.

Maha Elbayad, Jiatao Gu, Edouard Grave, and Michael Auli. 2020. Depth-adaptive transformer. In *International Conference on Learning Representations*.

Cristobal Eyzaguirre and Alvaro Soto. 2020. Differentiable adaptive computation time for visual reasoning. In *Proceedings of the IEEE/CVF Conference on Computer Vision and Pattern Recognition*, pages 12817–12825.

A. Graves. 2016. Adaptive computation time for recurrent neural networks. *ArXiv*, abs/1603.08983.

Chuan Guo, Geoff Pleiss, Yu Sun, and Kilian Q. Weinberger. 2017. On calibration of modern neural networks. In *Proceedings of the 34th International Conference on Machine Learning*, volume 70 of *Proceedings of Machine Learning Research*, pages 1321–1330. PMLR.

Yizeng Han, Gao Huang, Shiji Song, Le Yang, Honghui Wang, and Yulin Wang. 2021. Dynamic neural networks: A survey. *IEEE Transactions on Pattern Analysis and Machine Intelligence*.

Xiaoqi Jiao, Yichun Yin, Lifeng Shang, Xin Jiang, Xiao Chen, Linlin Li, Fang Wang, and Qun Liu. 2020. TinyBERT: Distilling BERT for natural language understanding. In *Findings of the Association for Computational Linguistics: EMNLP 2020*. Association for Computational Linguistics.

Yigitcan Kaya, Sanghyun Hong, and Tudor Dumitras. 2019. Shallow-deep networks: Understanding and mitigating network overthinking. In *International Conference on Machine Learning*, pages 3301–3310. PMLR.

Olga Kovaleva, Alexey Romanov, Anna Rogers, and Anna Rumshisky. 2019. Revealing the dark secrets of BERT. In *Proceedings of the 2019 Conference on Empirical Methods in Natural Language Processing and the 9th International Joint Conference on Natural Language Processing (EMNLP-IJCNLP)*, pages 4365–4374, Hong Kong, China. Association for Computational Linguistics.

Zhenzhong Lan, Mingda Chen, Sebastian Goodman, Kevin Gimpel, Piyush Sharma, and Radu Soricut. 2020. Albert: A lite bert for self-supervised learning of language representations. In *International Conference on Learning Representations*.

Weijie Liu, Peng Zhou, Zhiruo Wang, Zhe Zhao, Haotang Deng, and Qi Ju. 2020. FastBERT: a self-distilling BERT with adaptive inference time. In *Proceedings of the 58th Annual Meeting of the Association for Computational Linguistics*, pages 6035–6044, Online. Association for Computational Linguistics.

Yijin Liu, Fandong Meng, Jie Zhou, Yufeng Chen, and Jinan Xu. 2021. Faster depth-adaptive transformers.

Adam Paszke, Sam Gross, Soumith Chintala, Gregory Chanan, Edward Yang, Zachary DeVito, Zeming Lin, Alban Desmaison, Luca Antiga, and Adam Lerer. 2017. Automatic differentiation in pytorch.

Anna Rogers, Olga Kovaleva, and Anna Rumshisky. 2020. A primer in BERTology: What we know about how BERT works. *Transactions of the Association for Computational Linguistics*, 8:842–866.

Victor Sanh, Lysandre Debut, Julien Chaumond, and Thomas Wolf. 2020. Distilbert, a distilled version of bert: smaller, faster, cheaper and lighter.

Roy Schwartz, Jesse Dodge, Noah A Smith, and Oren Etzioni. 2020. Green ai. *Communications of the ACM*, 63(12):54–63.

Emma Strubell, Ananya Ganesh, and Andrew McCallum. 2019. Energy and policy considerations for deep learning in NLP. In *Proceedings of the 57th Annual Meeting of the Association for Computational Linguistics*. Association for Computational Linguistics.

Siqi Sun, Yu Cheng, Zhe Gan, and Jingjing Liu. 2019. Patient knowledge distillation for BERT model compression. In *Proceedings of the 2019 Conference on Empirical Methods in Natural Language Processing and the 9th International Joint Conference on Natural Language Processing (EMNLP-IJCNLP)*, pages 4323–4332, Hong Kong, China. Association for Computational Linguistics.

Ashish Vaswani, Noam Shazeer, Niki Parmar, Jakob Uszkoreit, Llion Jones, Aidan N Gomez, Łukasz Kaiser, and Illia Polosukhin. 2017. Attention is all you need. In *Advances in neural information processing systems*, pages 5998–6008.

Alex Wang, Amanpreet Singh, Julian Michael, Felix Hill, Omer Levy, and Samuel Bowman. 2018. GLUE: A multi-task benchmark and analysis platform for natural language understanding. In *Proceedings of the 2018 EMNLP Workshop BlackboxNLP: Analyzing and Interpreting Neural Networks for NLP*, pages 353–355, Brussels, Belgium. Association for Computational Linguistics.

Thomas Wolf, Lysandre Debut, Victor Sanh, Julien Chaumond, Clement Delangue, Anthony Moi, Pierric Cistac, Tim Rault, Remi Louf, Morgan Funtowicz, Joe Davison, Sam Shleifer, Patrick von Platen, Clara Ma, Yacine Jernite, Julien Plu, Canwen Xu, Teven Le Scao, Sylvain Gugger, Mariama Drame, Quentin Lhoest, and Alexander Rush. 2020. Transformers: State-of-the-art natural language processing. In *Proceedings of the 2020 Conference on Empirical Methods in Natural Language Processing: System Demonstrations*. Association for Computational Linguistics.

Ji Xin, Raphael Tang, Jaejun Lee, Yaoliang Yu, and Jimmy Lin. 2020. DeeBERT: Dynamic early exiting for accelerating BERT inference. In *Proceedings of the 58th Annual Meeting of the Association for Computational Linguistics*, pages 2246–2251, Online. Association for Computational Linguistics.

Ji Xin, Raphael Tang, Yaoliang Yu, and Jimmy Lin. 2021. BERxiT: Early exiting for BERT with better fine-tuning and extension to regression. In *Proceedings of the 16th Conference of the European Chapter of the Association for Computational Linguistics: Main Volume*, pages 91–104, Online. Association for Computational Linguistics.

Wangchunshu Zhou, Canwen Xu, Tao Ge, Julian McAuley, Ke Xu, and Furu Wei. 2020. Bert loses patience: Fast and robust inference with early exit. In *Advances in Neural Information Processing Systems*, volume 33, pages 18330–18341. Curran Associates, Inc.

Benchmarking Post-Hoc Interpretability Approaches for Transformer-based Misogyny Detection

Giuseppe Attanasio[1,2], **Debora Nozza**[1], **Eliana Pastor**[2], **Dirk Hovy**[1]

[1]Bocconi University, Milan, Italy
[2]Politecnico di Torino, Turin, Italy
{giuseppe.attanasio3,debora.nozza,dirk.hovy}@unibocconi.it,
eliana.pastor@polito.it

Abstract

Warning: This paper contains examples of language that some people may find offensive.

Transformer-based Natural Language Processing models have become the standard for hate speech detection. However, the unconscious use of these techniques for such a critical task comes with negative consequences. Various works have demonstrated that hate speech classifiers are biased. These findings have prompted efforts to explain classifiers, mainly using attribution methods. In this paper, we provide the first benchmark study of interpretability approaches for hate speech detection. We cover four post-hoc token attribution approaches to explain the predictions of Transformer-based misogyny classifiers in English and Italian. Further, we compare generated attributions to attention analysis. We find that only two algorithms provide faithful explanations aligned with human expectations. Gradient-based methods and attention, however, show inconsistent outputs, making their value for explanations questionable for hate speech detection tasks.

1 Introduction

The advent of social media has proliferated hateful content online – with severe consequences for attacked users even in real life. *Women* are often attacked online. A study by Data & Society[1] of women between 15 to 29 years showed that 41% self-censored to avoid online harassment. Of those, 21% stopped using social media, 13% stopped going online, and 4% stopped using their mobile phone altogether. These numbers demonstrate the need for automatic misogyny detection systems for moderation purposes.

	You	**are**	**a**	**smart**	**woman**
ΔP (10^{-2})	-0.1	1.1	-0.0	0.8	-47.6
G	0.11	0.10	0.09	0.25	0.27
IG	-0.17	0.18	-0.09	-0.35	-0.20
SHAP	0.00	-0.14	-0.04	-0.03	0.78
SOC	0.07	-0.13	0.03	0.03	0.52

Table 1: Explanations generated by benchmarked methods. A fine-tuned BERT wrongly classifies the text as misogynous. Darker colors indicate higher importance.

Various Natural Language Processing (NLP) models have been proposed to detect and mitigate misogynous content (Basile et al., 2019; Indurthi et al., 2019; Lees et al., 2020; Fersini et al., 2020a; Safi Samghabadi et al., 2020; Attanasio and Pastor, 2020; Guest et al., 2021; Attanasio et al., 2022). However, several papers already demonstrated that hate speech detection models suffer from unintended bias, resulting in harmful predictions for protected categories (e.g., *women*). Table 1 (top row) reports a very simple sentence that a state-of-the-art NLP model misclassifies as misogynous content.

This issue shows the need to understand the rationale behind a given prediction. A mature literature on model interpretability with applications to NLP-specific approaches exists (Ross et al., 2021; Sanyal and Ren, 2021; Rajani et al., 2019, inter-alia).[2] As explanations become part of legal regulations (Goodman and Flaxman, 2017), a growing body of work has focused on the *evaluation* of explanation approaches (Nguyen, 2018; Hase and Bansal, 2020; Nguyen and Martínez, 2020; Jacovi and Goldberg, 2020, inter-alia). However, little guidance on which interpretability method suits

[1]https://www.datasociety.net/pubs/oh/Online_Harassment_2016.pdf

[2]We refer the reader to Danilevsky et al. (2020) and Madsen et al. (2021) for a recent, thorough perspective on explanation methods for NLP models.

Proceedings of NLP Power! The First Workshop on Efficient Benchmarking in NLP, pages 100 - 112
May 26, 2022

best to the sensible context of misogyny identification has been given. For instance, some explanations in Table 1 hint to which token is wrongly driving the classification and even highlight a potential bias of the model. But not all of them.

We bridge this gap. We benchmark interpretability approaches to explain state-of-the-art Transformer classifiers on the task of automatic misogyny identification. We cover two benchmark Twitter datasets for misogyny detection in English and Italian (Fersini et al., 2018, 2020b). We focus on single-instance, post-hoc input attribution methods to measure the importance of each token for predicting the instance label. Our benchmark suite comprises gradient-based methods (Gradients (Simonyan et al., 2014) and Integrated Gradients (Sundararajan et al., 2017)), Shapley values-based methods (SHAP (Lundberg and Lee, 2017)), and input occlusion (Sampling-And-Occlusion (Jin et al., 2020)). We evaluate explanations in terms of plausibility and faithfulness (Jacovi and Goldberg, 2020). Table 1 reports an example of token-wise contribution computed with these methods. Furthermore, we study attention-based visualizations and compare them to token attribution methods searching for any correlation. To our knowledge, this is the first benchmarking study of feature attribution methods used to explain Transformer-based misogyny classifiers.

Our results show that SHAP and Sampling-And-Occlusion provide plausible and faithful explanations and are consequently recommended for explaining misogyny classifiers' outputs. We also find that, despite their popularity, gradient- and attention-based methods do *not* provide faithful explanations. Outputs of gradient-based explanation methods are inconsistent, while *attention does not provide any useful insights for the classification task.*

Contributions We benchmark four post-hoc explanation methods on two misogyny identification datasets across two languages, English and Italian. We evaluate explanations in terms of plausibility and faithfulness. We demonstrate that not every token attribution method provides reliable insights and that attention cannot serve as explanation. Code is available at `https://github.com/MilaNLProc/benchmarking-xai-misogyny`.

2 Benchmarking suite

In the following, we describe the scope (§2.1) of our benchmarking study, the included methods (§2.2), and the evaluation criteria (§2.2).

2.1 Scope

We consider *local* explanation methods (Lipton, 2018; Guidotti et al., 2019). Given a classification model, a data point, and a target class, these methods explain the probability assigned to the class by the model. *Global* explanations provide model- or class-wise explanations and are hence out of the scope of this work.

Among local explanation methods, we focus on *post-hoc* interpretability, i.e., we explain classification models that have already been trained. We leave out *inherently interpretable* models (Rudin, 2019) as they do not find widespread use in NLP-driven practical applications.

We restrict our study to input attribution methods. In Transformer-based language models, inputs typically correspond to the tokens' input embeddings (Madsen et al., 2021). We, therefore, refer to *token attribution* methods to generate a contribution score for each input token (or word, resulting by some aggregation of sub-word token contributions).

2.2 Methods

We benchmark three families of input token attribution methods. First, we derive token contribution using gradient attribution. These methods compute the gradient of the output with respect to each of the inputs. We compute simple gradient (G) (Simonyan et al., 2014) and integrated gradients (IG) (Sundararajan et al., 2017). Then, we attribute inputs using approximated Shapley values (SHAP) (Lundberg and Lee, 2017). Finally, following the literature on input perturbation via occlusion, we impute input contributions using Sampling-And-Occlusion (SOC) (Jin et al., 2020). See appendix A.2 for all implementation details.

Attention There is an open debate of whether attention is explanation or not (Jain and Wallace, 2019; Wiegreffe and Pinter, 2019; Bastings and Filippova, 2020). Our benchmarking study provides a perfect test-bed to understand if attention aligns with attribution methods. We compare standard self-attention with effective attention (Brunner et al., 2020; Sun and Marasović, 2021). Further, we measure attribution between input tokens and

Dataset	# Train	# Test	Hate %	F1
AMI-EN	4,000	1,000	45%	68.78
AMI-IT	5,000	1,000	47%	79.79

Table 2: Summary of datasets in terms of the number of training, validation and test tweets, percentage of hateful records within the training split, and F1-score of BERT models on test sets.

hidden representations using Hidden Token Attribution (HTA) (Brunner et al., 2020).

2.3 Evaluation criteria

We use *plausibility* and *faithfulness* as evaluation criteria (Jacovi and Goldberg, 2020). A "plausible" explanation should align with human beliefs. In our context, the provided explanation artifacts should *convince* humans that highlighted words are responsible for either misogynous speech or not.[3] A "faithful" explanation is a proxy for the true "reasoning" of the model. Gradient attributions are commonly considered faithful explanations as gradients provide a direct, mathematical measure of how variations in the input influences output. For the remaining attribution approaches, we measure faithfulness under the *linearity assumption* (Jacovi and Goldberg, 2020), i.e., the impact of certain parts of the input is independent of the rest. In our case, independent units correspond to input tokens. Following related work (Jacovi et al., 2018; Feng et al., 2018; Serrano and Smith, 2019, inter-alia), we evaluate faithfulness by erasing input tokens and measuring the variation on the model prediction. Ideally, faithful interpretations highlight tokens that change the prediction the most.

2.4 Data

Automatic misogyny identification is the binary classification task to predict whether a text is misogynous or not.[4] We focus on two recently-released datasets for misogynous content identification in English and Italian, released as part of the Automatic Misogyny Identification (AMI) shared tasks (Fersini et al., 2018, 2020b). Both datasets have been collected via keyword-based search on Twitter. Table 2 reports the dataset statistics.

[3] In this study, the human expectation corresponds to the authors'.

[4] Characterizing misogyny is a much harder task, possibly modeling complex factors such as shaming, objectification, or more. Here, we simplify the task to focus on benchmarking interpretability.

3 Experimental setup

Among the Transformer-based models, we focus on BERT (Devlin et al., 2019) due to its widespread usage. We fine-tuned pre-trained BERT-based models on the AMI-EN and AMI-IT datasets. We report full details on the training in appendix A.1. Table 2 reports the macro-F1 performance of BERT models on the test splits.

We explain BERT outputs on both tweets from test sets[5] and manually-generated data. On real data, we address two questions: 1) *Is it right for the right reason?*, i.e., we assess if the model relies on a plausible set of tokens; 2) *What is the source of error?*, i.e., we aim to identify tokens that wrongly drive the classification outcome. By explaining manually-defined texts, we can probe for model biases.

Tables 3-6 report token contributions computed with benchmarked approaches (§2.2). We report contributions for individual tokens.[6] We define table contents as follows. Separately by explanation method, we first generate raw contributions and then L1-normalize the vector. Finally, we use a linear color scale between solid blue (assigned for contribution -1), white (contribution 0), and solid red (contribution 1). For all reported examples, we explain the `misogynous` class. Hence, positive contributions indicate tokens *pushing* towards the misogynous class, while negative contributions push towards the non-misogynous one. Lastly, the second top row reports the variation on the probability assigned by the model when the corresponding token is erased (ΔP).

4 Discussion

Error analysis Table 3 shows the explanations for a tweet incorrectly predicted as misogynous. IG, SHAP, and SOC assign a negative contribution to the word *boy*. This matches our expectations since the target of the hateful comment is the male gender. These explanations are thus plausible. Still, the tweet is classified as misogynous. The tokens *pu* and *##ssy* mainly drive the prediction to the misogynous class, as revealed by all explainers (SHAP and SOC in a clearer way). Ex-

[5] We rephrase and explain rephrased versions of tweets to protect privacy.

[6] While several work average sub-word contributions for out-of-vocabulary words, there is no general agreement on whether this brings meaningful results. Indeed, an average would assume a model that leverages tokens as a single unit, while there is no clear evidence of that.

	You	pu	##ssy	boy
ΔP (10^{-2})	-0.3	-0.2	-35.6	0.8
G	0.11	0.19	0.32	0.18
IG	0.26	0.00	0.14	-0.60
SHAP	-0.03	0.52	0.28	-0.17
SOC	-0.01	0.03	0.51	-0.14

Table 3: Example from AMI-EN test set, anonymyzed text on first row. Ground truth: `non misogynous`. Prediction: `misogynous` ($P = 0.78$).

planations suggest the model is failing to assign the proper importance to the targeted gender of the hateful comment. These plausible explanations are also faithful. Removing the term *boy* increases the probability of the misogynous class while omitting tokens *pu* and *##ssy* decrease it.

We further analyze the term *p*ssy* and its role as a source of errors. Almost all tweets of the test set containing the term *p*ssy* are labeled by the model as misogynous. The false-positive rate on this set of tweets is 0.93 compared to the 0.49 of the overall test set. Similar considerations apply to English words typically associated with misogynous content as *b*tch* and *wh*re*.

Is it right for the right reason? Table 4 shows the explanation of a correctly predicted misogynous tweet. Gradient, SHAP, and SOC explanations assign a high positive contribution to slurs (*b*tch*, *s*ck*, and *d*ck*). These explanations align with human expectations. However, not all slurs impact the classification outcome. Explanations on *b*tch* are faithful but they are not for *s*ck* and *d*ck*. Differently, IG does not highlight any token with a positive contribution. This goes against expectations as the predicted class is misogynous and therefore we cannot draw conclusions.

Unintended bias We study explanations to search for errors caused by unintended bias, a known phenomenon affecting models for misogynous identification. A model suffering from unintended bias performs better (or worse) when texts mention specific identity terms (e.g., *woman*) (Dixon et al., 2018).

Table 1 reports the non-misogynous text "You are a smart woman" incorrectly labeled as misogynous. SHAP, SOC, and, to a lesser extent, Gradient explanations indicate the term *woman* as responsible for the prediction. This result matches with recent findings on the unintended bias of hateful detection models (Nozza et al., 2019; Dixon et al., 2018; Borkan et al., 2019) and therefore explanations are plausible. Removing the term *woman* causes a drop of 0.48 to the probability of the misogynous class. This validates the insight provided by the explanations. Similar to the previous examples, the explanation of IG is difficult to interpret.

Table 5 shows another example of unintended bias. The text "Ann is in the kitchen" is incorrectly labeled as misogynous. Gradients, SHAP, and SOC assign the highest positive contribution to the (commonly) female name *Ann*. Interestingly, the second most important word for Gradients and SHAP is *kitchen*, reflecting stereotypes learned by the classification model (Fersini et al., 2018). These explanations are faithful: the model prediction drops by a significant 0.40 and 0.24 when erasing the tokens *Ann* and *kitchen*, respectively. We substitute the name *Ann* with *David*, a common male name. We observe that the prediction and the explanations drastically change. The text is correctly assigned to the non-misogynous class and IG, SHAP, and SOC assign a high negative contribution to the word *David*. The all-positive contributions of Gradients do not provide useful insights.

Bias due to language-specific expressions Table 6 (left) shows an example of incorrectly predicted misogynous text in Italian: "p*rca p*ttana che gran pezzo di f*ga" ("holy sh*t what a nice piece of *ss"). The expression "*p*rca p*ttana*" (literally *pig sl*t*) is a taboo interjection commonly used in the Italian language and does not imply misogynous speech.

The interpretation of the gradient explanation is hard since all contributions are positive and associated with the misogynous class. All explanation methods assign a positive contribution to the word *f*ga* (**ss*). SHAP, SOC, and, to a lesser extent IG, indicate that the main reason behind the non-misogynous prediction is the term *p*rca*. The bias of the model towards this expression was firstly exposed in (Nozza, 2021) and it thus validates IG, SHAP, and SOC explanations as plausible. When one of the two terms of the expression is removed, the probability increases significantly. This suggests that explanations by IG, SHAP, and SOC are faithful. Further, we inspect the behavior of explanation methods when we erase one of the terms. We omit the word *p*rca* and we report its explanations on Table 6 (right). The text is correctly assigned to the misogynous class and the word

	s*ck	a	d*ck	and	choke	you	b*tch
ΔP (10^{-2})	-0.02	0.2	0.8	0.3	-0.1	0.03	-13.4
G	0.10	0.08	0.14	0.07	0.08	0.10	0.25
IG	-0.14	-0.16	-0.08	-0.05	-0.20	-0.22	-0.16
SHAP	0.24	-0.03	0.07	-0.05	0.05	-0.06	0.50
SOC	0.20	-0.02	0.26	-0.02	0.07	0.00	0.29

Table 4: Example from AMI-EN test set, anonymyzed text on first row. Ground truth: `misogynous`. Prediction: `misogynous` ($P = 0.90$).

	Ann	is	in	the	kitchen	David	is	in	the	kitchen
ΔP (10^{-2})	-40.4	15.4	12.7	-12.6	-24.3	-1.0	8.0	-1.3	-5.8	-6.7
G	0.25	0.16	0.08	0.10	0.21	0.19	0.18	0.09	0.09	0.28
IG	-0.15	0.18	0.12	-0.33	-0.22	-0.36	0.14	0.09	-0.25	-0.17
SHAP	0.27	-0.31	-0.15	-0.01	0.27	-0.29	-0.38	-0.19	-0.05	0.09
SOC	0.28	-0.19	-0.06	0.10	0.07	-0.25	-0.11	-0.03	0.04	0.05

Table 5: Manually-generated example. Text starts with a female (left) and male (right) name. Ground truth (both): `non-misogynous`. Prediction: `misogynous` ($P = 0.53$) (left), `non-misogynous` ($P = 0.14$) (right).

	p*rca	p*ttana	che	gran	pezzo	di	f*ga	p*ttana	che	gran	pezzo	di	f*ga
ΔP (10^{-2})	94.7	79.7	-0.8	-0.6	0.3	-0.7	-0.6	1.0	-2.3	-1.3	0.4	0.3	-22.9
G	0.17	0.15	0.06	0.07	0.11	0.07	0.13	0.20	0.08	0.10	0.14	0.08	0.21
IG	-0.25	-0.10	-0.09	-0.16	-0.04	0.21	0.13	-0.12	-0.03	-0.25	0.11	0.17	0.32
SHAP	-0.69	-0.01	0.01	0.05	0.05	0.05	0.14	0.15	0.10	0.13	0.10	0.10	0.43
SOC	-0.56	-0.07	0.00	0.04	0.05	-0.05	0.22	0.00	0.05	0.07	0.04	-0.12	0.57

Table 6: Manually-generated example. Complete text (left) and text without initial "p*rca" (right). Non-literal translation: "*holy sh*t what a nice piece of *ss*". Ground truth (both): `misogynous`. Prediction: `non-misogynous` ($P = 0.03$) (left), `misogynous` ($P = 0.97$) (right).

*f*ga* (**ss*) has the highest positive contribution for all the approaches.

4.1 Is attention explanation?

We follow up on the open debate on attention used as an explanation, providing examples on the misogyny identification task. Figure 1 shows self-attention maps in our fine-tuned BERT at different layers and heads for the already discussed sentence "You are a smart woman". Based on our previous analysis (§4), we know that the model has an unintended bias towards the token "woman".

We cannot infer the same information from attention maps. Raw attention weights differ significantly for different layers and heads. In this example, there is a vertical pattern (Kovaleva et al., 2019) on the token "a" in layer 3 (Figure 1a). However, the pattern disappears from heads in the same layer (Figure 1b) and from the same head on deeper layers, where, instead, a block pattern characterizes "smart" and "woman" (Figure 1c). This variability hinders interpretability as no unique behavior emerges. Effective Attention (Brunner et al., 2020) is based on attention and shares the same issue.[7] These results further motivate the idea that attention gives only a *local* perspective on token contribution and contextualization (Bastings and Filippova, 2020). However, this does not provide any useful insight for the classification task. To further validate this limited scope, we use Hidden Token Attribution (Brunner et al., 2020) and measure the contribution of each input token (i.e., its first-layer token embedding) to hidden representations. On lower layers, there is a marked diagonal contribution, meaning that tokens mainly contribute to their own representation. Interestingly, on the upper layers, a strong contribution to "smart" and "woman" appears for all the tokens in the sentence. Different patterns between HTA and attention suggest that, even in the locality of a layer and a single head, attention weights do not measure token contribution.

We observed similar issues on other examples and for Italian models (see appendix B). We there-

[7] In most of our experiments, Effective Attention brings no perceptually different maps than simple Attention. The two methods are hence equivalent for local attention inspection.

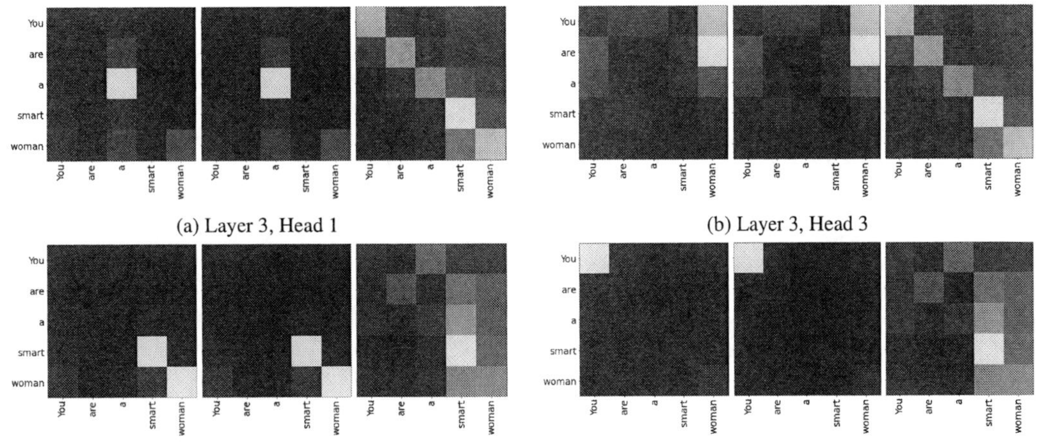

(a) Layer 3, Head 1 (b) Layer 3, Head 3

(c) Layer 10, Head 1 (d) Layer 10, Head 3

Figure 1: Attention (left), Effective Attention (center), and Hidden Token Attribution (right) maps at different layers in fine-tuned BERT. Lighter colors indicate higher weights. Sentence: "You are a smart woman".

fore cannot consider attention as a plausible nor a faithful explanation method and *discourage the use of attention to explain BERT-based misogyny classifiers*.

5 Related Work

Few works applied interpretability approaches to hate speech detection. Wang (2018) proposes an adaptation of explainability techniques for computer vision to visualize and understand the CNN-GRU classifier for hate speech (Zhang et al., 2018). Mosca et al. (2021) study both local and global explanations. They use Shapley values (Lundberg and Lee, 2017) to quantify feature importance on a *local* level and feature space exploration for a *global* explanation. Risch et al. (2020) analyze multiple attribution-based explanation methods for offensive language detection. The analysis includes an interpretable model (Naïve Bayes), model-agnostic methods based on surrogate models (LIME (Ribeiro et al., 2016), layer-wise relevance propagation (LRP) (Bach et al., 2015), and a self-explanatory model (LSTM with an attention mechanism). SHAP explainer is applied (Wich et al., 2020) to investigate the impact of political bias on hate speech classification. Sample-And-Occlusion (SOC) explanation algorithm has been used in its hierarchical version in different papers for showing the results of hate speech detection (Nozza, 2021; Kennedy et al., 2020).

In this paper, we specifically focus on hate speech against women. In this context, Godoy and Tommasel (2021) apply SHAP to derive global explanations with the aim of exploring unintended bias of Random Forest-based misogyny classifier.

While growing efforts are made for evaluating interpretability approaches for NLP models (Atanasova et al., 2020; DeYoung et al., 2020; Prasad et al., 2021; Nguyen, 2018; Hase and Bansal, 2020; Nguyen and Martínez, 2020; Jacovi and Goldberg, 2020), the evaluation is not domain-specific. Therefore, the benchmarking miss to consider specific sensitive problems and biases that are proper of the hate speech domain on which the explanation validation must focus. This paper fills this gap by focusing on post-hoc feature attribution explanation methods on individual predictions for the task of hate speech against women.

6 Conclusion

In this paper, we benchmarked different explainability approaches on Transformer-based models for the task of hate speech detection against women in English and Italian. We focus on post-hoc feature attribution methods applied to fine-tuned BERT models. Our evaluation demonstrated that SHAP and SOC provide plausible and faithful explanations and are consequently recommended for explaining misogyny classifiers' outputs. In contrast, gradient- and attention-based approaches failed in providing reliable explanations.

As future work, we plan to add to the benchmarking suite a systematic evaluation involving human annotators. We also plan to include recently introduced token attribution methods (Sikdar et al., 2021) as well as new families of approaches, like natural language explanations (Rajani et al., 2019; Narang et al., 2020) and input editing (Ross et al., 2021). Finally, we will assess explanations of the most problematic data subgroups (Goel et al., 2021; Pastor et al., 2021; Wang et al., 2021).

Acknowledgments

We would like to thank the anonymous reviewers and area chairs for their suggestion to strengthen the paper. This research is partially supported by funding from the European Research Council (ERC) under the European Union's Horizon 2020 research and innovation program (No. 949944, INTEGRATOR), and by Fondazione Cariplo (grant No. 2020-4288, MONICA). DN, and DH are members of the MilaNLP group, and of the Data and Marketing Insights Unit at the Bocconi Institute for Data Science and Analysis. EP is member of the DataBase and Data Mining Group (DBDMG) at Politecnico di Torino. GA did part of the work as a member of the DBDMG and is currently a member of MilaNLP. Computing resources were provided by the SmartData@PoliTO center on Big Data and Data Science.

Ethical Considerations

We explain BERT-based classifiers using a controlled subset of a large, fast-growing collection of explanation methods available in the literature. While replicating our experiments with different approaches, or on different data samples, from different datasets or explaining different models, we cannot exclude that some people may find the explanations offensive or stereotypical. Further, recent work has demonstrated gradient-based explanations are manipulable (Wang et al., 2020), questioning the reliability of this widespread category of methods.

We, therefore, advocate for responsible use of this benchmarking suite (or any product derived from it) and suggest pairing it with human-aided evaluation. Moreover, we encourage users to consider this work as a starting point for model debugging (Nozza et al., 2022) and the included explanation methods as baselines for future developments.

References

Pepa Atanasova, Jakob Grue Simonsen, Christina Lioma, and Isabelle Augenstein. 2020. A diagnostic study of explainability techniques for text classification. In *Proceedings of the 2020 Conference on Empirical Methods in Natural Language Processing (EMNLP)*, pages 3256–3274, Online. Association for Computational Linguistics.

Giuseppe Attanasio, Debora Nozza, Dirk Hovy, and Elena Baralis. 2022. Entropy-based attention regularization frees unintended bias mitigation from lists. In *Findings of the Association for Computational Linguistics: ACL2022*. Association for Computational Linguistics.

Giuseppe Attanasio and Eliana Pastor. 2020. PoliTeam @ AMI: Improving sentence embedding similarity with misogyny lexicons for automatic misogyny identificationin italian tweets. In Valerio Basile, Danilo Croce, Maria Maro, and Lucia C. Passaro, editors, *EVALITA Evaluation of NLP and Speech Tools for Italian - December 17th, 2020*, pages 48–54. Accademia University Press.

Sebastian Bach, Alexander Binder, Grégoire Montavon, Frederick Klauschen, Klaus-Robert Müller, and Wojciech Samek. 2015. On pixel-wise explanations for non-linear classifier decisions by layer-wise relevance propagation. *PLOS ONE*, 10(7):1–46.

Valerio Basile, Cristina Bosco, Elisabetta Fersini, Debora Nozza, Viviana Patti, Francisco Manuel Rangel Pardo, Paolo Rosso, and Manuela Sanguinetti. 2019. SemEval-2019 task 5: Multilingual detection of hate speech against immigrants and women in Twitter. In *Proceedings of the 13th International Workshop on Semantic Evaluation*, pages 54–63, Minneapolis, Minnesota, USA. Association for Computational Linguistics.

Jasmijn Bastings and Katja Filippova. 2020. The elephant in the interpretability room: Why use attention as explanation when we have saliency methods? In *Proceedings of the Third BlackboxNLP Workshop on Analyzing and Interpreting Neural Networks for NLP*, pages 149–155, Online. Association for Computational Linguistics.

Daniel Borkan, Lucas Dixon, Jeffrey Sorensen, Nithum Thain, and Lucy Vasserman. 2019. Nuanced metrics for measuring unintended bias with real data for text classification. In *Companion Proceedings of The 2019 World Wide Web Conference*, WWW '19, page 491–500, New York, NY, USA. Association for Computing Machinery.

Gino Brunner, Yang Liu, Damian Pascual, Oliver Richter, Massimiliano Ciaramita, and Roger Wattenhofer. 2020. On identifiability in transformers. In *8th International Conference on Learning Representations, ICLR 2020*. OpenReview.net.

Marina Danilevsky, Kun Qian, Ranit Aharonov, Yannis Katsis, Ban Kawas, and Prithviraj Sen. 2020. A survey of the state of explainable AI for natural language processing. In *Proceedings of the 1st Conference of the Asia-Pacific Chapter of the Association for Computational Linguistics and the 10th International Joint Conference on Natural Language Processing*, pages 447–459, Suzhou, China. Association for Computational Linguistics.

Jacob Devlin, Ming-Wei Chang, Kenton Lee, and Kristina Toutanova. 2019. BERT: Pre-training of deep bidirectional transformers for language understanding. In *Proceedings of the 2019 Conference of the North American Chapter of the Association for Computational Linguistics: Human Language Technologies, Volume 1 (Long and Short Papers)*, pages 4171–4186, Minneapolis, Minnesota. Association for Computational Linguistics.

Jay DeYoung, Sarthak Jain, Nazneen Fatema Rajani, Eric Lehman, Caiming Xiong, Richard Socher, and Byron C. Wallace. 2020. ERASER: A benchmark to evaluate rationalized NLP models. In *Proceedings of the 58th Annual Meeting of the Association for Computational Linguistics*, pages 4443–4458, Online. Association for Computational Linguistics.

Lucas Dixon, John Li, Jeffrey Sorensen, Nithum Thain, and Lucy Vasserman. 2018. Measuring and mitigating unintended bias in text classification. In *Proceedings of the 2018 AAAI/ACM Conference on AI, Ethics, and Society*, AIES '18, page 67–73, New York, NY, USA. Association for Computing Machinery.

Shi Feng, Eric Wallace, Alvin Grissom II, Mohit Iyyer, Pedro Rodriguez, and Jordan Boyd-Graber. 2018. Pathologies of neural models make interpretations difficult. In *Proceedings of the 2018 Conference on Empirical Methods in Natural Language Processing*, pages 3719–3728, Brussels, Belgium. Association for Computational Linguistics.

Elisabetta Fersini, Debora Nozza, and Giulia Boifava. 2020a. Profiling Italian misogynist: An empirical study. In *Proceedings of the Workshop on Resources and Techniques for User and Author Profiling in Abusive Language*, pages 9–13, Marseille, France. European Language Resources Association (ELRA).

Elisabetta Fersini, Debora Nozza, and Paolo Rosso. 2018. Overview of the EVALITA 2018 task on automatic misogyny identification (AMI). volume 12, page 59, Turin, Italy. CEUR.org.

Elisabetta Fersini, Debora Nozza, and Paolo Rosso. 2020b. AMI @ EVALITA2020: Automatic misogyny identification. In *Proceedings of the 7th evaluation campaign of Natural Language Processing and Speech tools for Italian (EVALITA 2020)*, Online. CEUR.org.

Daniela Godoy and Antonela Tommasel. 2021. Is my model biased? exploring unintended bias in misogyny detection tasks. In *AIofAI'21: 1st Workshop on Adverse Impacts and Collateral Effects of Artificial Intelligence Technologies*, pages 97–111.

Karan Goel, Nazneen Fatema Rajani, Jesse Vig, Zachary Taschdjian, Mohit Bansal, and Christopher Ré. 2021. Robustness gym: Unifying the NLP evaluation landscape. In *Proceedings of the 2021 Conference of the North American Chapter of the Association for Computational Linguistics: Human Language Technologies: Demonstrations*, pages 42–55, Online. Association for Computational Linguistics.

Bryce Goodman and Seth Flaxman. 2017. European union regulations on algorithmic decision-making and a "right to explanation". *AI magazine*, 38(3):50–57.

Ella Guest, Bertie Vidgen, Alexandros Mittos, Nishanth Sastry, Gareth Tyson, and Helen Margetts. 2021. An expert annotated dataset for the detection of online misogyny. In *Proceedings of the 16th Conference of the European Chapter of the Association for Computational Linguistics: Main Volume*, pages 1336–1350, Online. Association for Computational Linguistics.

Riccardo Guidotti, Anna Monreale, Salvatore Ruggieri, Franco Turini, Fosca Giannotti, and Dino Pedreschi. 2019. A survey of methods for explaining black box models. *ACM Computing Surveys*, 51(5):93:1–93:42.

Xiaochuang Han, Byron C. Wallace, and Yulia Tsvetkov. 2020. Explaining black box predictions and unveiling data artifacts through influence functions. In *Proceedings of the 58th Annual Meeting of the Association for Computational Linguistics*, pages 5553–5563, Online. Association for Computational Linguistics.

Peter Hase and Mohit Bansal. 2020. Evaluating explainable AI: Which algorithmic explanations help users predict model behavior? In *Proceedings of the 58th Annual Meeting of the Association for Computational Linguistics*, pages 5540–5552, Online. Association for Computational Linguistics.

Vijayasaradhi Indurthi, Bakhtiyar Syed, Manish Shrivastava, Nikhil Chakravartula, Manish Gupta, and Vasudeva Varma. 2019. FERMI at SemEval-2019 task 5: Using sentence embeddings to identify hate speech against immigrants and women in Twitter. In *Proceedings of the 13th International Workshop on Semantic Evaluation*, pages 70–74, Minneapolis, Minnesota, USA. Association for Computational Linguistics.

Alon Jacovi and Yoav Goldberg. 2020. Towards faithfully interpretable NLP systems: How should we define and evaluate faithfulness? In *Proceedings of the 58th Annual Meeting of the Association for Computational Linguistics*, pages 4198–4205, Online. Association for Computational Linguistics.

Alon Jacovi, Oren Sar Shalom, and Yoav Goldberg. 2018. Understanding convolutional neural networks for text classification. In *Proceedings of the 2018 EMNLP Workshop BlackboxNLP: Analyzing and Interpreting Neural Networks for NLP*, pages 56–65, Brussels, Belgium. Association for Computational Linguistics.

Sarthak Jain and Byron C. Wallace. 2019. Attention is not Explanation. In *Proceedings of the 2019 Conference of the North American Chapter of the Association for Computational Linguistics: Human Language Technologies, Volume 1 (Long and Short Papers)*, pages 3543–3556, Minneapolis, Minnesota. Association for Computational Linguistics.

Xisen Jin, Zhongyu Wei, Junyi Du, Xiangyang Xue, and Xiang Ren. 2020. Towards hierarchical importance attribution: Explaining compositional semantics for neural sequence models. In *8th International Conference on Learning Representations, ICLR 2020, Addis Ababa, Ethiopia, April 26-30, 2020*. OpenReview.net.

Brendan Kennedy, Xisen Jin, Aida Mostafazadeh Davani, Morteza Dehghani, and Xiang Ren. 2020. Contextualizing hate speech classifiers with post-hoc explanation. In *Proceedings of the 58th Annual Meeting of the Association for Computational Linguistics*, pages 5435–5442, Online. Association for Computational Linguistics.

Narine Kokhlikyan, Vivek Miglani, Miguel Martin, Edward Wang, Bilal Alsallakh, Jonathan Reynolds, Alexander Melnikov, Natalia Kliushkina, Carlos Araya, Siqi Yan, et al. 2020. Captum: A unified and generic model interpretability library for PyTorch. *arXiv preprint arXiv:2009.07896*.

Olga Kovaleva, Alexey Romanov, Anna Rogers, and Anna Rumshisky. 2019. Revealing the dark secrets of BERT. In *Proceedings of the 2019 Conference on Empirical Methods in Natural Language Processing and the 9th International Joint Conference on Natural Language Processing (EMNLP-IJCNLP)*, pages 4365–4374, Hong Kong, China. Association for Computational Linguistics.

Alyssa Lees, Jeffrey Sorensen, and Ian Kivlichan. 2020. Jigsaw @ AMI and HaSpeeDe2: Fine-Tuning a Pre-Trained Comment-Domain BERT Model. In *Proceedings of Seventh Evaluation Campaign of Natural Language Processing and Speech Tools for Italian. Final Workshop (EVALITA 2020)*, Bologna, Italy. CEUR.org.

Zachary C. Lipton. 2018. The mythos of model interpretability: In machine learning, the concept of interpretability is both important and slippery. *Queue*, 16(3):31–57.

Scott M Lundberg and Su-In Lee. 2017. A unified approach to interpreting model predictions. In *Advances in Neural Information Processing Systems*, volume 30. Curran Associates, Inc.

Andreas Madsen, Siva Reddy, and Sarath Chandar. 2021. Post-hoc Interpretability for Neural NLP: A Survey. *arXiv preprint arXiv:2108.04840*.

Edoardo Mosca, Maximilian Wich, and Georg Groh. 2021. Understanding and interpreting the impact of user context in hate speech detection. In *Proceedings of the Ninth International Workshop on Natural Language Processing for Social Media*, pages 91–102, Online. Association for Computational Linguistics.

Sharan Narang, Colin Raffel, Katherine Lee, Adam Roberts, Noah Fiedel, and Karishma Malkan. 2020. WT5?! Training Text-to-Text Models to Explain their Predictions. *arXiv preprint arXiv:2004.14546*.

An-phi Nguyen and María Rodríguez Martínez. 2020. On quantitative aspects of model interpretability. *arXiv preprint arXiv:2007.07584*.

Dong Nguyen. 2018. Comparing automatic and human evaluation of local explanations for text classification. In *Proceedings of the 2018 Conference of the North American Chapter of the Association for Computational Linguistics: Human Language Technologies, Volume 1 (Long Papers)*, pages 1069–1078, New Orleans, Louisiana. Association for Computational Linguistics.

Debora Nozza. 2021. Exposing the limits of zero-shot cross-lingual hate speech detection. In *Proceedings of the 59th Annual Meeting of the Association for Computational Linguistics and the 11th International Joint Conference on Natural Language Processing (Volume 2: Short Papers)*, pages 907–914, Online. Association for Computational Linguistics.

Debora Nozza, Federico Bianchi, , and Dirk Hovy. 2022. Pipelines for Social Bias Testing of Large Language Models. In *Proceedings of the First Workshop on Challenges & Perspectives in Creating Large Language Models*. Association for Computational Linguistics.

Debora Nozza, Claudia Volpetti, and Elisabetta Fersini. 2019. Unintended bias in misogyny detection. In *IEEE/WIC/ACM International Conference on Web Intelligence*, WI '19, page 149–155, New York, NY, USA. Association for Computing Machinery.

Eliana Pastor, Luca de Alfaro, and Elena Baralis. 2021. Looking for trouble: Analyzing classifier behavior via pattern divergence. In *Proceedings of the 2021 International Conference on Management of Data*, page 1400–1412, New York, NY, USA. Association for Computing Machinery.

Grusha Prasad, Yixin Nie, Mohit Bansal, Robin Jia, Douwe Kiela, and Adina Williams. 2021. To what extent do human explanations of model behavior align with actual model behavior? In *Proceedings of the Fourth BlackboxNLP Workshop on Analyzing and Interpreting Neural Networks for NLP*, pages 1–14, Punta Cana, Dominican Republic. Association for Computational Linguistics.

Nazneen Fatema Rajani, Bryan McCann, Caiming Xiong, and Richard Socher. 2019. Explain yourself! leveraging language models for commonsense reasoning. In *Proceedings of the 57th Annual Meeting of the Association for Computational Linguistics*, pages 4932–4942, Florence, Italy. Association for Computational Linguistics.

Marco Túlio Ribeiro, Sameer Singh, and Carlos Guestrin. 2016. "Why Should I Trust You?": Explaining the Predictions of Any Classifier. In *Proceedings of the 22nd ACM SIGKDD International Conference on Knowledge Discovery and Data Mining, San Francisco, CA, USA, August 13-17, 2016*, pages 1135–1144. ACM.

Julian Risch, Robin Ruff, and Ralf Krestel. 2020. Offensive language detection explained. In *Proceedings of the Second Workshop on Trolling, Aggression and Cyberbullying*, pages 137–143, Marseille, France. European Language Resources Association (ELRA).

Alexis Ross, Ana Marasović, and Matthew Peters. 2021. Explaining NLP models via minimal contrastive editing (MiCE). In *Findings of the Association for Computational Linguistics: ACL-IJCNLP 2021*, pages 3840–3852, Online. Association for Computational Linguistics.

Cynthia Rudin. 2019. Stop explaining black box machine learning models for high stakes decisions and use interpretable models instead. *Nature Machine Intelligence*, 1(5):206–215.

Niloofar Safi Samghabadi, Parth Patwa, Srinivas PYKL, Prerana Mukherjee, Amitava Das, and Thamar Solorio. 2020. Aggression and misogyny detection using BERT: A multi-task approach. In *Proceedings of the Second Workshop on Trolling, Aggression and Cyberbullying*, pages 126–131, Marseille, France. European Language Resources Association (ELRA).

Soumya Sanyal and Xiang Ren. 2021. Discretized integrated gradients for explaining language models. In *Proceedings of the 2021 Conference on Empirical Methods in Natural Language Processing*, pages 10285–10299, Online and Punta Cana, Dominican Republic. Association for Computational Linguistics.

Sofia Serrano and Noah A. Smith. 2019. Is attention interpretable? In *Proceedings of the 57th Annual Meeting of the Association for Computational Linguistics*, pages 2931–2951, Florence, Italy. Association for Computational Linguistics.

Sandipan Sikdar, Parantapa Bhattacharya, and Kieran Heese. 2021. Integrated directional gradients: Feature interaction attribution for neural NLP models. In *Proceedings of the 59th Annual Meeting of the Association for Computational Linguistics and the 11th International Joint Conference on Natural Language Processing (Volume 1: Long Papers)*, pages 865–878, Online. Association for Computational Linguistics.

Karen Simonyan, Andrea Vedaldi, and Andrew Zisserman. 2014. Deep inside convolutional networks: Visualising image classification models and saliency maps. In *2nd International Conference on Learning Representations, ICLR 2014*.

Kaiser Sun and Ana Marasović. 2021. Effective attention sheds light on interpretability. In *Findings of the Association for Computational Linguistics: ACL-IJCNLP 2021*, pages 4126–4135, Online. Association for Computational Linguistics.

Mukund Sundararajan, Ankur Taly, and Qiqi Yan. 2017. Axiomatic attribution for deep networks. In *Proceedings of the 34th International Conference on Machine Learning - Volume 70*, ICML'17, page 3319–3328. JMLR.org.

Cindy Wang. 2018. Interpreting neural network hate speech classifiers. In *Proceedings of the 2nd Workshop on Abusive Language Online (ALW2)*, pages 86–92, Brussels, Belgium. Association for Computational Linguistics.

Junlin Wang, Jens Tuyls, Eric Wallace, and Sameer Singh. 2020. Gradient-based analysis of NLP models is manipulable. In *Findings of the Association for Computational Linguistics: EMNLP 2020*, pages 247–258, Online. Association for Computational Linguistics.

Xiao Wang, Qin Liu, Tao Gui, Qi Zhang, Yicheng Zou, Xin Zhou, Jiacheng Ye, Yongxin Zhang, Rui Zheng, Zexiong Pang, Qinzhuo Wu, Zhengyan Li, Chong Zhang, Ruotian Ma, Zichu Fei, Ruijian Cai, Jun Zhao, Xingwu Hu, Zhiheng Yan, Yiding Tan, Yuan Hu, Qiyuan Bian, Zhihua Liu, Shan Qin, Bolin Zhu, Xiaoyu Xing, Jinlan Fu, Yue Zhang, Minlong Peng, Xiaoqing Zheng, Yaqian Zhou, Zhongyu Wei, Xipeng Qiu, and Xuanjing Huang. 2021. TextFlint: Unified multilingual robustness evaluation toolkit for natural language processing. In *Proceedings of the 59th Annual Meeting of the Association for Computational Linguistics and the 11th International Joint Conference on Natural Language Processing: System Demonstrations*, pages 347–355, Online. Association for Computational Linguistics.

Maximilian Wich, Jan Bauer, and Georg Groh. 2020. Impact of politically biased data on hate speech classification. In *Proceedings of the Fourth Workshop on Online Abuse and Harms*, pages 54–64, Online. Association for Computational Linguistics.

Sarah Wiegreffe and Yuval Pinter. 2019. Attention is not not explanation. In *Proceedings of the 2019 Conference on Empirical Methods in Natural Language Processing and the 9th International Joint Conference on Natural Language Processing (EMNLP-IJCNLP)*, pages 11–20, Hong Kong, China. Association for Computational Linguistics.

Thomas Wolf, Lysandre Debut, Victor Sanh, Julien Chaumond, Clement Delangue, Anthony Moi, Pierric Cistac, Tim Rault, Remi Louf, Morgan Funtowicz, Joe Davison, Sam Shleifer, Patrick von Platen, Clara Ma, Yacine Jernite, Julien Plu, Canwen Xu, Teven Le Scao, Sylvain Gugger, Mariama Drame, Quentin Lhoest, and Alexander Rush. 2020. Transformers: State-of-the-art natural language processing. In *Proceedings of the 2020 Conference on Empirical Methods in Natural Language Processing: System Demonstrations*, pages 38–45, Online. Association for Computational Linguistics.

Ziqi Zhang, David Robinson, and Jonathan A. Tepper. 2018. Detecting hate speech on twitter using a convolution-GRU based deep neural network. In *The Semantic Web - 15th International Conference, ESWC 2018, Heraklion, Crete, Greece, June 3-7, 2018, Proceedings*, volume 10843 of *Lecture Notes in Computer Science*, pages 745–760. Springer.

A Experimental setup

A.1 Training hyper-parameters

All our experiments use the Hugging Face transformers library (Wolf et al., 2020). We base our models and tokenizers on the `bert-base-cased` checkpoint for English tasks and on the `dbmdz/bert-base-italian-cased` checkpoint for Italian. We pre-process and tokenize our data using the standard pre-trained BERT tokenizer, with a maximum sequence length of 128 and right padding. We train all models for 3 epochs with a batch size of 64, a linearly decaying learning rate of $5 \cdot 10^{-5}$ and 10% of the total training step as a warmup, and full precision. We use 10% of training data for validation. We evaluate the model every 50 steps on the respective validation set. At the end of the training, we use the checkpoint with the best validation loss. We re-weight the standard cross-entropy loss using the inverse of class frequency to account for class imbalance.

A.2 Explanation methods

We used the Captum library (Kokhlikyan et al., 2020) with default parameters to compute gradients (G) and integrated gradients (IG). Following (Han et al., 2020), for IG we multiply gradients by input word embeddings. For Shapley values estimation (SHAP), we use the shap library[8] with Partition-SHAP as approximation method. For Sampling-And-Occlusion (SOC), we used the implementation associated with Kennedy et al. (2020).[9] Please refer to our repository (`https://github.com/MilaNLProc/benchmarking-xai-misogyny`) for further technical details.

A.3 Attention maps

We used attention weights provided by the transformers library for visualization. We implemented Effective Attention and Hidden Token Attribution following Brunner et al. (2020). We release the implementation on our repository.

B Attention plots

Figure 2 shows attention visualizations for the sentence "p*rca p*ttana che gran pezzo di f*ga" (Non-literal translation: *"holy sh*t what a nice piece of *ss"*). As discussed in §4 (**Bias due to language-specific expressions**), the text is misclassified as `non-misogynous` and most of explanation methods correctly highlight the Italian interjection "p*rca p*ttana".

Similar to results reported in §2.2, we cannot find useful insights in attention plots. Attention in layer 3 has a diagonal pattern in head 1, and a diagonal pattern in head 3 on the word *che* ("*what*"). However, these patterns disappear in layer 10 where attention is focused on *p*rca*. At layer 10, HTA is more spread than attention, suggesting that the latter measures only a *local* token contribution.

[8] `https://github.com/slundberg/shap`

[9] `https://github.com/BrendanKennedy/contextualizing-hate-speech-models-with-explanations`

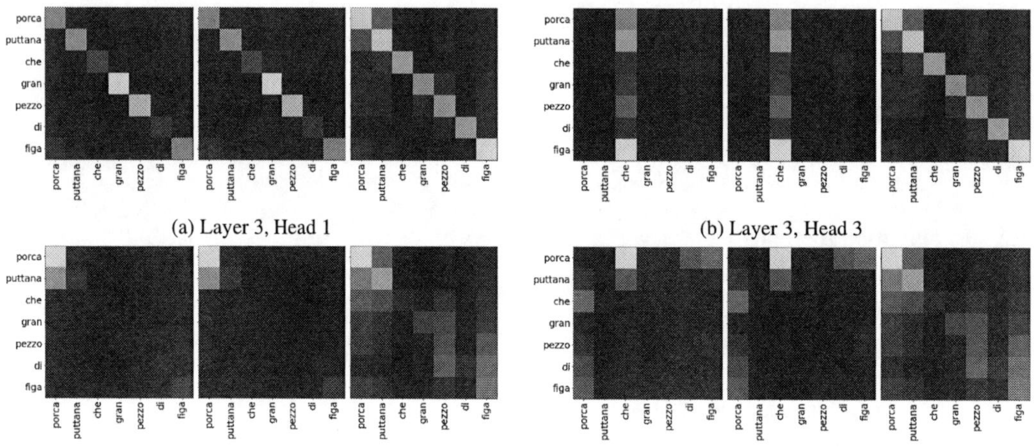

(a) Layer 3, Head 1 (b) Layer 3, Head 3

(c) Layer 10, Head 1 (d) Layer 10, Head 3

Figure 2: Attention (left), Effective Attention (center), and Hidden Token Attribution (right) maps at different layers in fine-tuned BERT. Lighter colors indicate higher weights. Sentence: "p*rca p*ttana che gran pezzo di f*ga", non-literal translation: "*holy sh*t what a nice piece of *ss*".

Characterizing the Efficiency vs. Accuracy Trade-off for Long-Context NLP Models

Phyllis Ang
Duke University
Durham, North Carolina, USA
phyllis.ang@duke.edu

Bhuwan Dhingra
Duke University
Durham, North Carolina, USA
bdhingra@cs.duke.edu

Lisa Wu Wills
Duke University
Durham, North Carolina, USA
lisa@cs.duke.edu

Abstract

With many real-world applications of Natural Language Processing (NLP) comprising of long texts, there has been a rise in NLP benchmarks that measure the accuracy of models that can handle longer input sequences. However, these benchmarks do not consider the trade-offs between accuracy, speed, and power consumption as input sizes or model sizes are varied. In this work, we perform a systematic study of this accuracy vs. efficiency trade-off on two widely used long-sequence models – Longformer-Encoder-Decoder (LED) and Big Bird – during fine-tuning and inference on four datasets from the SCROLLS benchmark. To study how this trade-off differs across hyperparameter settings, we compare the models across four sequence lengths (1024, 2048, 3072, 4096) and two model sizes (base and large) under a fixed resource budget. We find that LED consistently achieves better accuracy at lower energy costs than Big Bird. For summarization, we find that increasing model size is more energy efficient than increasing sequence length for higher accuracy. However, this comes at the cost of a large drop in inference speed. For question answering, we find that smaller models are both more efficient and more accurate due to the larger training batch sizes possible under a fixed resource budget.

1 Introduction

Over the past few years, advances in sequence modeling have led to impressive results on several NLP benchmarks (Wang et al., 2019, 2020). A closer look at these results reveals that higher accuracies are typically achieved by increasingly larger and computationally intensive models, which have large carbon footprints that can have an adverse effect on the environment (Strubell et al., 2019).

This has led to the Green AI initiative, which urges researchers to consider energy and computational efficiency when evaluating models in order to promote those which achieve high accuracies with smaller carbon footprints (Schwartz et al., 2020). However, although it has been a few years since Green AI was introduced, efficiency metrics have still not been integrated into many recently proposed benchmarks such as the Long Range Arena (LRA) (Tay et al., 2020a) and SCROLLS (Shaham et al., 2022). These benchmarks serve as a strong basis for comparison between Transformer models in terms of accuracy. However, improved accuracy is often obtained by either increasing the input sequence length or the model size, and the energy cost of these improvements is not clear. Moreover, previous characterizations of model efficiency in terms of speed (e.g., in LRA) only focus on *inter*-model comparisons, keeping model sizes and input sequence lengths fixed. Here, we argue that the accuracy-vs-efficiency trade-off also has implications for *intra*-model comparisons when selecting hyperparameters – e.g., increasing the sequence length might positively impact accuracy but may also negatively impact efficiency metrics. As a result, when faced with a fixed resource budget, it is not clear whether practitioners should opt for increasing the model size or increasing the input length for the most efficient use of resources.

In this work, we perform a systematic study of the trade-off between efficiency and accuracy for two widely used long-context NLP models – Big Bird (Zaheer et al., 2020) and Longformer-Encoder-Decoder (LED) (Beltagy et al., 2020) – on four datasets from the SCROLLS benchmark.[1] We characterize efficiency using several metrics, including the total energy consumption during training, training speed, inference speed, and power efficiency. We compare the models across several different input lengths and two different model sizes (base and large). Overall, for summarization, we find that, perhaps surprisingly, increasing model size is a more energy efficient way of increasing accu-

[1]Code available at `https://github.com/phyllisayk/nlp-efficiency-tradeoff`.

Proceedings of NLP Power! The First Workshop on Efficient Benchmarking in NLP, pages 113 - 121
May 26, 2022 ©2022 Association for Computational Linguistics

racy as compared to increasing sequence length. However, if inference speed is the main efficiency metric of interest, then smaller models should be preferred. For question answering, on the other hand, we find that using smaller models is more efficient in terms of all metrics *and* more accurate due to the larger training batch sizes allowed under a fixed resource budget.

2 Background

2.1 NLP Benchmarks

Benchmarks such as SuperGLUE (Wang et al., 2019) and SQuAD (Rajpurkar et al., 2018) have served as the gold standard in the development of NLP models. However, these benchmarks only capture model performance on short text sequences while many NLP tasks of interest, such as question answering and summarization, involve long contexts. Recently, several efficient Transformer models have been introduced which require sub-quadratic memory and time complexity with respect to the input length (Tay et al., 2020b). Consequently, new standardized benchmarks have been introduced specifically focusing on the long sequence modeling capabilities of these models, including the Long Range Arena (LRA) (Tay et al., 2020a) and SCROLLS (Shaham et al., 2022).

Although LRA evaluates long-sequence models, it only contains two language datasets which artificially elongate the input sequences through byte tokenization. The SCROLLS benchmark, on the other hand, focuses on language tasks which naturally require synthesizing information from long sequences, including summarization, question answering, and classification. SCROLLS does not compare models in terms of efficiency at all, and while LRA compares model speeds, it only does so across different model architectures, ignoring the impact of hyperparameter choices. For our analysis, we utilize three summarization tasks and one question answering task from SCROLLS.

2.2 Energy Considerations

As deep learning models grow more complex to meet increasing demands, the computation required to run these models generates an increasingly larger energy cost (Strubell et al., 2019). This has led to the Green AI initiative (Schwartz et al., 2020) which demands higher energy efficiency while maintaining state-of-the-art accuracies. A benchmark of the performance and energy efficiency of AI accelerators has been performed during training, but it only examined 2-layer LSTMs and vanilla Transformers (Wang et al., 2020). HULK (Zhou et al., 2021) is an NLP benchmark that evaluates the energy efficiency of several Transformer models (e.g., BERT (Devlin et al., 2019) and RoBERTa (Liu et al., 2019)) during pre-training, fine-tuning, and inference, but it does not consider long-range models. Additionally, neither of the benchmarks consider the effects of different sequence lengths on both energy efficiency and accuracy. However, we confirm the observation from HULK that larger model sizes do not always imply lower efficiency.

Dataset	Task	Avg Input Length
GovReport	Summ	7,897
SumScreenFD	Summ	5,639
QMSum	Summ	10,396
Qasper	QA	3,671

Table 1: An overview of the datasets from SCROLLS that were used in this paper. This is an abbreviated version of the table shown in the original SCROLLS paper (Shaham et al., 2022). *Summ* indicates summarization and *QA* indicates Question Answering. See Appendix A for more information.

3 Methodology

Our main contribution is an analysis of how different sequence lengths affect the trade-off between accuracy, power, and speed in long-context Transformer models during fine-tuning and inference. Since our focus is on long-context NLP tasks, we investigated the following four input sequence lengths: 1024, 2048, 3072, and 4096.

3.1 Datasets

We conduct our analyses on four datasets from the SCROLLS benchmark: GovReport (Huang et al., 2021), SummScreenFD (Chen et al., 2021), QMSum (Zhong et al., 2021), and Qasper (Dasigi et al., 2021). These datasets span two different tasks – summarization and question answering – which frequently involve long inputs. We provide a summary of these datasets in Table 1 with more details provided in Appendix A. We cast these datasets in a unified sequence-to-sequence format using the same procedure as done in SCROLLS.

3.2 Models

Following standard practice, we start with pretrained models and restrict our analysis to the fine-tuning and inference stages. Since our tasks are cast in a sequence-to-sequence format, we pick two widely used encoder-decoder models for long-context NLP – the Longformer-Encoder-Decoder (LED) and Big Bird. To mimic a typical use-case, we obtained these two pre-trained models from the HuggingFace library[2] – hence our analysis can be easily extended to any HuggingFace model.

Longformer-Encoder-Decoder (LED). We analyzed both the base and large version of the LED model released with the original paper (Beltagy et al., 2020). This version of the LED model utilized the `Longformer-chunks` implementation that achieves high compute efficiency at the cost of higher memory by chunking the key and query matrices such that only a single matrix multiplication operation from PyTorch is needed. The two versions of the model are stored on HuggingFace as `allenai/led-base-16384` and `allenai/led-large-16384`.

Big Bird. Following the encoder-decoder setup in the original Big Bird paper (Zaheer et al., 2020), we utilized the version of Big Bird-large that has been pretrained on the PubMed dataset starting from Pegasus-large. This model is stored on HuggingFace as `google/bigbird-pegasus-large-pubmed`. We only performed experiments on the large version of this model as the base version is not released on HuggingFace.

3.3 Hardware Resources Provisioned

Our initial experiments with the LED-base model suggest that large batch sizes are imperative for obtaining high accuracies on the question answering task but less so for the summarization tasks (see Table 2). Quadrupling the batch sizes on the Qasper question answering dataset – through the use of gradient accumulation step size of four – resulted in a two to four point increase in the F1 scores across the input sequence lengths. Take the input sequence length of 1024 as an example (i.e., first row of Table 2), we were able to fit a batch size of 24 on one GPU (labeled *1 GPU*) without suffering an out-of-memory error when performing fine-tuning, obtaining a modest F1 score of 17.68. When we quadrupled the batch size to 96 by using gradient accumulation with step size of four (labeled *1 GPU - Accum*), the model accuracy went up to an F1 score of 21.39. When the batch sizes were further increased through the use of more GPUs (labeled *8 GPUs - Accum*), the increase in F1 scores becomes more prominent at four to seven points. The same trends hold for all sequence lengths on the Qasper dataset. On the other hand, quadrupling the batch sizes for the GovReport summarization dataset resulted in negligible increases in Rouge scores while the further increase via multiple GPUs actually resulted in (slightly) lower Rouge scores.

These initial experiments informed our decision to use a fixed resource budget of 1 Nvidia RTX A6000 GPU for both fine-tuning and inference of all models on the summarization tasks, since increasing the number of GPUs does not have a positive effect on the model accuracy. On the other hand, for the question answering task, we used a much larger fixed resource budget of 8 Nvidia RTX A6000 GPUs (on the same server) for both fine-tuning and inference to allow for larger batch sizes that can obtain much better model accuracy.

3.4 Fine-tuning

All pre-trained models mentioned in Section 3.2 are fined-tuned without mixed precision or gradient checkpointing on all datasets until convergence. A model has converged when the accuracy metric of interest for that specific task stays the same or has worsened for 3 validation calls. In our case, since we perform validation every 500 steps for summarization tasks and every 10 steps for the question answering task, a model has converged when the metric has stayed the same or worsened for 1500 steps for summarization tasks and 30 steps for the question answering task.

In terms of hyperparameters, we used the same hyperparameters that the SCROLLS benchmark utilized for the LED-base model except for the batch sizes. To control for the effects of memory on our metrics, for each sequence length and model, we selected the largest batch size that can fit on the 48GB A6000 GPU. For the question answering task, the batch sizes were selected so that the minibatches on each of the 8 GPUs were maximized. To further increase the effective size of each of minibatches in the question answering task, we set gradient accumulation steps to four. More information about the hyperparameters is outlined in Appendix B.

3.5 Inference

Since we do not have access to the labels in the test sets of SCROLLS, inference is run on the vali-

[2] `https://huggingface.co/`

Dataset	Seq Len	1 GPU		1 GPU - Accum		8 GPUs - Accum	
		Batch Size	Acc	Batch Size	Acc	Batch Size	Acc
Qasper	1024	24	17.68	96	21.39	704	25.30
	2048	12	22.74	48	27.87	352	29.97
	3072	8	29.57	32	33.75	224	33.94
	4096	6	32.88	24	34.20	160	36.36
GovReport	1024	24	49.53	96	49.53	704	48.78
	2048	12	51.15	48	51.28	352	50.18
	3072	8	51.67	32	52.09	224	50.60
	4096	6	51.71	24	52.27	160	50.95

Table 2: Accuracy of the LED-base model with varying batch sizes across different hardware configurations. *Accum* indicates that a gradient accumulation step size of four was used to obtain the larger batch sizes. On the Qasper question answering task, where *Acc* represents the F1 score of the predicted answers, increasing the batch sizes significantly improves the accuracy for all sequence lengths. On the GovReport summarization task, where *Acc* represents the Rouge score, increasing the batch sizes has a negligible effect.

dation set using the fine-tuned models. All of our inferences were performed with a batch size of 16.

3.6 Evaluation Criteria

Accuracy. Our evaluation metrics for accuracy of the models on each dataset follow those mentioned in the SCROLLS paper. GovReport, SummScreenFD, and QMSum are evaluated using Rouge, as is standard for summarization; Qasper is evaluated using a token-level F1 score after normalizing both the predicted and ground-truth answer strings.[3] For Rouge, following SCROLLS, we calculated the geometric mean of three different types of rouge to provide a single value: Rouge-1 (unigram overlap), Rouge-2 (bigram overlap), and Rouge-L (longest sequence overlap).

Efficiency. For efficiency metrics, we explored the training power efficiency (number of samples trained per second per Watt), total training energy required (average power $\times$ training time), training speed (number of samples trained per second), and inference speed (number of samples inferenced per second). The training and inference speeds are provided by the HuggingFace library while the total energy consumed and the power efficiency of the GPU(s) were collected with the help of the Weights and Biases (wandb) tool.[4]

We chose power efficiency as one of our metrics because it is one of the most important industry standard metrics used for machine learning platforms (TPU uses performance per Watt, MLPerf (Reddi et al., 2020; Mattson et al., 2020) measures the number of samples inferenced per second per Watt) as it is a key component of TCO (Total Cost of Ownership). Cloud providers routinely spend 40-50% of the cost towards electricity as well as powering and cooling the servers, and this cost is increasing. Hence, maximizing the utility of this spent power by increasing the number of samples processed per watt is crucial for reducing the carbon footprint of NLP research.

4 Results

4.1 Summarization Datasets

Figure 1 depicts the power efficiency of each summarization dataset vs. its corresponding training accuracy for input lengths ranging from 1024 to 4096 tokens. We make the following observations: First, power efficiency has a strong inverse correlation with the size of the input sequence lengths, with small variations across datasets. Second, the Big Bird-large model has similar power efficiency to LED-large model across the input sequence lengths, but Big Bird's Rouge scores are much lower, making one of the LED models a better choice to select when training summarization tasks.

Figure 2 shows the total energy consumed during training on each of the three summarization datasets. Interestingly, we observe that on GovReport and QMSum, LED-large with sequence length 1024 is more efficient *and* has higher accuracy than each of the LED-base models with larger sequence lengths. Increasing the sequence length for LED-large further increases this accuracy while still often being more efficient than LED-base models

[3] Normalization is done in the same manner as Squad (Rajpurkar et al., 2018)).

[4] `https://wandb.ai/site`

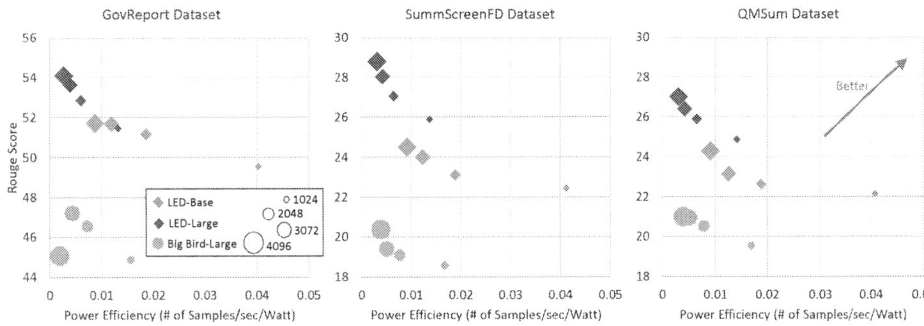

Figure 1: Power efficiency measured in number of samples per second per watt vs. model accuracy in Rouge score for the three summarization datasets – GovReport (Left), SummScreenFD (Middle), QMSum (Right) – while varying input sequence lengths.

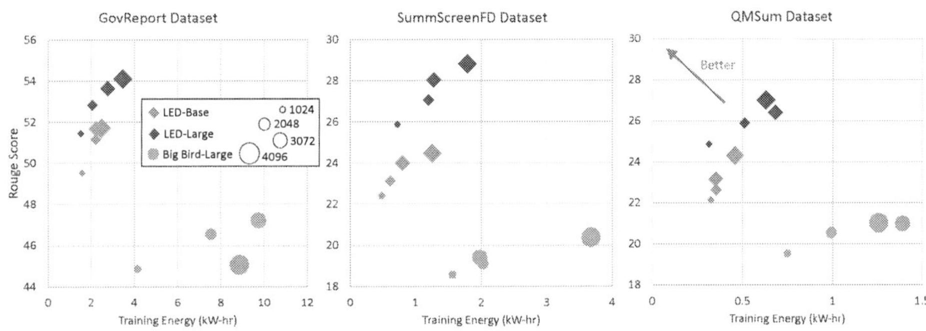

Figure 2: Total training energy consumption measured in kiloWatt-hour vs. model accuracy in Rouge score for the three summarization datasets – GovReport (Left), SummScreenFD (Middle), QMSum (Right) – while varying input sequence lengths.

with greater sequence lengths. This suggests that, for summarization, using larger models with short sequence lengths is a more energy friendly way to get higher accuracies (as compared to small models with larger sequence lengths). We find Big Bird to both consume more energy and achieve lower Rouge scores.

The training speed (Figure 3) and the inference speed (Figure 4) of the summarization datasets show similar trends. As the input sequence lengths increase, the training and inference speeds decrease due to the sub-quadratic runtime complexity (with respect to the input sequence lengths) exhibited in the attention mechanisms employed in these efficient Transformer models. Unlike training energy, inference speed increases when the model size is smaller at the cost of lower accuracy. However, sometimes (such as the datapoints exhibited in the GovReport dataset) a similar accuracy can be obtained by LED-base model with a larger input length (2048) as opposed to LED-large with a smaller input length (1024).

4.2 Qasper Dataset and Scaling Up Resources

Figure 5 shows all four efficiency metrics for the Qasper question answering task. Once again, the LED models outperform Big Bird in the overall F1 score. Interestingly, we observe that under fixed resources, LED-base also outperforms LED-large on this dataset.[5] We suspect this is due to the larger batch sizes we can fit for LED-base as compared to LED-large, which we found to be particularly important for this dataset. Hence, we found it to be more efficient and more accurate to use the smaller model on this task. Increasing sequence length brings large gains in accuracy with a small increased cost in training energy but a large slowdown in terms of speed.

[5]We note that our LED-base model with input sequence length 4096 achieves an F1 score of approximately 10 points higher than what was reported in the SCROLLS paper.

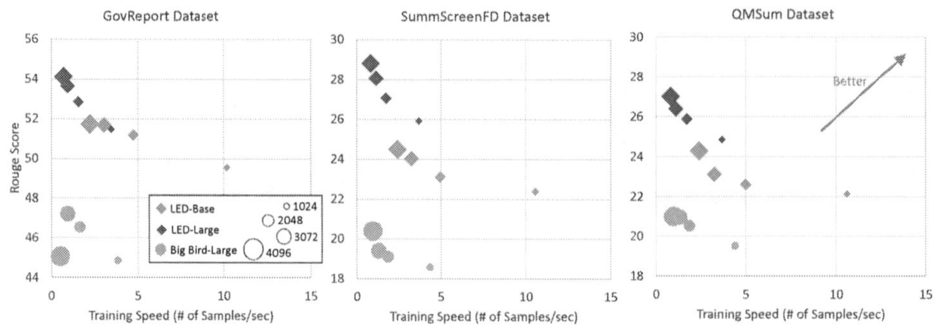

Figure 3: Model training speed measured in number of samples per second vs. model accuracy in Rouge score for the three summarization datasets – GovReport (Left), SummScreenFD (Middle), QMSum (Right) – while varying input sequence lengths.

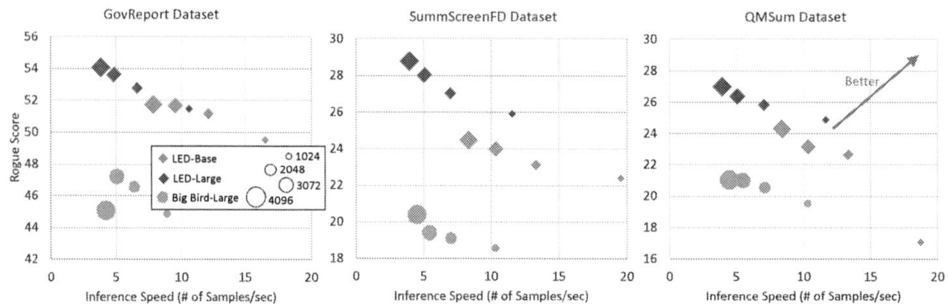

Figure 4: Model inference speed measured in number of samples per second vs. model accuracy in Rouge score for the three summarization datasets – GovReport (Left), SummScreenFD (Middle), QMSum (Right) – while varying input sequence lengths.

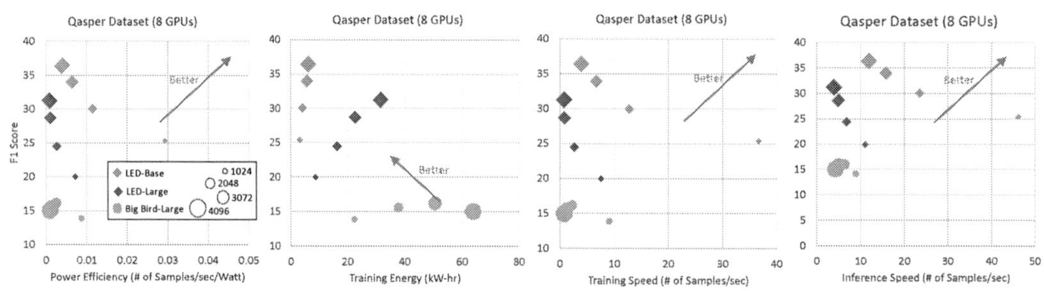

Figure 5: Power efficiency measured in number of samples per second (Left), training energy estimated in kiloWatt-hour (Center Left), training speed (Center Right) and inference speed (Right) in number of samples per second vs. model accuracy in F1 score for the Qasper question answering dataset while varying input sequence lengths.

4.3 Energy Consumption Deep Dive

To understand the energy consumption of the hardware platform, we present a deeper analysis on the GovReport dataset. We plot the GPU utilization (as an average over the entire training run), the GPU memory usage (as an average over the entire training run), and the training time (in seconds) in Figure 6. From the GPU utilization plot, we observe that the single GPU is pretty well utilized for the LED models while Big Bird seems to not saturate the GPU especially when the input sequence length is 4096. This would suggest that Big Bird would incur a smaller energy cost because not all GPU resources are online. However, Big Bird took about 48 hours to train for a sequence length of 4096 while LED-large took 14 hours to train at the same sequence length. The almost four times in training time contributed to Big Bird's high en-

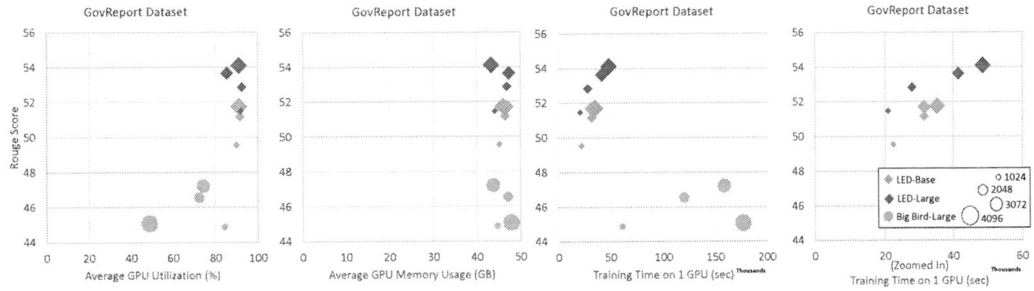

Figure 6: Average GPU utilization (Left), average GPU memory usage (Center Left), and total training time in seconds (Center Right and Right) vs. model accuracy for the GovReport summarization dataset while varying input sequence lengths.

ergy consumption in Figure 2, making it the least carbon-friendly model to train for GovReport. In general, the training time on the GPU (depicted in Figure 6-right) exhibits a similar trend as the total energy consumed. The average GPU utilization is therefore not an indicative metric in predicting the energy consumption of model training in this case, but the training time is, as energy is calculated using power consumed over time (or the area under the curve when plotting power over time).

5 Conclusion

We have presented a systematic study of the accuracy vs. efficiency trade-offs involved in four long-context NLP tasks across two model architectures. In addition to comparing model architectures as commonly done in NLP benchmarks, our focus was on comparing models of two different sizes and four different sequence lengths. We highlight several key findings which we hope practitioners can utilize to select hyperparameters under a resource constrained setting. One such key finding is that using a larger model instead of larger input sequence lengths is a more energy friendly way to achieve higher accuracies on summarization tasks if inference speed is not a concern. On the other hand, utilizing a longer input sequence length with a smaller model for question answering task results in higher accuracies with higher efficiency.

References

Iz Beltagy, Matthew E. Peters, and Arman Cohan. 2020. Longformer: The Long-Document Transformer. *arXiv:2004.05150 [cs]*. ArXiv: 2004.05150.

Mingda Chen, Zewei Chu, Sam Wiseman, and Kevin Gimpel. 2021. SummScreen: A Dataset for Abstractive Screenplay Summarization. *arXiv:2104.07091 [cs]*. ArXiv: 2104.07091.

Pradeep Dasigi, Kyle Lo, Iz Beltagy, Arman Cohan, Noah A. Smith, and Matt Gardner. 2021. A dataset of information-seeking questions and answers anchored in research papers. In *Proceedings of the 2021 Conference of the North American Chapter of the Association for Computational Linguistics: Human Language Technologies*, pages 4599–4610, Online. Association for Computational Linguistics.

Jacob Devlin, Ming-Wei Chang, Kenton Lee, and Kristina Toutanova. 2019. BERT: Pre-training of deep bidirectional transformers for language understanding. In *Proceedings of the 2019 Conference of the North American Chapter of the Association for Computational Linguistics: Human Language Technologies, Volume 1 (Long and Short Papers)*, pages 4171–4186, Minneapolis, Minnesota. Association for Computational Linguistics.

Luyang Huang, Shuyang Cao, Nikolaus Parulian, Heng Ji, and Lu Wang. 2021. Efficient attentions for long document summarization. In *Proceedings of the 2021 Conference of the North American Chapter of the Association for Computational Linguistics: Human Language Technologies*, pages 1419–1436, Online. Association for Computational Linguistics.

Yinhan Liu, Myle Ott, Naman Goyal, Jingfei Du, Mandar Joshi, Danqi Chen, Omer Levy, Mike Lewis, Luke Zettlemoyer, and Veselin Stoyanov. 2019. Roberta: A robustly optimized bert pretraining approach. *arXiv preprint arXiv:1907.11692*.

Peter Mattson, Christine Cheng, Gregory Diamos, Cody Coleman, Paulius Micikevicius, David Patterson, Hanlin Tang, Gu-Yeon Wei, Peter Bailis, Victor Bittorf, David Brooks, Dehao Chen, Debo Dutta, Udit Gupta, Kim Hazelwood, Andy Hock, Xinyuan Huang, Daniel Kang, David Kanter, Naveen Kumar, Jeffery Liao, Deepak Narayanan, Tayo Oguntebi, Gennady Pekhimenko, Lillian Pentecost, Vijay Janapa Reddi, Taylor Robie, Tom St John, Carole-Jean Wu, Lingjie Xu, Cliff Young, and Matei Zaharia. 2020. Mlperf training benchmark. In *Pro-*

ceedings of Machine Learning and Systems, volume 2, pages 336–349.

Pranav Rajpurkar, Robin Jia, and Percy Liang. 2018. Know what you don't know: Unanswerable questions for SQuAD. In *Proceedings of the 56th Annual Meeting of the Association for Computational Linguistics (Volume 2: Short Papers)*, pages 784–789, Melbourne, Australia. Association for Computational Linguistics.

Vijay Janapa Reddi, Christine Cheng, David Kanter, Peter Mattson, Guenther Schmuelling, Carole-Jean Wu, Brian Anderson, Maximilien Breughe, Mark Charlebois, William Chou, Ramesh Chukka, Cody Coleman, Sam Davis, Pan Deng, Greg Diamos, Jared Duke, Dave Fick, J. Scott Gardner, Itay Hubara, Sachin Idgunji, Thomas B. Jablin, Jeff Jiao, Tom St John, Pankaj Kanwar, David Lee, Jeffery Liao, Anton Lokhmotov, Francisco Massa, Peng Meng, Paulius Micikevicius, Colin Osborne, Gennady Pekhimenko, Arun Tejusve Raghunath Rajan, Dilip Sequeira, Ashish Sirasao, Fei Sun, Hanlin Tang, Michael Thomson, Frank Wei, Ephrem Wu, Lingjie Xu, Koichi Yamada, Bing Yu, George Yuan, Aaron Zhong, Peizhao Zhang, and Yuchen Zhou. 2020. MLPerf Inference Benchmark. *arXiv:1911.02549 [cs, stat]*. ArXiv: 1911.02549.

Roy Schwartz, Jesse Dodge, Noah A. Smith, and Oren Etzioni. 2020. Green ai. *Commun. ACM*, 63(12):54–63.

Uri Shaham, Elad Segal, Maor Ivgi, Avia Efrat, Ori Yoran, Adi Haviv, Ankit Gupta, Wenhan Xiong, Mor Geva, Jonathan Berant, and Omer Levy. 2022. SCROLLS: Standardized CompaRison Over Long Language Sequences. *arXiv:2201.03533 [cs, stat]*. ArXiv: 2201.03533.

Emma Strubell, Ananya Ganesh, and Andrew McCallum. 2019. Energy and policy considerations for deep learning in NLP. In *Proceedings of the 57th Annual Meeting of the Association for Computational Linguistics*, pages 3645–3650, Florence, Italy. Association for Computational Linguistics.

Yi Tay, Mostafa Dehghani, Samira Abnar, Yikang Shen, Dara Bahri, Philip Pham, Jinfeng Rao, Liu Yang, Sebastian Ruder, and Donald Metzler. 2020a. Long Range Arena: A Benchmark for Efficient Transformers. *arXiv:2011.04006 [cs]*. ArXiv: 2011.04006.

Yi Tay, Mostafa Dehghani, Dara Bahri, and Donald Metzler. 2020b. Efficient Transformers: A Survey. *arXiv:2009.06732 [cs]*. ArXiv: 2009.06732.

Alex Wang, Yada Pruksachatkun, Nikita Nangia, Amanpreet Singh, Julian Michael, Felix Hill, Omer Levy, and Samuel Bowman. 2019. Superglue: A stickier benchmark for general-purpose language understanding systems. *Advances in neural information processing systems*, 32.

Y. Wang, Q. Wang, S. Shi, X. He, Z. Tang, K. Zhao, and X. Chu. 2020. Benchmarking the Performance and Energy Efficiency of AI Accelerators for AI Training. In *2020 20th IEEE/ACM International Symposium on Cluster, Cloud and Internet Computing (CCGRID)*, pages 744–751.

Manzil Zaheer, Guru Guruganesh, Kumar Avinava Dubey, Joshua Ainslie, Chris Alberti, Santiago Ontanon, Philip Pham, Anirudh Ravula, Qifan Wang, Li Yang, and Amr Ahmed. 2020. Big bird: Transformers for longer sequences. In *Advances in Neural Information Processing Systems*, volume 33, pages 17283–17297. Curran Associates, Inc.

Ming Zhong, Da Yin, Tao Yu, Ahmad Zaidi, Mutethia Mutuma, Rahul Jha, Ahmed Hassan Awadallah, Asli Celikyilmaz, Yang Liu, Xipeng Qiu, and Dragomir Radev. 2021. QMSum: A new benchmark for query-based multi-domain meeting summarization. In *Proceedings of the 2021 Conference of the North American Chapter of the Association for Computational Linguistics: Human Language Technologies*, pages 5905–5921, Online. Association for Computational Linguistics.

Xiyou Zhou, Zhiyu Chen, Xiaoyong Jin, and William Yang Wang. 2021. HULK: An Energy Efficiency Benchmark Platform for Responsible Natural Language Processing. In *Proceedings of the 16th Conference of the European Chapter of the Association for Computational Linguistics: System Demonstrations*, pages 329–336, Online. Association for Computational Linguistics.

A SCROLLS Dataset

Table 3 gives an overview of the datasets used in this paper, and we provide a brief description of each dataset below.

GovReport. (Huang et al., 2021) A summarization dataset comprised of reports published by the U.S. Government Accountability Office (GAO) and Congressional Research Service (CRS).

SummScreenFD. (Chen et al., 2021) A summarization dataset where the goal is to generate a summary of an episode of a TV show when given a transcript of the episode.

QMSum. (Zhong et al., 2021) A query-based summarization dataset composed of meeting notes from various sources such as academic group meetings, industrial product meetings, and public policy meetings. Models have to be able summarize specific sections of meetings when given a query.

Qasper. (Dasigi et al., 2021) A question answering dataset over NLP papers from Semantic Scholar Open Research Corpus (S2ORC). Given the title

Dataset	Task	Domain	Metric	Avg #Words		#Examples
				Input	Output	
GovReport	Summ	Government	ROUGE	7,897	492.7	19,402
SummScreenFD	Summ	TV	ROUGE	5,639	100.0	4,348
QMSum	QB-Summ	Meetings	ROUGE	10,396	69.7	1,810
Qasper	QA	Science	F1	3,671	11.5	5,692

Table 3: An overview of the datasets the SCROLLS dataset with their statistics that was recreated from the original SCROLLS paper (Shaham et al., 2022). *Summ* indicates summarization, *QB-Summ* means query-based summarization and *QA* means question answering. The number of examples for each dataset includes all the examples from train, validation, and test sets.

Hyperparameter	Value
Validation Accumulation Steps	10
Learning Rate (all other dataset)	2e-5
Learning Rate Scheduler	Linear
Learning Rate Warm-up Ratio	0.1
Adam Optimizer Epsilon	1e-6
Adam Optimizer Beta1	0.9
Adam Optimizer Beta2	0.98
Dataloader Workers	1
Maximum Epoch	50
Early Stopping	3

Table 4: Hyperparameters used during fine-tuning of the pre-trained models. For any hyperparameters that are not listed in this table, we used the default values provided from the HuggingFace Trainer Library [7].

and abstract of a paper, models have to be able to generate the answer to a question about the paper.

B SCROLLS Model Hyperparameters

All the experiments conducted in this project were built upon the pre-trained models from the HuggingFace library. Many of the hyperparameters used here are the same as those used for the LED-base model in SCROLLS. Unless specified in Table 4, hyperparameters take on default values from the HuggingFace Trainer library.[6]

As mentioned in Section 3.4, we selected the largest batch sizes that can fit on the NVIDIA RTX A6000 GPU(s) during fine-tuning for each model and dataset in order to control for the effects of memory on our metrics. Table 5 shows the batch sizes used for fine-tuning each model on the different datasets at different input sequence lengths.

Task	Model	Seq Len	Batch
Summ	LED-base	1024	24
		2048	12
		3072	8
		4096	6
	LED-large	1024	8
		2048	4
		3072	3
		4096	2
	Big Bird-large	1024	7
		2048	4
		3072	2
		4096	2
QA	LED-base	1024	704
		2048	352
		3072	224
		4096	160
	LED-large	1024	256
		2048	128
		3072	64
		4096	64
	Big Bird-large	1024	224
		2048	96
		3072	64
		4096	32

Table 5: Batch sizes used for fine-tuning the different models for each of the tasks at each input sequence length. *Summ* indicates summarization, and *QA* means question answering. The batch sizes listed for the QA task is the total batch size across the 8 GPUs with gradient accumulation step set to four.

[6] https://huggingface.co/docs/transformers/main_classes/trainer

[7] See previous note.

Author Index